Critical Acclaim for *Persuasive Technology*

It is rare for books to be published that define a new discipline or that fundamentally change how we think about technology and our jobs. This book does all of this. You MUST read this book, whether to grow your business or to teach your children how to overcome manipulation.

— Jakob Nielsen, Ph.D.
Principal, Nielsen Norman Group

B.J. Fogg has created an important new discipline, one that is of vital importance to everyone: the person in the street, the ethicist, the marketing and advertising person, and of course those who build, deploy, and use modern technology. Today's technology is used to change attitudes and behavior. This creates powerful opportunities, multiple challenges, and severe ethical issues. This powerful, yet easy to read book addresses the issues critically, with insight, and in depth.

— Donald A. Norman
Professor of Computer Science, Northwestern University
Cofounder, Nielsen Norman Group

Any medium has the potential to do great good or harm. Learn how to use design to intervene and make our interaction with technology more humane. A must read for those who are serious about designing the future.

— Clement Mok
Designer and CEO of CMCD

What you, dear reader, hold in your hands is the very first book on a totally new field of intellectual inquiry, one that has important practical implications for a host of people across many different domains, all centered around persuasion.

— Philip G. Zimbardo, Ph.D.
Professor of Psychology, Stanford University
President of the American Psychological Association, 2002

Persuasive Technology

*Using Computers to Change
What We Think and Do*

The Morgan Kaufmann Series in Interactive Technologies

Series Editors:
Stuart Card, Xerox PARC ∎ Jonathan Grudin, Microsoft
Jakob Nielsen, Nielsen Norman Group

Persuasive Technology

*Using Computers to Change
What We Think and Do*

B.J. Fogg, Ph.D.
Stanford University

MORGAN KAUFMANN PUBLISHERS

An Imprint of Elsevier

AMSTERDAM   BOSTON   LONDON   NEW YORK
OXFORD   PARIS   SAN DIEGO   SAN FRANCISCO
SINGAPORE   SYDNEY   TOKYO

Publishing Director   Diane D. Cerra
Publishing Services Manager   Edward Wade
Developmental Editor   Jeannine Drew
Project Management   Yonie Overton
Editorial Coordinator   Mona Buehler
Text Design, Composition, and
Illustration   Rebecca Evans, Evans & Associates
Cover Design   Lee Friedman
Cover Image   Getty Images
Copyeditor   Ken DellaPenta
Proofreader   Sharilyn Hovind
Indexer   Steve Rath
Interior Printer   The Maple-Vail Book Manufacturing Group
Cover Printer   Phoenix Color Corporation

Morgan Kaufmann Publishers
An Imprint of Elsevier
340 Pine Street, Sixth Floor
San Francisco, CA 94104–3205
www.mkp.com

Library of Congress Control Number: 2002110617
ISBN-13: 978-1-55860-643-2
ISBN-10: 1–55860–643–2

*To those who have taught me
at home, in the classroom,
and beyond*

Foreword

by Philip G. Zimbardo, Ph.D.
Professor of Psychology, Stanford University
President of the American Psychological Association, 2002

Captivated by Captology

I like to think that I am the midwife of this extraordinary brainchild of B.J. Fogg's. A few years ago, B.J. was my teaching associate in a novel course I had created on the psychology of mind control. In the section he designed, B.J. decided to structure his course activities around a set of new concepts that he was developing for his dissertation. He was engaged in original research exploring the parallels between the persuasive influence of computers and human agents. His thinking extended the recent work of Byron Reeves and Cliff Nass, who along with Terry Winograd and myself, comprised his dissertation committee. Reeves and Nass were among the first communications researchers to identify the ways in which people treat computers and other media similarly to the ways they deal with real—nonvirtual—people.

B.J.'s experimental research convincingly demonstrated that basic principles of social psychology operated in creating "charismatic computers" that were perceived as likeable and credible. His students were fascinated by the work they did under his supervision, as was I. The more he taught me about the breadth and depth of the ideas emerging from his new perspective, the more I was convinced he was onto something really hot. When we discussed publication of his ideas, I urged him to go beyond burying these vital messages in academic journals, which might have limited and surely delayed impact on the field. Instead, I urged B.J. to think on a grander scale and write this book.

What you, dear reader, hold in your hands is the very first book on a totally new field of intellectual inquiry, one that has important practical implications for a host of people across many different domains, all centered around persuasion. You will find it a wonderfully rich mine of novel insights and potentially powerful applications written in a clear, compelling, readable style. And, of course, you can trust what you read and learn, because B.J. Fogg is *The* credible communicator on this topic. His expertise soon will become evident to you, and I will vouch for his trustworthiness until you can establish it on your own.

The audience for this book goes well beyond social scientists to all those involved in human-computer interactions, in health care delivery, in marketing any product, in civic affairs, and, of course, the general public. Why? Because B.J. Fogg informs us all of the many new uses of computer-centered persuasive influences that can be more effective in some circumstances than human agents of persuasion.

"Captology" is the term that B.J. coined to capture the domain of research, design, and applications of persuasive computers. It is an acronym for *computers as persuasive technologies.* I predict it soon will be coin of the realm for all those interested in how interactive technologies can operate to change opinions, attitudes, and values and to affect the behavior of people—in short, for understanding how these new machines can change old minds in specific, predictable ways.

Much of my professional life has been devoted to documenting the tremendous influence that social factors exert on people's thoughts, feelings, and actions. But psychology, like many other domains of study, has promoted an approach focused on the individual in order to understand how people change, thus biasing the search for antecedents on dispositional attributes, on qualities inside the person. We fail to recognize the power and pervasiveness of a range of subtle situational variables that may operate on us in subtle ways to transform behavioral options. Roles, rules, uniforms, groups, situational norms, social models, prevailing ideologies, labels, terminology, signs, symbols, and more can induce, initiate, and seduce us to do things we think of as ego-alien. I have seen this first hand in my research on cults, deindividuation, cognitive dissonance, and my Stanford Prison Experiment. Yet, the power of social factors has not ceased to amaze me. Smart people can be led to make stupid decisions, normal people to behave abnormally, and good people to engage in evil deeds—all at the flick of a situational switch.

This research and the classic studies on blind obedience to authority by Stanley Milgram, my Bronx high school classmate, reveal the amazing extent to which behavior can be brought under situational control. Although these examples of controlled laboratory experiments are limited in duration and venue, there are an endless number of "real-world experiments" being conducted every day, in many places around our nation and the globe, without oversight or even evaluation of their continued effectiveness. The social experiment of U.S. prisons is one example of a continuing failed hypothesis for controlling crime and reducing criminal behavior. The same could be said of other government-inspired attempts at societal interventions, among them the "war on poverty," "the war on drugs," and "the war on terrorism."

Our world and technology have evolved dramatically since my Yale University mentor, Carl Hovland, first began the systematic investigation of communication and persuasion in the 1950s. Although groundbreaking at the time, that work never advanced technologically beyond paper-and-pencil questionnaires. The time has come for us to pay attention to how technology can—and will—be designed to change how people think and what they do. Not to do so would be at our peril. We would miss opportunities to bring about positive, desired changes in people's lives. We would be slow to take necessary steps against unwanted persuasion by unethical agencies using this new technology for profit or political advantage. And, we would lose time in understanding more fully the dynamics of attitude and value formation, as well as their change.

Twenty-first-century technology is already replacing people deemed in many spheres of the workplace as little more than "the human burden on profits, due to personal inefficiencies"—bank tellers, gas station attendants, information operators, check-out cashiers, to start. Such workers will be replaced by interactive technology media that are more efficient, never complain or get sick, persist despite boring tasks, are not unionized, and expect neither vacations nor raises. This model will be extended to every domain where people are seen as expendable. Their knowledge will be incorporated by systems technologies, their expertise mimicked by robots or smart software, their personal time limitations eliminated through accessibility 24/7. The bottlenecks they create—by being too few for the needs of too many—will be resolved by less highly credentialed staff who will serve as the centralized resource in a technology-based delivery system.

If all of us, professionals and citizens alike, comprehend how computers can be used to persuade us to take control over the decisions affecting our health and well being, we can harness this power for the good it can impart, while sounding alarms against the dark side of this force of persuasive influence. Understanding the deep nature of *captology* is essential to prepare us to appreciate how persuasive technologies can work to get a message across to change thoughts, feelings, and actions.

In many ways this book is about the future of influence—how people are persuaded, how people are motivated to take actions. B.J. Fogg asserts that the future of influence lies in digital technology, and I believe he is on the right path. We are still inculcated with the old model framed by Niccolo Machiavelli that human beings are the effective agents of influence; we ignore the alternative model first outlined by George Orwell in *1984* that technology could be corrupted by Big Brother to control the minds of the masses.

How effective will the new computer technology become as a source of influence to modify our decisions and behaviors? It is too soon to know, but the emerging evidence from research laboratories and from products already being tested and used in the marketplace informs us that computers do indeed influence people.

I think of myself as a low-tech guy, but nevertheless I strongly believe in the substantial power that new computer technologies will have to influence us. These emerging interactive technologies will have undeniably impressive capabilities to influence certain people to take designated actions to achieve specific outcomes in particular realms of their lives. In my mind, it's not a matter of *whether* computers can influence us, that's been demonstrated by B.J. and others. Instead, it's now a matter of understanding the scope of that influence—how far and how effectively will persuasive technologies reach into our lives?

Consider a single example: the explosion of obesity and adult onset diabetes in the United States, now approaching an epidemic. Computer technologies may offer the only reasonable behavior modification program that can reach millions of people every day with persistent messages about dieting, recording weight, and being part of a social support group; bypass shame and guilt through anonymous participation; give rewards and incentives; and provide convenience and economy once you own the equipment.

Yes, of course, there will be undesirable applications for persuasive technology, and we must be on guard to identify and expose them, as we would for negative human persuasive sources. Yet, our focus as concerned citizens, psychologists, and creators of computer systems should be on discovering how to utilize this new power of persuasive technology wisely and well!

I know you will learn much from reading this remarkable book that can serve as the starting point for a new conversation about the place of computers as influence agents in our everyday lives. This collective conversation about how technology can motivate and persuade us starts today but will last for decades. Be sure also to review B.J.'s informative Notes and References at the end of each chapter. Finally, check out his Web site (*www.persuasivetech.info*) for additional materials, graphic illustrations, and updates on captology. Perhaps we can persuade him to facilitate the national dialogue on new persuasive technologies on his Web site. In the meantime, your next step is a small one on the path of this exciting new discovery—turn one page and meet the creator of captology. I give you Dr. B.J. Fogg. Take it away, B.J.!

Contents

---

chapter 7   **Credibility and the World Wide Web**   **147**

---

chapter 9   The Ethics of Persuasive Technology   211

chapter 10   Captology: Looking Forward   241

Preface

When I was 10 years old, I studied propaganda. Each week my fifth grade class would meet with a teaching intern from Fresno State University. He showed us how the media and politicians use techniques to change what people think and do. I learned names for the various propaganda techniques, and I could soon identify them in magazine ads and TV commercials. I felt empowered.

I thought it strange to be learning about propaganda in a rural bungalow classroom surrounded by fig orchards, but I also found the topic fascinating. I marveled at how words, images, and songs could get people to donate blood, buy new cars, or join the Army.

This was my first formal introduction to persuasion. After that, everywhere I looked I started seeing what I called "propaganda," used for good purposes and bad.

While my interest in persuasion was growing, so was my exposure to technology, thanks to my father. In the late 1960s, we got a phone call at home. It was Dad. "I'm driving down the street now," he said. "I'll be home in about one minute." He'd installed some sort of phone in his car, obviously well ahead of the curve. Later, an enormous microwave oven would find a home in our garage (the only place where the beast would fit). Soon we'd enjoy a device that could display images on our TV; we'd sit as a family and watch the eye surgeries Dad had performed. Later, before computer systems were commercially available, Dad built his own computer with parts he'd ordered, spending many evenings soldering computer chips onto a circuit board.

It seems strange now, but it was not at all unusual for my parents to take vacations to Las Vegas with their Fresno friends. The purpose wasn't gambling; instead, they made their annual pilgrimage to the Consumer Electronics Show (CES) to experience the latest and greatest in the world of consumer technology. Sometimes they would take a few of their seven children with them. For me, this was just about the best vacation ever. At that time I did not suspect that someday I would be paid to participate in CES and similar trade shows.

My early exposure to persuasive techniques and technology clearly shaped my interests. After a long career (seven years) as an undergraduate, studying most anything that struck my fancy, I discovered an area that pulled together the interests I'd been developing since I was a child. The area was document design (now more widely known as information design). As described by Karen Schriver,[1] a leading thinker on the topic of communicating information, document design was all about making information "accessible, usable, and persuasive."

I was enthralled by the topic and devoured everything I could find about it, from the readability of fonts, to models of text structure, to conceptual arguments about programmed instruction. With PageMaker 1.0 as my partner, I started a company named "Avatar" to provide document design services to software companies, direct marketing firms, and anyone else who needed better ways to inform and persuade an audience.

While completing my master's degree in 1992, I created a document design curriculum and taught honors students in what I still believe was the first undergraduate course ever in information design. In the two years that I taught this course, as my students and I explored how to make documents "accessible, usable, and persuasive," it became clear to me that my real interest was in the third aspect: persuasion.

I could see that the future of information design, specifically in creating artifacts to persuade people, lay in digital technology, in online environments, and in interactive computing products. So, with the vision of understanding how computer systems can be designed to persuade people, I began my doctoral work at Stanford University, in the process becoming a social scientist—specifically an experimental psychologist.

---

1. The article by Karen Schriver that brought together so many of my interests and gave this area a name was Document design from 1980 to 1989: Challenges that remain, *Technical Communication*, 36(4), 316–331 (1989).

   Later, Dr. Schriver published a book in this area: *Dynamics in Document Design: Creating Texts for Readers* (New York: Wiley, 1996).

To my surprise, after searching through the literature and asking thought leaders in related areas such as psychology, human-computer interactions (HCI), and marketing, I concluded that no one had yet paid special attention to the role of computers in persuasion. A few pioneering products existed, but there was no examination of the potentials and pitfalls of computer systems created to change people's attitudes and behaviors.

My doctoral thesis would examine how computers could be persuasive. I titled my dissertation "Charismatic Computers." It included experimental studies on how to make computers more likable and persuasive, as well as outlining a vision for a new domain that I referred to as "captology," an acronym based on the phrase *computers as persuasive technologies*. My vision of captology has inevitably deepened and expanded over the years as technology has evolved and I've learned more about the ways in which computers can influence people.

Persuasive technology is a fast-growing area of research and development. Computing systems of many types, from Web sites to productivity applications to mobile devices, are becoming increasingly focused on motivating and influencing users.

One of the assertions in this book is that in the future we'll see more and more computing products designed for the primary purpose of persuasion. In addition, software applications—desktop or Web-based—designed mainly for other purposes (such as productivity, creativity, or collaboration) will increasingly incorporate elements of persuasion, ideally motivating users to make better use of the application and supporting them in achieving their goals.

In my view, it will become important for most people designing end-user computing products to understand how principles of motivation and influence can be designed into interactive experiences with computers. As end-user computing matures, understanding captology may become as important as understanding usability.

For the past nine years at Stanford, I've been investigating how interactive technologies can change people's attitudes and behaviors. Although captology is still an emerging area of research and design, the time has come to share this work with a larger audience and to bring some order to this domain. The purpose of this book is precisely that: to lay the groundwork for better understanding current and future persuasive technologies.

My goal in writing this book is to provide insight into the current state of computers and persuasion and foresight into the likely future of persuasive technology. The book was written primarily for professionals interested in researching, analyzing, or designing persuasive technologies. But it is not a technical book, and based on my teaching experience at Stanford, I believe it has relevance for a broad range of readers. That includes technology watchers as well as executives who want to understand how they might use persuasive technology to develop new products, win new customers and markets, or strengthen brand identity and loyalty.

I hope that all readers will appreciate the importance of ethics in creating persuasive technology products. I've devoted a chapter of the book to this topic. In my view, the evolution of persuasive technology systems should not be left to accident or to market forces alone. The power to persuade via computing systems comes with the responsibility to use the technology for appropriate, ethical ends. This is my ultimate hope for this book: that it will contribute to the responsible design and application of persuasive technology.

Acknowledgments

Many people contributed invaluable help and support for this book. First, I want to acknowledge my debt to all of those who, over the years, have helped me design studies and conduct research relating to captology. I could not have completed this research—or this book—without your help. Thank you.

The four people on my dissertation committee at Stanford University deserve special acknowledgment. Each of them continued to support me long after my thesis was signed and delivered. Special thanks to Clifford Nass for advising me throughout my doctoral work during the mid-1990s. Without his influence and help, this book would not exist. Thanks also to Byron Reeves, for teaching me about quantitative research methods and for being an advocate of my work since my arrival at Stanford. In the area of human-computer interaction, I feel fortunate to have worked with Terry Winograd off and on over the years. I still strive to make good on the confidence Terry has placed in me and my work. In the area of psychology, I'm deeply grateful to Phil Zimbardo for seeing the potential for persuasive technology, for making time in his hectic schedule to advise me, for giving me the first opportunity to test my material in a classroom — and for being the first to encourage me to write a book on captology.

Others at Stanford have also played a key role in supporting my work and in making this book a reality. I thank John Perry for making a personal sacrifice to give my lab physical space at Stanford's CSLI. Thanks also to Decker Walker for advocating that I teach graduate students in Stanford's Learning, Design, and

Technology Program. And many thanks to CSLI's Michele King for helping me on innumerable tasks, big and small, making my life easier in the process.

Research done in my Stanford lab has given this book greater richness. I'm grateful to the dozens of people who have worked with me over the years. I owe a special debt of gratitude to those students who joined my lab at the beginning, showing confidence in captology and in me. These people helped to shape my thinking and contributed many unpaid and uncredited hours to the cause: Daniel Berdichevsky, John Bruck, Jared Kopf, Erik Neuenschwander, Jason Tester, and Shawn Tseng. Researchers who subsequently joined the lab have also expanded our understanding of persuasive technology. These people include John Boyd, Tami Kameda, Jonathan Marshall, Rupa Patel, Josh Solomon, Peter Westen, Peter Dodd, and Nina Kim, among others. Those who commented on early drafts of the book or contributed directly to the research you'll find here also deserve acknowledgment. They include Meghann Evershed, George Slavich, Cathy Soohoo, Tracy Trowbridge, Ling Kong, Akshay Rangnekar, Johnnie Manzari, Katherine Woo, Kim Rice, Phil King, and Ramit Sethi.

In my industry work, I was fortunate to interact with many people who supported my research in captology. I am especially grateful to Janice Bradford (H-P), Debby Hindus (Interval Research), Bob Glass (Sun Microsystems), and Rick Kinoshita (Casio U.S. R&D). Other friends and colleagues in industry have helped to sharpen my thinking and improve the quality of this book, including Andy Cargile, Denise Caruso, Peter and Trudy Johnson-Lenz, John Lilly, Brenda Laurel, Jakob Nielsen, Youngme Moon, and Nathan Shedroff.

Thanks to various reviewers who made time to comment on different versions of my manuscript, some of whom remained anonymous. There is one person on the review team to whom I am enormously grateful: Chauncey Wilson. His critiques and suggestions were excellent; this is a much better book thanks to him.

I wish to acknowledge my editor at Morgan Kaufman Publishers, Diane Cerra, for recognizing the importance of captology and for championing my book. Thanks, Diane!

No person contributed more to this book in its final phases than did my developmental editor, Jeannine Drew. Although the book's content is attributed to me as the author, evidence of Jeannine's expert assistance appears on every page. As we worked together, she offered challenging critiques of my ideas and examples, created solutions to difficult problems, and never faltered in any of her commitments. Her input and guidance have made this book better in so many ways. I look forward to the next opportunity to work with Jeannine.

The people I've mentioned by name above represent only a partial list of those to whom I am grateful. So many colleagues, professors, students, clients, and friends have made an impact on my thinking, my research, and this book. Any shortcomings you may find in these pages are not due to those who offered help and support to me, but are solely my responsibility.

Finally, thanks to my family for being patient about the many evenings, weekends, and holidays I've devoted to researching and writing this book rather than being with them. My deep appreciation to my parents, Gary and Cheryl, and to Linda, Steve, Mike, Kim, and Becky and their families. I am also extremely grateful to Denny for clearing my path so I could make progress on my many commitments, including this book.

Introduction
Persuasion in the Digital Age

Computers weren't initially created to persuade; they were built for handling data—calculating, storing, and retrieving. But as computers have migrated from research labs onto desktops and into everyday life, they have become more persuasive by design. Today computers are taking on a variety of roles as persuaders, including roles of influence that traditionally were filled by teachers, coaches, clergy, therapists, doctors, and salespeople, among others. We have entered an era of persuasive technology, of *interactive computing systems designed to change people's attitudes and behaviors.*

The earliest signs of persuasive technology appeared in the 1970s and 1980s, when a few computing systems were designed to promote health and increase workplace productivity. One of the earliest examples is a computer system named Body Awareness Resource Network (BARN), developed in the late 1970s. This pioneering program was designed to teach adolescents about health issues such as smoking, drugs, exercise, and more, with an ultimate focus on enhancing teens' behaviors in these areas.[1] Gradually other interactive programs of this nature followed, most designed to address adolescent health issues or to treat psychological disorders.[2] But it wasn't until the late 1990s—specifically, the emergence of the Internet—that more than a handful of people began creating persuasive technology.

> **I define *persuasive technology* as** any interactive computing system designed to change people's attitudes or behaviors.

1

Persuasion on the Web

The emergence of the Internet has led to a proliferation of Web sites designed to persuade or motivate people to change their attitudes and behavior. Web sites are the most common form of persuasive technology today. Consider a few examples:

- Amazon.com doesn't just process orders; it attempts to persuade people to purchase more products. It does so by offering suggestions based on user preferences gathered during previous visits and feedback from others who ordered the product, and by presenting compelling promotions, such as the Gold Box offers and the "Share the Love" program.

- Iwon.com wants visitors to make it their default search engine and awards prizes to persuade them to do so.

- Classmates.com, the leading online service for reuniting people, successfully leverages social influence principles (a topic discussed in Chapters 5 and 8) to persuade people to give up their personal information, from maiden name to birth year. In some cases, the site is able to persuade people to post personal histories and recent photographs online.

- The *New York Times* online tries to persuade readers to give up their personal information, including household income, when they sign up for the free online version of the newspaper.

- The auction site eBay has developed an online exchange system with sufficient credibility (a topic discussed in Chapters 6 and 7) that users are persuaded to make financial transactions, big and small, with strangers who have screen names like "punnkinhead" and "bodyheat2."

Beyond the Web

Beyond the Web, persuasive technology can take on many forms, from mobile phones to "smart" toothbrushes to the computerized trailers that sit by the roadside and post the speed of passing cars in an attempt to persuade drivers to abide by the speed limit. In some cases, the technology may not even be visible to the user. With the emergence of embedded computing, the forms of persuasive technology will likely become more diverse, "invisible," and better integrated into everyday life. The Web, which is so prominent today, will be just one of many forms of persuasive technology within another 10 years.

The uses for persuasive technology also will expand in the coming decade, extending far beyond the primary applications we see today, such as advertising, marketing, and sales. At work, persuasive technology might be used to motivate teams to set goals and meet deadlines. At home, it could encourage kids to develop better study habits. In civic life, it could persuade people to vote on election day. Wherever the need for persuasion exists, I believe that interactive technology can play a role.

Throughout this book, you'll see plenty of examples of current and emerging persuasive technology applications. Table 1 suggests some of the domains and potential applications. Some of these examples are explored in more detail in later chapters.

Table 1   Persuasive Technology: Domains and Applications

Domain	Example application	Persuades users to
Commerce	Amazon.com's recommendation system	Buy more books and other products
Education, learning, and training	CodeWarriorU.com	Engage in activities that promote learning how to write code
Safety	Drunk driving simulator	Avoid driving under the influence of alcohol
Environmental preservation	Scorecard.org	Take action against organizations that pollute
Occupational effectiveness	"In My Steps" VR system	Treat cancer patients with more empathy
Preventive healthcare	Quitnet.com	Quit smoking
Fitness	Tectrix VR bike	Exercise and enjoy it

continued

Table 1   Continued

Domain	Example application	Persuades users to
Disease management	Bronki the bronchia-saurus game	Manage asthma more effectively
Personal finance	FinancialEngines.com	Create and adhere to a retirement plan
Community involvement/ activism	CapitolAdvantage.com	Get ordinary citizens in-volved in public affairs
Personal relationships	Classmates.com	Reconnect with former classmates
Personal manage-ment and self-improvement	MyGoals.com	Set goals and take the needed steps to achieve them

We are still in the early stages of persuasive technology development. The potential for using (or, unfortunately, abusing) such technology is enormous. Those who are early to understand this emerging field will be in the best position to benefit from it, personally and professionally. By understanding the ideas in this book, readers will be in a better position to

- Recognize when Web sites and computing products are designed to influence people

- Identify the persuasion strategies these interactive systems use

- Understand the dynamics behind the persuasive elements in Web sites and other products

- Identify new opportunities for influence in computing systems

- Create interactive experiences that motivate and persuade people

- Address the ethical issues of persuading via computing systems

- Predict what the future holds for persuasion via computing products

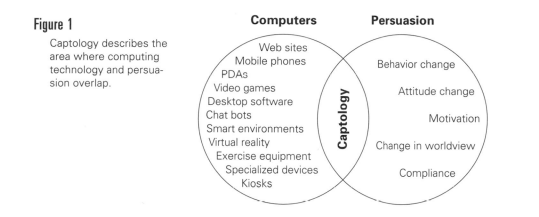

Figure 1

Captology describes the area where computing technology and persuasion overlap.

The Emergence of "Captology"

The study of computers as persuasive technologies is relatively new. As noted in the preface, to describe this emerging area, I coined the term "captology"—an acronym based on the phrase "computers as persuasive technologies." Briefly stated, captology focuses on the *design, research, and analysis of interactive computing products created for the purpose of changing people's attitudes or behaviors*. It describes the area where technology and persuasion overlap (Figure 1).

Potential and Pitfalls

Interactivity **gives computing technology a strong advantage over other persuasive media.**

When I first began sharing my experimental research on computers and persuasion, I received radically different responses. Some colleagues became upset over the potential misuses of persuasive technology. Some, in peer reviews and at conferences, even declared my research immoral. Other people were excited about the potential of persuasive technology for marketing and sales: rather than using static media or costly human beings, these people glimpsed how computing technology could grow their businesses. Still others saw the potential for applying persuasive technology to promote positive social goals, such as preventing teen pregnancy or reducing world hunger.

Both positive and negative reactions to captology have merit. Perhaps more than anyone else, I've investigated both the potential and the pitfalls of persuasive technology. Although I don't find captology immoral, I acknowledge that persuasive technology can be used in unethical ways in an attempt to change people's attitudes and behaviors. For example, an online game could be used to persuade children to give up personal information.

In this book I focus primarily on the positive, ethical applications of persuasive technology. But I also highlight the pitfalls, and I explore the ethics of such technology in Chapter 9.

Advantage over Traditional Media: Interactivity

Traditional media, from bumper stickers to radio spots, from print ads to television commercials, have long been used to influence people to change their attitudes or behaviors. What's different about computers and persuasion? The answer, in a word, is *interactivity*.

As a general rule, persuasion techniques are most effective when they are interactive, when persuaders adjust their influence tactics as the situation evolves. Skilled salespeople know this and adjust their pitches according to feedback from the prospect.

Persuasive technologies can adjust what they do based on user inputs, needs, and situations. An interactive program to help someone quit smoking can tailor its approach to how much the person smokes (physical addiction) and address the often-powerful psychological issues (psychological addiction) that compel the person to smoke. Over time, as the person reports progress or failures, the system can use its knowledge about the smoker's demographic variables as well as physical and psychological addiction issues to make suggestions (such as alternatives to smoking when the urge is strong), lead the person through activities (such as interactive scenarios), or provide the right kind of encouragement to help the person quit. Traditional media cannot easily deliver such a tailored program.

Today computer technology is being designed to apply traditional human techniques of interactive persuasion, to extend the reach of humans as interactive persuaders. This is new territory, both for computing technology and for human beings.

Advantages over Human Persuaders

When it comes to persuasion, computers not only have an advantage over traditional media. They also have six distinct advantages over human persuaders. Specifically, they can do the following:

1. Be more persistent than human beings

2. Offer greater anonymity

3. Manage huge volumes of data

4. Use many modalities to influence

5. Scale easily

6. Go where humans cannot go or may not be welcome

1. Computers Are Persistent

You've probably experienced how some software registration programs persist in asking you to register. If you don't register at installation, from time to time the program reminds you—or nags you—to share your personal information (Figure 2). Not everyone does, of course, but the persistent reminders undoubtedly increase the rate of registration. People get tired of saying no; everyone has a moment of weakness when it's easier to comply than to resist.

Figure 2

Eudora registration
screen.

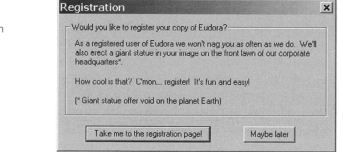

No human can be as persistent as a machine. Computers don't get tired, discouraged, or frustrated. They don't need to eat or sleep. They can work around the clock in active efforts to persuade, or watch and wait for the right moment to intervene. As the software registration example suggests, when it comes to persuasion, this higher level of persistence can pay off.

2. Computers Allow Anonymity

Another advantage computers have in persuasion is that they allow anonymity. The option of remaining anonymous is important in sensitive areas such as sexual behavior, substance abuse, or psychological problems.[3] It's often easier (and less embarrassing) to get information or help anonymously, via an interactive computing program, than it is to face another human being.

Anonymity also is important when people are experimenting with new attitudes and behaviors. You may have sensed this phenomenon in anonymous chat rooms: shy people can try being bold, those with conservative values can test liberal waters, and those who normally guard their privacy can open up and speak their minds. For better and for worse, anonymity helps overcome social forces that lock people into ruts and routines.[4] At times anonymity makes it easier for people to change.

3. Computers Can Store, Access, and Manipulate Huge Volumes of Data

Another advantage: Computers can store, access, and manipulate large quantities of data, far beyond the capabilities of human beings. This gives interactive technology the potential to be more persuasive than human beings.

In some situations, the sheer quantity of information presented will change what people believe and perhaps what they do.[5] In such situations, the computer's ability to draw on a vast storehouse of information will give it greater powers of persuasion. In other cases, the computer's ability to find and present precisely the right fact, statistic, or reference from that volume of data can help to persuade more effectively than a human could.

The ability of computers to access and manipulate large volumes of information also enables them to make suggestions—another form of persuasion (I'll discuss suggestion technology in Chapter 3). Using collaborative filtering or Bayesian networks—automated methods for making inferences—computers can predict what a user is likely to buy or do and make recommendations to the user based on that. Sometimes I go to Amazon to buy a single CD and end up buying a few different titles because the site made excellent recommendations. (To me, getting targeted recommendations feels like a service, not a hard sell, but others may find this "service" intrusive.)

4. Computers Can Use Many Modalities

Often people are influenced not by information itself but by how it's presented—the modality. Human beings can convey information in many modes, but we cannot match the variety of modes available to a computing system.

To persuade, computers can present data and graphics, rich audio and video, animation, simulation, or hyperlinked content.[6] The ability to use various modalities enables technology to match people's preferences for visual, audio, or textual experiences. Technology can also create a synergistic effect by combining modes, such as audio, video, and data, during an interaction to produce the optimum persuasive impact.

One example of combining computing modalities emerged in the wake of the terrorist attacks of September 11, 2001. In the days that followed, as the United States and other countries debated how to respond, Alternet.org, whose mission is to "engage our community of readers in problem solving, community action and awareness of current events in the United States and abroad," created a Web-based experience to affect this response.[7] In seeking to persuade, the creators drew on at least three modalities available to computers. First, most people learned about the site through a text email from a friend, which included a link to the Web page.[8] Once at the site, the user saw an animation unfold, combining moving text, images, and a soundtrack. At the conclusion of this minute-long animation, the text read, "Urge President Bush to exercise sober restraint in responding. Click here." When users clicked the button, they were presented with a specific call to action and a template email they could modify and send to the White House.

Computing technology is the only media that could combine this range of modalities into a seamless experience, starting with a friend's email, leading to an emotionally charged animation, and ending with the means to take immediate action on the issue. That's the power of leveraging modalities to persuade.

The computer-based intervention "Alcohol 101" provides another example of how persuasive technology can leverage multiple modalities.[9] As first-year college students use this product to explore the negative consequences of excessive drinking at college parties, they find many types of experiences: interactive stories, TV-like video footage, simulations that calculate blood alcohol content, an interactive text-based game, and more. It's a rich interactive product, with something that is likely both to appeal to the wide range of people who use the product and to affect their attitudes and behavior.

5. Computer Software Can Scale

The next advantage technology has over human persuaders is the ability to scale—to grow quickly when demand increases. If a human persuader is effective, it's difficult to scale the experience so that it reaches millions of people around the world quickly. How can you replicate a top sales rep, an influential personal trainer, or a charismatic religious figure? You can increase the person's scope of influence through print, audio, or video communications, but the original experience may get lost along the way, particularly if the original experience was interactive.

By contrast, when it comes to software-based experiences—especially those delivered over the Internet—the ability to scale is relatively easy. You can replicate and distribute persuasive technology experiences that work just like the original.

6. Computers Can Be Ubiquitous

The final advantage that technology has over human persuaders is ubiquity—the ability to be almost everywhere. With the growth of embedded computers, computing applications are becoming commonplace in locations where human persuaders would not be welcomed, such as the bathroom or bedroom, or where humans cannot go (inside clothing, embedded in an automotive system, or implanted in a toothbrush).

When interactive computing systems are embedded in everyday objects and environments, they can intervene at precisely the right time and place, giving them greater persuasive power. (Chapters 3 and 8 address the persuasive impact of intervening at the right time and place.) Rather than having parents nag their kids to brush their teeth, a smart toothbrush could help motivate kids to do the job by reminding them at the appropriate time and place. Likewise, an embedded car system can be more effective than a classroom discussion in promoting safe driving, by intervening at just the right moments, such as after a reckless driver has barely avoided an accident. The system might sense the driver has slammed on the brakes, didn't use a turn signal, or otherwise was negligent, and communicate to the driver via an audio signal, verbal message, or other means.

With the rise of ubiquitous computing, we'll see a growing number of technologies that attempt to motivate and influence. In the coming years we are likely to see computers playing new persuasive roles in promoting health, safety, and eco-friendly behavior, in addition to selling products and services (the most frequent application of persuasive technology today).

How to Read This Book

In the following chapters, I will provide frameworks and principles for understanding persuasive technology. Along the way, I'll discuss studies I've conducted at Stanford, as well as share many examples of computing products—from Web sites to mobile systems—designed to change what people think and do. I'll also outline possibilities for new types of persuasive technologies.

The plan of the book is straightforward: The first five chapters lay the groundwork for understanding captology. Subsequent chapters address computer credibility, Web credibility, mobile and networked persuasion, and ethics. The last chapter provides a glimpse into the future of persuasive technology.

Throughout this book, my goal is to provide understanding and insight and some general "how to" guidelines. Whether you are a designer, researcher, or user of persuasive technology, I'm confident you can apply the insights offered here to your own work and life. By providing a framework for understanding persuasive technology and for designing responsible, ethical applications, it's my hope that I can help others to leverage the power of technology to improve the lives of individuals and communities.

The field of captology is evolving. With that in mind, I have established a Web site, *www.persuasivetech.info,* where readers can go to find the latest information about this emerging area. At the site I'll also post errata sheets for this book, as well as comments, corrections, and suggestions from readers. I would welcome your feedback.

Notes and References

For updates on the topics presented in this chapter, visit *www.persuasivetech.info.*

1. K. Bosworth, D. H. Gustafson, R. P. Hawkins, B. Chewning, and P. M. Day, BARNY: A computer based health information system for adolescents, *Journal of Early Adolescence,* 1(3): 315 321 (1981).

2. For example, see G. Lawrence, Using computers for the treatment of psychological disorders, *Computers in Human Behavior,* 2(1): 43–62 (1986).

   See the following for more on early examples of persuasive technology:

   a. S. J. Schneider, Trial of an on-line behavioral smoking cessation program, *Computers in Human Behavior,* 2: 277–286 (1986).

   b. M. L. Tombari, S. J. Fitzpatrick, and W. Childress, Using computers as contingency managers in self-monitoring interventions: A case study, *Computers in Human Behavior,* 1: 75–82 (1985).

   c. J. Woodward, D. Carnine, and L. Davis, Health ways: A computer simulation for problem solving in personal health management, Special issue: Technological advances in community health, *Family & Community Health,* 9(2): 60–63 (1986).

   d. C. Muehlenhard, L. Baldwin, W. Bourg, and A. Piper, Helping women "break the ice": A computer program to help shy women start and maintain conversations with men, *Journal of Computer-Based Instruction,* 15(1): 7–13 (1988).

   e. S. W. Demaree, Interactive technology: The greatest sales tool ever invented? *Magazine of Bank Administration,* 63(1): 16 (1987).

3. For an example of how anonymity is helpful when dealing with sexual issues, see Y. M. Binik, C. F. Westbury, and D. Servan-Schreiber, Case histories and shorter communications: Interaction with a "sex-expert" system enhances attitudes towards computerized sex therapy, *Behavioral Research Therapy,* 27: 303–306 (1989).

4. For one of the early studies showing that people who are anonymous break from their socially induced behaviors, see

   P. G. Zimbardo, The human choice: Individuation, reason, and order versus deindividuation, impulse, and chaos, *Nebraska Symposium on Motivation,* 17: 237–302 (1969).

   For recent research on the effects of anonymity in computer environments, see

   T. Postmes, R. Spears, K. Sakhel, and D. De Groot, Social influence in computer-mediated communication: The effects of anonymity on group behavior, *Personality and Social Psychology Bulletin,* 27: 1243–1254 (2001).

   Also, see the ongoing work of Dr. Martin Lea, a psychologist at the University of Manchester: *http://www.psy.man.ac.uk/staff/mlea/index.htm.*

5. When people aren't deeply involved in an issue or are not able to think deeply (in other words, when they are using peripheral processing, rather than central processing), they rely more heavily on the number of arguments in favor of an idea rather than the quality of arguments. This is one of the basic assertions of the Elaboration Likelihood Model. Richard Petty and John Cacioppo have published widely in this area. For example, see

   R. E. Petty and J. T. Cacioppo, The elaboration likelihood model of persuasion, in L. Berkowitz (ed.), *Advances in Experimental Social Psychology* (San Diego, CA: Academic Press, 1986), vol. 19, pp. 123–205.

6. For a discussion of how graphics can be persuasive, see W. King, M. Dent, and E. Miles, The persuasive effect of graphics in computer-mediated communication, *Computers in Human Behavior,* 7(4): 269–279 (1991).

7. The online experience related to the events of September 11, 2001, was created by free-rangegraphics.com.

8. You can find the online experience related to the events of September 11, 2001, at *http://www.alternet.org/break_cycle.html.*

9. For information about the Alcohol 101 program, see *www.alcohol101.org.*

chapter 1

Overview of Captology

Defining Persuasion

> For purposes of captology, *persuasion* is defined as the attempt to change attitudes or behaviors or both.

Although philosophers and scholars have been examining persuasion for at least 2,000 years, not everyone agrees on what the term really means.[1] For purposes of captology, I define persuasion as *an attempt to change attitudes or behaviors or both* (without using coercion or deception). This is a broad definition, and one on which many persuasion professionals, such as academic researchers, marketers, and clinical psychologists, would agree. It also fits with how the word is used in everyday life.

It's important to note the difference between *persuasion* and *coercion*, terms that are sometimes confused. Coercion implies force; while it may change behaviors, it is not the same as persuasion, which implies voluntary change—in behavior, attitude, or both.[2]

Similarly, *persuasion* and *deception* may be confused. For instance, when I ask my students to find examples of persuasion on the Web, invariably some of them come to class with screen shots of Internet banner ads that report false emergencies ("Your systems resources are low. Click here!") or that misinform users ("Pornography is downloading to your computer. Click here to stop.") While such ads might change what people think and do, they do so through deception, not persuasion. Computer-based coercion and deception are topics in their own right,[3] but they are not covered under the umbrella of captology because they do not depend on persuasion.[4]

Focus on the Human-Computer Relationship

Captology focuses on attitude or behavior change resulting from *human-computer interaction.*

In the premier issue of the academic journal *Interacting with Computers,* an editorial posed an important question: Do we interact *with* computers or do we interact *through* them?[5] While a good rhetorician could argue either side of this question, it seems clear that people interact both *with* and *through* computers, depending on the situation.

Captology—the study of computers as persuasive technology—focuses on human-computer interaction (HCI), not on computer-mediated communication (CMC). Specifically, captology investigates how people are motivated or persuaded when interacting *with* computing products rather than *through* them. CMC is a separate area of research and design, with interesting intellectual questions to answer and big dollars at stake.[6] But it falls outside the realm of captology.

Under the CMC model, the computer is a channel that allows humans to interact with each other. For example, people in different locations may use computer tools, such as instant messaging and electronic whiteboards, to collaborate with one another. In this scenario, the computer facilitates communication; it does not persuade.

By contrast, in a human-computer interaction, the computing product is a participant in the interaction and can be a source of persuasion. The computer can proactively seek to motivate and influence users, drawing on strategies and routines programmed into it. It can encourage, provide incentives, and negotiate, to name a few strategies. In later chapters you'll find examples of technology products that use such proactive persuasion techniques.

Persuasion Is Based on Intentions, Not Outcomes

Captology focuses on *planned* persuasive effects of technology, not on side effects.

At the start of this chapter, I defined persuasion as an attempt to change attitudes or behaviors or both. This definition implies that true persuasion—whether brought about by humans or computers—requires intentionality. Captology focuses on the *planned persuasive effects* of computer technologies.

This point about intentionality may seem subtle, but it is not trivial. Intentionality is what distinguishes between a planned effect and a side effect of a technology.[7]

If you examine the history of computing technologies, you find that many high-tech products have changed the way people think, feel, and act. But most of these changes were not planned persuasive effects of the technology; they were side effects. Once people started using email, most probably changed how they used "snail mail": they bought fewer stamps and went to the post office less often. Similarly, when video games came onto the market, kids started watching less television and played outside less often.[8]

Captology does not include such unintended outcomes; it focuses on the attitude and behavior changes *intended* by the designers of interactive technology products. These planned effects can range widely, from persuading people to buy things online, to motivating people to take stretch breaks after extended periods of desk work, to convincing people that bioterrorism is a serious threat.

Captology focuses on endogenous, or "built-in," persuasive intent, not on exogenous intent.

One other point about intentions: Captology focuses on *endogenous* intent, that is, the persuasive intent that is designed into a computing product. A product also could acquire *exogenous* persuasive intent from users or another source—that is, if a product is adopted for a persuasive goal the designers hadn't planned. For example, the Palm computer is not a persuasive product by design, but a student might buy it to motivate herself to do homework more regularly. The Sony CD Discman wasn't designed to be persuasive, but a friend of mine bought one because she thought that the ability to listen to music during her workouts would motivate her to run more often. Captology does not focus on such exogenous intent but only on the endogenous persuasive intent built into a product.

Levels of Persuasion: Macro and Micro

Technology can persuade on two levels: macro and micro.

Attitude and behavior changes that result from successful persuasion can take place on two levels: macro and micro. Understanding these two levels of persuasion will make it easier to identify, design, or analyze persuasion opportunities in most computing products.

A game called HIV Roulette, which I'll describe in more detail in Chapter 4, is designed to persuade users to avoid risky sexual behavior. Baby Think It Over, also detailed in Chapter 4, is designed to persuade teenage girls to avoid becoming pregnant. Persuasion and motivation are the sole reasons such products exist. I use the term *macrosuasion* to describe this overall persuasive intent of a product.

Some computing products, such as email programs or image manipulation software, do not have an overall intent to persuade, but they could incorporate smaller persuasive elements to achieve a different overall goal. I refer to this approach as *microsuasion*.

Microsuasion elements can be designed into dialogue boxes, icons, or interaction patterns between the computer and the user.[9] For example, in educational software applications, microsuasion techniques—such as offering praise or giving gold stars for completing a task—can lead to staying on task longer, getting a better understanding of the material, or strengthened brand loyalty.

Quicken, the personal finance application created by Intuit, provides a good example of how microsuasion can make a product more effective. The overall goal of the product is to simplify the process of managing personal finances. But note how the program uses microsuasion to achieve this goal. At the simplest level, the software reminds people to pay bills on time, helping them be financially responsible. The program also tracks personal spending habits and shows results in graphs, highlighting the financial consequences of past behavior and allowing projections into future financial scenarios. In addition, the software praises users for doing menial but necessary tasks, such as balancing their online check registry. These microsuasion elements—reminders, visualizations, and praise—are influence strategies embedded in the Quicken experience to change what users think and how they act.

Consider a few ways that microsuasion is used in CodeWarriorU.com, a site designed to teach people how to use the CodeWarrior tools to develop software applications. To convince users that its teaching methods are effective, the site uses testimonials, easily accessible from the homepage. To persuade users to enroll, the homepage extols the benefits of at least a dozen courses, casting a wide net in making the sales pitch to prospects. In addition, no matter where users go on the site, on every page they see invitations to enroll, in the form of prominent buttons that say "Register" and "Enroll now." Furthermore, the site reduces barriers to enroll: it's free and easy to do.

The site also uses microsuasion techniques to motivate users to continue making progress in their chosen course. Each course has a schedule with a firm ending date, which serves both to set work expectations and a deadline. Each lesson has tracking features that help users see how much they've completed and how much work remains. The CodeWarriorU.com system also tracks students by maintaining a transcript that includes completion dates of assignments and performances on quizzes. To further motivate users to continue progressing, the site makes enrollment public to other students through a class roster and discussion area, as well as by sending preprogrammed emails that prompt users to complete their work. All of these microsuasion elements contribute to the overall learning goal of CodeWarriorU.com.[10]

Microsuasion on the Web

Examples of Web sites that use microsuasion are plentiful and sometimes subtle. For example, eBay has created a rating system—what it calls "feedback"—whereby buyers and sellers evaluate each other after a transaction is completed. This system motivates people to be honest, responsive, and courteous in their interactions. Similarly, the survival of epinions.com, a site that "helps people make informed buying decisions,"[11] hinges on persuading people to share their opinions online. To encourage this, epinions hands out highly visible titles of status ("Top Reviewer" and "Editor") when people contribute many reviews that are valued by readers. Classmates.com uses the lure of curiosity—finding out more about high school classmates—to persuade browsers to register their personal information at the site. Once registered, users have access to the information about others in their class who have registered. In their overall macrosuasive goal of motivating people to quit smoking, Quitnet.com uses public commitment (announcing your quit date) as a microsuasion strategy. All of these techniques involve persuasion on a micro level.

Microsuasion in Video Games

Video games are exceptionally rich in microsuasion elements. The overall goal of most games is to provide entertainment, not to persuade. But during the entertainment experience, players are bombarded with microsuasion elements, sometimes continuously, designed to persuade them to keep playing.

WarCraft III is a real-time strategy (RTS) game that uses microsuasion elements to make the game compelling (if not addictive for some). Throughout the game, as players kill enemies, the player hears a dying sound, an audio reinforcement for succeeding. If players kill monsters, who are neither friend nor foe in this game, the dying monsters drop gold or other items of value that the player can use later as resources. The prospect of gaining new powers also serves as microsuasion. Specifically, if a "hero" belonging to one of the players progresses to the next level, the player can select a new power for that individual, such as the ability to heal others. And of course, players are motivated by the challenge of getting themselves ranked on the high score list.

As the previous discussion suggests, designers of products such as Baby Think It Over must understand macrosuasion techniques to succeed in their overall goal of persuasion. But even designers of products such as productivity software—products that do not have persuasion as their primary goal—must understand how persuasion techniques can be used at the micro level in order to make their products more effective and successful.

Captology: Summary of Key Terms and Concepts

1. For purposes of captology, persuasion is defined as an *attempt to change attitudes or behaviors or both* (without using coercion or deception).

2. Captology focuses on attitude or behavior change resulting from *human-computer interaction* (HCI), not from *computer-mediated communication* (CMC).

3. Captology focuses on *planned* persuasive effects of technology, not on side effects of technology use.

4. Captology focuses on the *endogenous,* or "built-in," persuasive intent of interactive technology, not on *exogenous* persuasive intent (i.e., intent from the user or another outside source).

5. Captology recognizes that technology can persuade on two levels, macro and micro.

Notes and References

For updates on the topics presented in this chapter, visit *www.persuasivetech.info.*

1. Persuasion scholars don't agree on a single definition of persuasion. For example, Reardon defines persuasion as "the activity of attempting to change the behavior of at least one person through symbolic interaction" (Reardon 1991, p. 3). Other scholars (including myself) view persuasion more broadly. For example, see D. Forsythe, *Our Social World,* (New York: Brooks/Cole, 1995). Also, in their definition of persuasion, Zimbardo and Leippe (1991) extend persuasion to encompass changing a person's "behaviors, feelings, or thoughts about an issue, object, or action" (p. 2). Other scholars expand persuasion beyond the idea of "changing"; persuasion includes shaping and reinforcing (Stiff 1994).

If you are interested in investigating the definition of persuasion further, these sources are a good starting point:

a. K. K. Reardon, *Persuasion in Practice* (Newbury Park, CA: Sage, 1991).

b. P. G. Zimbardo and M. Leippe, *Psychology of Attitude change and Social Influence* (New York: McGraw-Hill, 1991).

c. J. B. Stiff, *Persuasive Communication* (New York: Guilford, 1994).

2. The line between persuasion and coercion can be a fine one. Consider dialog boxes that won't go away until you've answered the questions they pose; sites that require you to provide personal information before you can view their "free" content; and ads that pop up right over the part of the page you are trying to read. These and other "persuasive" techniques may be viewed as subtly coercive and may have a cumulatively negative effect on users.

3. C. Castelfranchi, Artificial liars: Why computers will (necessarily) deceive us and each other, *Ethics and Information Technology*, 2:113–119 (2000).

4. For example, both Reardon (1991) and Zimbardo and Leippe (1991) discuss distinctions in persuasion, coercion, and deception. See

a. K. K. Reardon, *Persuasion in Practice* (Newbury Park: Sage, 1991).

b. P. G. Zimbardo and M. Leippe, *Psychology of Attitude change and Social Influence* (New York: McGraw-Hill, 1991).

5. T. J. M. Bench Capon and A. M. McEnery, People interact through computers, not with them, *Interacting with Computers*, 1(1): 48–52 (1989).

6. Computer-mediated communication (CMC) is a large area, so it's difficult to single out one article or person to represent the work in this domain. For a broad picture of CMC, visit John December's online resource about computer-mediated communication at *http://www.december.com/cmc/info/* (note: this is a for-profit effort). His site gives pointers to more specific areas in CMC, such as conferences, journals, and organizations.

7. Stanford professor Donald Roberts was the first to help me clearly see the distinction between effects and effectiveness, including the key role intention plays in interpreting outcomes. I use different terms in my writing (planned effects versus side effects), but the concept is the same. Don Roberts and Nathan Maccoby address the issue of intended and unintended outcomes in the following:

D. F. Roberts and N. Maccoby, Effects of mass communication, in G. Lindzey and E. Aronson (eds.), *The Handbook of Social Psychology*, 3rd ed., vol. II (New York: Random House, 1985), pp. 539–598.

8. A 1999 study by Nielsen Media Research documents that kids are watching less TV and proposes that one factor is competition from video games. For a brief summary of this research, see *http://www.ncpa.org/pd/social/pd120299h.html*.

A longer article, drawing on various studies, that talks about the decline in kids' TV watching and suggests that computer games are a factor, is Lauren Rublin's "Tuning Out," published in *Barron's* on November 8, 1999.

9. Many common interaction patterns found in human-human interactions can be applied to HCI. For example, the "door in the face" technique involves asking a big favor to which a person is likely to say no, then exploiting the guilt the person feels in order to persuade him or her to do a smaller favor.

10. One could argue that the real purpose of CodeWarriorU.com is not to help students to learn but to sell them books and software for each course. Even so, my main point still applies: the microsuasion elements I outline contribute to a larger overall goal.

11. This quote about the purpose of epinions comes from *http://www.epinions.com/about/.*

chapter 2

The Functional Triad
Computers in Persuasive Roles

Based on my experience in teaching and speaking about captology, I've learned that the quickest way to help people grasp the subject is to introduce what I call the "functional triad." This is a conceptual framework that illustrates the different roles that computing technology can play.

The functional triad overarches the various perspectives and theories on persuasion that have been developed since the days of Aristotle (see sidebar on page 24), while highlighting the potential of computing products to persuade and motivate. Having this framework makes it easier to design or study computers as persuasive technologies.

This brief chapter will provide an overview of the three key elements in the functional triad. The next three chapters will examine each element in more detail.

The Functional Triad: Roles Computers Play

The functional triad is a framework for thinking about the roles that computing products play, from the perspective of the user. In its simplest form, the functional triad shows that interactive technologies can operate in three basic ways: as tools, as media, and as social actors (Figure 2.1). These three functions capture how people use or respond to virtually any computing product, from simple products like a portable electronic pedometer to sophisticated products

A Brief History of Persuasion Studies

The study of persuasion has a long history. In classical Greece, Aristotle was the leading thinker on the topic of *rhetoric—the art of determining how to persuade in any given situation.*[1] In Aristotle's day, rhetoricians were mainly concerned with giving public speeches that influenced their listeners. As part of their education, privileged Greek males studied how to use public speaking skills to change people's moods, influence their opinions, or motivate them to action. The Greeks felt the art of speaking persuasively was key to maintaining a healthy democracy.

Today the formal study of persuasion continues to be advanced, primarily through research in social psychology, which began during the early part of the 1900s. Inspired largely by the U.S. government's need to persuade citizens to support war efforts, social psychologists established ambitious research programs to determine what caused people to change their attitudes and behaviors.[2] Later, marketers and advertisers built on the insights gleaned from social psychology, systematically investigating how influence works and often applying their findings to help corporations prosper.

Despite the work of classical philosophers, modern psychologists, and contemporary marketers, there is no single definition of persuasion. Many theories and perspectives have come from the fields of rhetoric, psychology, marketing, and others.[3] All of these approaches contribute to our understanding of persuasion, but each has limitations. No single set of principles fully explains what motivates people and what causes them to adopt certain attitudes or to behave in certain ways.

such as TurboTax for the Web. Most computing products are a mix of these three functions, blending tool with social actor, or medium with tool, and so on.

Computers as Tools

One basic function of computers is to serve as tools. This is the first corner of the functional triad. In their role as tools, the goal of computing products is to make activities easier or more efficient to do (for example, math calculations or text manipulation), or to do things that would be virtually impossible without

Tool
Increases capability

A tool can be persuasive by

- Making target behavior easier to do
- Leading people through a process
- Performing calculations or measurements that motivate

Medium
Provides experience

Social actor
Creates relationship

A social actor can be persuasive by

- Rewarding people with positive feedback
- Modeling a target behavior or attitude
- Providing social support

A medium can be persuasive by

- Allowing people to explore cause-and-effect relationships
- Providing people with vicarious experiences that motivate
- Helping people rehearse a behavior

Figure 2.1   Computing technologies persuade in different ways, depending on their functional roles.

technology (such as tracking the location of a package you've sent or comparing a partial fingerprint with the thousands of criminal fingerprints on file).

When acting as tools, computers can influence and motivate people in specific ways. I'll return to this topic after explaining the next two corners of the functional triad.

Computers as Media

Computers also function as media—a role that has grown in recent years as processing power has increased and networking has become common. There are two categories of computers as media: symbolic and sensory. Computers function as symbolic media when they use symbols to convey information (for example, text, graphics, charts, and icons). They function as sensory media when they provide sensory information—audio, video, and (rarely) even smell[4] and touch sensations.[5] Virtual reality and virtual environments fit into this category, as do a range of other computer simulations.

While both symbolic and sensory media can influence people, captology focuses primarily on computers functioning as sensory media—especially, as computer simulations—because in this role, computers have unique capabilities to provide interactive experiences that motivate and persuade. (In truth, the symbolic and the sensory are often intertwined in computer systems, making it difficult to draw a clear line between the two categories.)

Computers as Social Actors

The third corner of the functional triad depicts the role that computers play as *social actors* or living entities. When people use an interactive technology, they often respond to it as though it were a living being. Digital pets, such as Tamagotchis, a fad product of the mid-1990s, are a well-known example of this phenomenon. In some respects, Tamagotchi owners interacted with these digital life forms as though they actually were alive.

The popularity of Tamagotchis made it evident that people can respond to computing technologies as though they were living creatures. But there is plenty of other evidence that people respond to computers as social actors. You hear it in the language of computer users. Computers are put to "sleep," they "wake up," and sometimes they "die." And people get emotionally involved with computer products. You've probably seen people get angry or swear at the computer when it doesn't deliver as expected, or offer thanks when the computer comes through in a pinch.

The evidence goes beyond these little quirks in our language and emotions. In the 1990s, my colleagues and I performed controlled lab studies at Stanford University showing that people do indeed respond socially to computer technology.[6] In a series of experiments, we brought students into the lab and had them interact with computers on a specific task. Sometimes the computers gave advice for completing a part of the task, sometimes the computers praised people for doing work, and other times the computers needed favors and asked for compliance.

In all cases, the computers used simple dialogue boxes and never referred to themselves as "I" or as a living entity. Nevertheless, the students who participated in these experiments responded to the computers much like they would respond to another human being. Among other things, they treated their computers as teammates, they were motivated by praise from the computers, and they repaid favors the computers did for them. (I'll present more details about these studies in Chapter 5.)

I should note that the participants in these experiments were computer savvy. In fact, a few of the studies included only graduate students in engineering, who know very well that computing devices are not living entities. Yet even these engineers responded in ways that indicated they were using the norms found in interactions between humans as they interacted with the computers. In summary, whether they mean to or not, people often treat computing products as though they were alive in some way.

Applying the Functional Triad to Captology

Understanding the functional triad is essential to leveraging or analyzing the persuasive power of computers. Persuasion strategies will differ depending on whether a computing technology is functioning as a tool, a medium, or a social actor. Each corner of the functional triad comes with its own set of persuasion techniques, which will be explored in the next three chapters.

In functioning as tools, computers can influence people in a number of ways. For example, they can make a target behavior easier to perform, lead users through a process, or perform calculations or measurements that motivate. These and other approaches will be explored in Chapter 3.

When functioning as sensory media, computing technology can persuade people by providing compelling experiences through simulations. These computer simulations persuade by enabling people to explore cause-and-effect relationships, by providing vicarious experiences that motivate, or by helping people rehearse a behavior. These persuasive approaches are explored in Chapter 4.

> Persuasion strategies differ depending on the role being played by the computer: tool, medium, or social actor.

Finally, when computing products adopt the role of social actor, they persuade people by applying the same persuasion principles that humans use to influence others; as social actors, computers can persuade people to change their attitudes or behaviors by rewarding them with positive feedback, modeling a target behavior or attitude, or providing social support. Chapter 5 discusses computers as persuasive social actors in more detail.

Research and Design Applications

For those with an interest in researching or designing persuasive technologies, the functional triad provides a framework for sorting out the elements in the overall user experience of a product. For researchers, identifying which elements of the product are acting as a tool, medium, social actor, or some combination of the three roles, makes it easier to understand the nature of the product's persuasive power. In my experience, this simple step often brings clarity to a research or analysis project and provides a basis for further exploration.

The functional triad also can help designers of persuasive technologies. When exploring ideas for a new product, designers can ask themselves how the product might persuade as a tool, medium, social actor, or through a combination of roles. Answering these questions in depth should produce many ideas about design options for Web sites, desktop applications, or mobile devices.

As an example, consider the task of designing a Web site to motivate people to get more physically fit. This online system could act as a persuasive tool, medium, social actor, or some combination of the three. As a designer steps through the three corners of the functional triad, different strategies for motivation and influence will become apparent.

As a tool, the system could lead a person through a step-by-step process of identifying personal barriers to eating better and exercising regularly. It could then take into account the person's preferences, family situation, and work constraints in suggesting realistic ways to overcome those barriers to better health. Furthermore, it could track and visually display how well the person is progressing toward fitness goals.

As a medium, the system could allow the person to rehearse in a virtual context healthier eating behaviors, such as choosing to eat only half of what's served while dining out and packaging up the other half to go before starting to eat. Also functioning as a medium, the system could allow the person to experiment with different diet and exercise routines to view the probable effect they would have on losing weight and increasing cardiovascular fitness over weeks and months, making more apparent key cause-and-effect relationships related to health.

Finally, as a social actor, the online system could be designed to take on the role of a knowledgeable and supportive health counselor. In this role, the system could use language to instruct, encourage, and praise users as they progress in their efforts to become healthier.

As this example suggests, the functional triad has practical applications for designers of persuasive technology products and for those who want to understand how computers can persuade. In the next three chapters, each corner of the functional triad will be explored in depth.

Notes and References

For updates on the topics presented in this chapter, visit *www.persuasivetech.info*.

1. Specifically, in Book 1, Chapter 2, of Aristotle's *Rhetoric*, rhetoric is defined as "the faculty of observing in any given case the available means of persuasion."

2. For an accounting of persuasion studies to support war efforts, see C. I. Hovland, I. L. Janis, and H. H. Kelley, *Communication and Persuasion* (New Haven, CT: Yale University Press, 1953). For more on the history of modern persuasion research, see W. J. McGuire, Attitudes and attitude change, in G. Lindzey and E. Aronson (eds.), *The Handbook of Social Psychology* (New York: Random House, 1985), vol. 2, pp. 238–241.

3. M. E. Ford, *Motivating Humans: Goals, Emotions, Personal Agency Beliefs* (Newbury Park, CA: Sage, 1992).

4. After the demise of the much-celebrated Digiscents, two companies are now vying to be the market leader in digital scent technologies: Savannah, Georgia–based Trisenx (see *www.trisenx.com*) and Plano, Texas–based AromaJet (see *www.aromajet.com*).

5. One company that is innovating computer systems that leverage the sense of touch is Immersion Corporation in San Jose, California (see *www.Immersion.com*).

6. To read about multiple experiments supporting the idea that people respond socially to computers, see the following:

    a. B. Reeves and C. Nass, *The Media Equation: How People Treat Computers, Television, and New Media Like Real People and Places* (New York: Cambridge University Press, 1996).

    b. B. J. Fogg, *Charismatic Computers: Creating More Likable and Persuasive Interactive Technologies by Leveraging Principles from Social Psychology*, doctoral dissertation, Stanford University, 1997.

chapter 3

Computers as Persuasive Tools

Three months out of college and into a job that required him to sit at a desk most of the day, Jeff realized he was gaining weight. He resolved to start an exercise program.

A friend suggested that Jeff buy a heart rate monitor, a wrist-worn computer that looks like a watch and receives heart rate signals from a chest strap. The system would make it easier for him to track his heart rate and stay within his target zone while exercising.

Jeff had never paid much attention to his heartbeat before, but this device made it easy. He wore the device while working out at the corporate gym. He also wore it during the day and sometimes even to bed. That way, he could have the system store readings at periodic intervals while he slept. Jeff figured his resting heart rate while sleeping would be a good indicator of how much progress he was making in getting aerobically fit.

From the beginning of modern computing,[1] computers were created to be tools that had two basic functions: storing data and performing calculations. The early view of computers was a narrow one. In 1943, Thomas Watson, then chairman of IBM, infamously projected that "there is a world market for maybe five computers."[2] The idea of a *personal* computer probably seemed outlandish, if anyone thought of it at all.

Figure 3.1

Computers as persuasive tools.

Tool
Increases capability

A tool can be persuasive by
- Making target behavior easier to do
- Leading people through a process
- Performing calculations or measurements that motivate

Social actor

Medium

Computers as tools have come a long way in just over 50 years, as the opening anecdote illustrates. They perform so many functions, from word processing to bookkeeping to health monitoring, that many of us would feel lost without them. In the future, it will become increasingly clear that computers can be used as *persuasive* tools, designed to change attitudes and behaviors—to motivate people to exercise, buy more products, donate to charity, stay in touch with family members, or pursue a new career, to name a few potential applications. This chapter focuses on the use of computers as persuasive tools—the first corner of the functional triad (Figure 3.1).

Seven Types of Persuasive Technology Tools

> A persuasive technology tool is an interactive product designed to change attitudes or behaviors or both by making desired outcomes easier to achieve.

For purposes of captology, I define a persuasive technology tool as an interactive product designed to change attitudes or behaviors or both by making a desired outcome easier to achieve. I have identified seven types of persuasive technology tools:

- Reduction
- Tunneling
- Tailoring
- Suggestion
- Self-monitoring
- Surveillance
- Conditioning

This chapter describes each of the seven types of persuasive technology tools, discusses the principles underlying them, and provides examples of actual or potential uses of each. Each type of tool applies a different strategy to change attitudes or behaviors. Although I list the seven types as separate categories, in reality a persuasive technology product usually incorporates two or more tool types to achieve a desired outcome.

Reduction Technology: Persuading through Simplifying

When a long-distance phone company tries to persuade you to change your carrier, it doesn't make you fill out forms, cancel your previous service, or sign any documents. You simply give your approval over the phone, and the new company takes care of the details. This is an example of a reduction strategy—making a complex task simpler.

I once used a reduction strategy to persuade my family to write letters to me when I moved to Europe. Before leaving, I presented a gift to each of my family members: a set of stamped envelopes with my new address already written on them—a primitive reduction technology. I hoped that reducing the number of steps required to drop me a note would persuade my family to write to me regularly. It worked.

Principle of Reduction

> Using computing technology to reduce complex behavior to simple tasks increases the benefit/cost ratio of the behavior and influences users to perform the behavior.

Reduction technologies make target behaviors easier by reducing a complex activity to a few simple steps (or ideally, to a single step). If you purchase products on Amazon.com, you can sign up for "one-click" shopping. With one click of a mouse, the items you purchase are billed automatically to your credit card, packed up, and shipped off. The reduction strategy behind "one-click" shopping is effective in motivating users to buy things.[3]

Psychological and economic theories suggest that humans seek to minimize costs and maximize gains.[4] The theory behind reduction technologies is that making a behavior easier to perform increases the benefit/cost ratio of the behavior. Increasing the perceived benefit/cost ratio increases a person's motivation to engage in the behavior more frequently.[5]

In the process of simplifying a behavior or activity, reduction technologies also may increase a person's self-efficacy, or the person's belief in his or her ability to perform a specific behavior. This, in turn, can help the person to develop a more positive attitude about the behavior, try harder to adopt the behavior, and perform it more frequently.[6]

Simplifying Political Input

At capitoladvantage.com, we can find a more detailed example of a reduction strategy. Suppose you wanted to increase grassroots participation in policy making, how news gets written, and the political process in general. That's what the people behind capitoladvantage.com wanted. So they created an online system that makes it simpler for people in the United States to share their views with their elected leaders. The leading product in "cyberadvocacy," the "CapWiz" system takes the complexity out of sharing your views (Figure 3.2).

The goal of CapWiz is "to empower, activate, educate, and mobilize constituencies to influence policymakers and the media to achieve public affairs objectives"[7]—in other words, to get ordinary citizens involved in public affairs. And apparently, this approach is working. On any given day (at the time of this writing), the system sends out between 20,000 and 45,000 constituent messages.[8]

You don't have to search for a name, address, paper, or stamps. You simply go to a site using the CapWiz system (at the time of this writing these included AOL, Yahoo!, MSN, and USA Today, among others) and enter your zip code. "Write all your elected officials with just one click," the Capitol Advantage site tells users.

When I wrote my representatives, I found it takes more than one click, but the CapWiz system has reduced the complexity significantly. To further reduce complexity (perhaps too much), organizations can use CapWiz to provide a template letter for their members to send to government officials.

Tunneling Technology: Guided Persuasion

Another way that computers act as persuasive tools is by leading users through a predetermined sequence of actions or events, step by step. I refer to this strategy as "tunneling." Using a tunneling technology is like riding a roller coaster at an amusement park: once you board the ride, you are committed to experiencing every twist and turn along the way.

When you enter a tunnel, you give up a certain level of self-determination. By entering the tunnel, you are exposed to information and activities you may not have seen or engaged in otherwise. Both of these provide opportunities for persuasion.

People often put themselves into tunnel situations voluntarily to change their attitudes or behaviors. They may hire personal trainers who direct them

Figure 3.2

CapWiz simplifies the process of writing to elected officials.

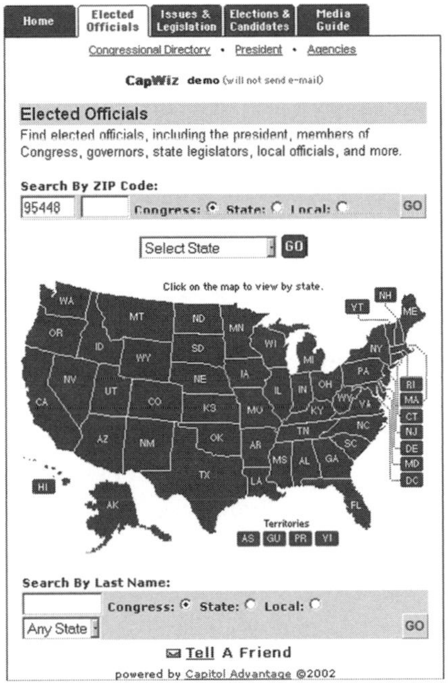

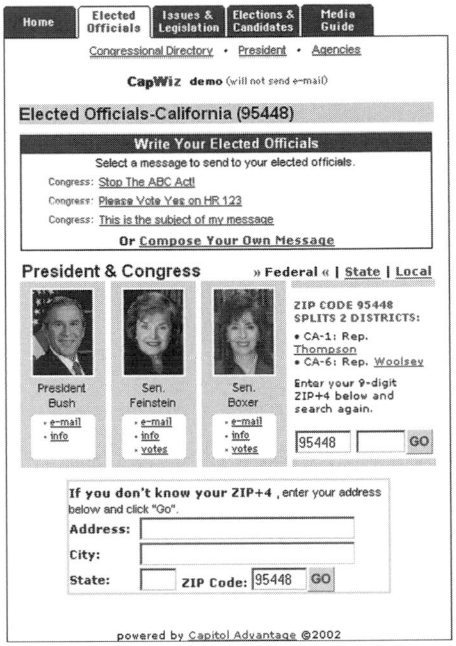

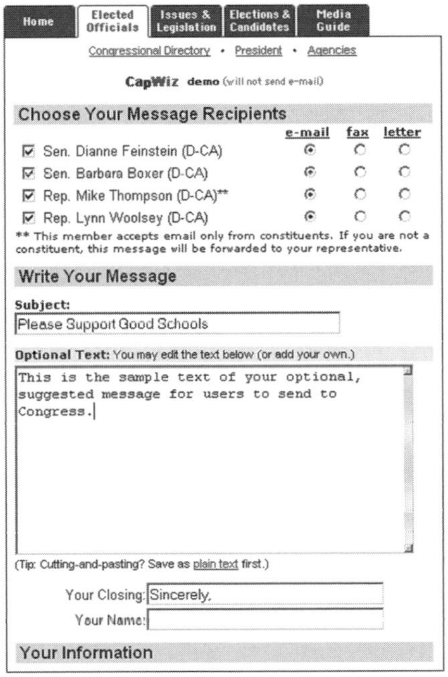

through workouts, sign up for spiritual retreats that control their daily schedules, or even check themselves into drug rehab clinics.

Tunneling technologies can be quite effective. For users, tunneling makes it easier to go through a process. For designers, tunneling controls what the user experiences—the content, possible pathways, and the nature of the activities. In essence, the user becomes a captive audience. If users wish to remain in the tunnel, they must accept, or at least confront, the assumptions, values, and logic of the controlled environment.

Finally, tunneling technologies are effective because people value consistency. Once they commit to an idea or a process, most people tend to stick with it, even in the face of contrary evidence.[9] This is particularly true in the case of tunnel situations that people have freely chosen.

Software installation provides a good example of tunneling technology. For the most part, installing software today is simple; the computer takes you through the process, step by step. At a few points in the installation tunnel, you can choose which aspects of the application to install and where, but you are still in the tunnel.

This is where the potential to persuade comes in. To persuade you that the application is a great product with many features you'll appreciate, an installation program may give you a promotional tour while the software is being copied onto your hard drive. The tour may congratulate you for making a smart choice, point out how the software will help you, and show people happily using the features. It may even advertise other company products. Because you're in the installation tunnel, you are a captive audience, seeing information you would not have seen otherwise.

Registration on Web sites is another form of tunneling. To gain access to many sites' services or content, users must go through a registration process.

Principle of Tunneling

> Using computing technology to guide users through a process or experience provides opportunities to persuade along the way.

During the registration process at eDiets.com, currently the leading diet Web site, the Web page gathers information about you while making offers about premium services or other products. After the program asks questions about your attitude toward weight loss ("I find I often eat in response to tension and stress"—strongly agree, agree, slightly agree, and so on), it then offers you an audiotape program designed "to create the mental changes needed for success."[10] The point is that through the tunneling process the eDiets system leads users through a step-by-step process that enables them to identify weaknesses in resolve, creating a need that is immediately filled by the audiotape offer.

Ethical Concerns

Tunneling can be an ethical and useful persuasion strategy. A retirement software program could lead users through the various steps of analyzing their financial situation, setting financial goals, and taking action to meet these goals. A health site could lead users through a series of questions designed to identify poor health habits and take steps to improve them.

On the other hand, tunneling can include negative or even unethical elements. Back to our software installation example: Many software programs include product registration as part of the installation procedure. At some point the program asks you to enter your personal information—your name, company, and other contact information. Often, it seems there is no easy way to avoid giving away your personal information and still successfully complete the software installation. Depending on the nature and scope of the personal information demanded to complete the installation, some programs might be considered unethical since they essentially put you into a corner where you have little choice: either give up the personal information or risk a faulty installation. (One unintended consequence is that some users who want to maintain their privacy simply give false information.)

In the worst-case scenarios, tunneling technologies may border on coercion, depending on how they are designed. To avoid coercion, designers of tunneling technology must make clear to users how they can exit the tunnel at any time without causing any damage to their system.

Tailoring Technology: Persuasion through Customization

A tailoring technology is a *computing product that provides information relevant to individuals to change their attitudes or behaviors or both.* Tailoring technologies make life simpler for computer users who don't want to wade through volumes of generic information to find what's relevant to them.

Psychology research has shown that tailored information is more effective than generic information in changing attitudes and behaviors.[11] Much of the research has taken place in the area of health interventions, in which information has been tailored to match people's education level, type and stage of disease, attitude toward the disease, and other factors.

Tailoring technology can be embedded in a variety of persuasive technology products. One example: A word processing application might suggest that you increase your working vocabulary by learning a word each day (the program has noticed that you use a relatively small set of words). You might be more motivated to follow up on this suggestion if the application provided tailored information showing the limited range of your working vocabulary, as well as a comparison chart that shows that you are well below the vocabulary level of others in your profession.

The Web offers some good examples of tailoring information to individuals to achieve a persuasive result. Consider Chemical Scorecard (Figure 3.3) found at scorecard.org. Created by Environmental Defense (formerly known as the Environmental Defense Fund), this site encourages users to take action against polluting organizations and makes it easy to contact policy makers to express concerns.[12]

When users enter their zip code, the site lists names of the polluting institutions in their area, gives data on chemicals being released, and outlines the possible health consequences. The technology can also generate a map that enables you to see the location of pollution sources relative to where you live, work, or attend school.

This tailored information can be compelling. The report I generated for my area of Silicon Valley identified hazards I didn't know about, and it identified the companies that were the major offenders. To my surprise, the polluters included a few companies with stellar reputations, including one of my former employers.

Principle of Tailoring

> Information provided by computing technology will be more persuasive if it is tailored to the individual's needs, interests, personality, usage context, or other factors relevant to the individual.

I also learned from Chemical Scorecard that exercising in the neighborhood of my YMCA may not be a good idea. A company located next to my running path emits almost 10,000 pounds of dichlorolfluoroethane each year; this chemical is a suspected cardiovascular toxicant. Such tailored information can influence people to change attitudes and behavior. It certainly changed mine; after consulting the site, I began to run on a treadmill inside the gym, rather than outside.

Many sites provide tailored information for commercial purposes. More and more e-commerce Web sites are suggesting additional items for consumers to buy, based on information gathered in previous visits. This form of tailoring can be effective. Not only can a site recommend more products to buy when the customer revisits the site, if the customer opts in, it can email discount coupons, offer newsletters to keep customers informed of new products and promotions, or use other online techniques to persuade customers to do more business with the site.

Figure 3.3

The Web site *www. scorecard.org* provides tailored information in order to persuade visitors to take action against polluters.

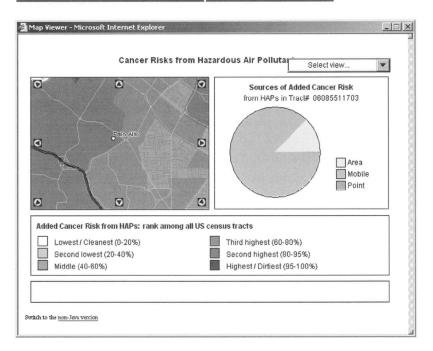

Ethical Concerns

It's not surprising that tailored information is more effective. But what may be surprising is that the mere *perception* that information has been tailored is likely to make a difference, according to some scholars.[13] In other words, information doesn't have to *be* personally relevant; it just has to *appear* that way.

Why does this work? When people believe messages are tailored for them, they pay more attention.[14] They will then process the information more deeply, and—if the information stands up to scrutiny—they will be more likely to be persuaded.[15]

Unfortunately, the fact that people are more likely to be persuaded if they simply perceive that information has been tailored for them enables designers to apply tailoring techniques in unethical ways. Suppose an interactive financial planning product gathers information about the user, then recommends that he invest mostly in tax-free bonds. The research on tailoring suggests the user will consider this path seriously. In reality, the advice engine may give everyone the same information—or, even worse, it may advise potential investors according to what would provide the greatest profit to the company behind the service. But the appearance of taking the user's special needs into account will make the advice more compelling.

Tailoring Information for Context

Chemical Scorecard tailors information to individuals, but it does not tailor information for *context*. That's the next big step for this and other tailoring technologies. In the case of Chemical Scorecard, tailoring information for context would mean taking the information from the system's databases and providing it to people during the normal routines of life.

Imagine a young couple shopping for a home. A tailoring technology in their car could inform them about the environmental status of the neighborhoods they are considering. Or a portable tailoring technology could inform me about toxic chemicals anywhere I jog.

Conceptually, it's easy to make the leap from personalized information to contextualized information. But from a technology and practical standpoint, there's a long way to go to make this a reality. To deliver contextualized information, the technology would have to not only locate you but also determine, among other things, whether you are alone or with others, what task you were performing, whether you are in a rush or at leisure, and what kind of mood you are in. All of these are important elements in determining an effective persuasion strategy. Then there are practical and social issues such as who will pay for the required technology and how privacy will be maintained. As such hurdles are overcome, tailoring technologies will have a greater impact on attitudes and behavior.

Suggestion Technology: Intervening at the Right Time

One soggy winter day, 15 students stood on the edge of a bridge that spans Highway 101 in Palo Alto, California. Each student held a poster painted with a bold orange letter. Lined up in order, the letters spelled out a simple but provocative message for the Silicon Valley drivers below: "W-H-Y N-O-T C-A-R-P-O-O-L-?" The automobiles below were moving at a snail's pace, bumper to bumper. However, one lane was nearly empty: the carpool lane. It's hard to imagine a driver trapped in the rush hour crawl who didn't—at least for a moment—reconsider his or her commute strategy. "Yeah, why not carpool? I could be home by now."

Principle of Suggestion

A computing technology will have greater persuasive power if it offers suggestions at opportune moments.

This anecdote illustrates the potential impact of making a suggestion at the most appropriate time. That's the principle behind another type of persuasive tool that I call "suggestion technology," which I define as *an interactive computing product that suggests a behavior at the most opportune moment.* To be viable, a suggestion technology must first cause you to think, "Should I take the course suggested here, or should I continue along my current path?"

The dynamics underlying suggestion technology date back at least 2,000 years, to a principle of persuasion called *kairos.* Discussed by ancient Greek rhetoricians, kairos means finding the opportune moment to present your message.[16] (In Greek mythology Kairos was the youngest son of Zeus and the "god of the favorable moment."[17])

Suggestion technologies often build on people's existing motivations—to be financially stable, to be healthy, to be admired by others. The suggestion technology simply serves to cue a relevant behavior, essentially saying, "Now would be a good time to do X"—to get out of growth stocks and into government bonds, to change the air filter in your home's heating system, to send a card to a friend you haven't seen in a while, to call a customer to see if she needs more of your product. For the technology to be successful, the suggested action must be compelling and timely enough that you implement it.

One familiar example of a suggestion technology is the Speed Monitoring Awareness and Radar Trailer (SMART),[18] a portable trailer (Figure 3.4) that can be placed at the side of the road to monitor the speed of oncoming vehicles. If you've seen SMART before, you've likely seen it in school zones and neighborhoods where drivers tend to exceed the posted speed limit.

As a driver approaches the trailer, SMART senses how fast the car is traveling, as far away as about 90 yards. It then displays the car's speed on a large output device, big enough that the driver can read it from afar. In most versions of this device, the trailer also shows the speed limit for the street, allowing drivers to compare their actual speed with the posted limit.

The goal of SMART is to suggest that drivers reevaluate their driving behavior. It creates a decision point about driving speed at the right time—when people are driving too fast.

SMART doesn't make an explicit suggestion; the suggested behavior is implicit: drive within the posted speed limit. The motivation to act on the suggestion comes from within the driver—either a fear of getting a speeding ticket or a sense of duty to drive safely.

Timing Is Critical

Timing is critical for a suggestion technology to be effective. The technology must identify the right time to make the suggestion. But what is the "right" time?

Although classical rhetoricians emphasized the importance of kairos in persuasion, they did not leave behind practical guidelines on how to recognize or create moments that would be most opportune. However, psychologists have identified some characteristics that define opportune moments of persuasion: When people are in a good mood, they are more open to persuasion.[19] When they find their current world view no longer makes sense, people are more open to adopting new attitudes and opinions.[20] In addition, people are more likely to be persuaded to comply with a request when they can take action on it immediately or when they feel indebted because of a favor they've received,[21] a mistake they have made,[22] or a request they recently denied.[23]

These are simple examples of opportune moments. In reality, the timing issues in persuasion are not easily reduced to guidelines. Timing involves many elements in the environment (ranging from the physical setting to the social context) as well as the transient disposition of the person being persuaded (such as mood, feelings of self-worth, and feelings of connectedness to others).

To illustrate the difficulty of creating opportune moments of persuasion, consider a concept that two students in my Stanford lab[24] explored, using Global Positioning System (GPS) technology to identify a person's location. Theoretically, by using GPS you could create a suggestion technology to persuade a person to do something when she is at a specific location.

The students created a prototype of a stuffed bear that McDonald's could give away to children or sell at a low price. Whenever the bear came near a McDonald's, it would begin singing a jingle about French fries—how delicious they are and how much he likes to eat them.

The toy was never implemented, but you can imagine how kids could be cued by the bear's song and then nag the parent driving the car to stop by McDonald's. You could also imagine how the technology might backfire, if the parent is in a hurry, in a bad mood, or doesn't have the money to spend on fast food. The point is, while the geography may be opportune for persuasion, the technology doesn't have the ability to identify other aspects of an opportune moment: the parent's state of mind, financial situation, whether the family has already eaten, and other variables. (In this example, there also are obvious ethical concerns related to manipulating children—a topic I'll explore in Chapter 9.)

Suggestion technology can be used for macrosuasion, as in the case of SMART, whose purpose is to promote safe driving. It also can be used for microsuasion—persuasion that's part of a larger interactive system. A personal finance application may suggest that you pay your utility bill today, a software management system could suggest that you back up your data soon, or an electronic reminder service may suggest that you buy and ship your mother's birthday gift early next week. The key to the success of such technology applications is creating a decision point at or near the time when it's appropriate to take action.

Self-Monitoring Technology: Taking the Tedium Out of Tracking

The next type of persuasive technology tool is self-monitoring technology. This type of tool *allows people to monitor themselves to modify their attitudes or behaviors to achieve a predetermined goal or outcome.* Ideally, self-monitoring technologies work in real time, giving users ongoing data about their physical state (or inferences about their mental state, based on physical feedback), their location, or their progress on a task. The goal is to eliminate the tedium of measuring and tracking performance or status. This makes it easier for people to know how well they are performing the target behavior, increasing the likelihood that they will continue to produce the behavior.[25]

In addition, self-monitoring technologies feed the natural human drive for self-understanding.[26] Like personality inventories or aptitude tests, self-monitoring technologies can help people learn about themselves. For this reason, using self-monitoring technologies may be intrinsically motivating.[27]

Heart rate monitors (Figure 3.5) are a good example of a self-monitoring technology designed to change behavior. Often worn directly on the body, these devices monitor a person's heart rate during exercise. By using these wearable computers, users can track their heart rate accurately and easily.

Heart rate monitors help people modify their physical behavior so their heart rate stays within a predetermined zone. The more advanced devices make it easier to stay within your desired zone by sounding an audio signal when your heart beats too fast or too slow, so you know whether to decrease or increase your level of exertion.

Figure 3.5

Heart rate monitors allow people to modify their exercise levels to achieve a target heart rate.

Figure 3.6

The HealthyJump product tracks calories burned while jumping rope.

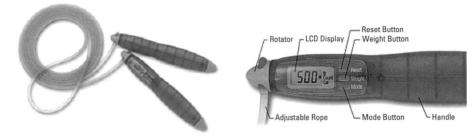

Heart rate monitors not only help people modify their behaviors, they also change attitudes in two ways. First, because the technology makes it easy to track your heart rate, you no longer need to focus on how far you've jogged or how fast you're going; you simply monitor your heart rate, which is the best indicator of an effective workout. Using a heart rate monitor shifted my attitude about exercise; I became more concerned about my heart rate than about adhering to a specific exercise regimen. Having a tool like a heart rate monitor can also change a person's general attitude about exercise. Because the device provides information on the person's physiological status, working out can be more interesting and, for some people, more fun.

Sometimes self-monitoring tools can be quite specialized. Tanita Corporation markets a jump rope (Figure 3.6) with a built-in monitor that lets users know how many calories they've burned as well as how many jumps they've completed.[28] Not only does the device make it easier to track a person's level of exercise, but getting concrete feedback from the device likely provides motivation to perform the activity.

Principle of Self-Monitoring

Applying computing technology to eliminate the tedium of tracking performance or status helps people to achieve predetermined goals or outcomes.

Eliminating a Language Quirk

A team of my students[29] created a conceptual design that illustrates how self-monitoring technology could work to change language behavior. They targeted a behavior that they themselves had problems with: using the word "like" too often ("I went to class and it was, like, so crowded" and "I was, like, 'Wow, I can't find a place to sit.'"). The student team knew they and most people in their age group had this language quirk. They were worried about speaking this way in job interviews or on the job: "It's, like, I've almost completed the presentation for tomorrow's client meeting."

In my students' conceptual design, they showed how someone could use next-generation mobile phone systems to self-monitor and eliminate or reduce this language quirk. While their conceptual design included various facets, the essence of the idea is that a word recognition system would listen to them as they talked on the mobile phone. Whenever they used the word "like," the phone would give a signal, making them aware of it. The signal could be a vibration or a faint audio signal that only the speaker could hear. In this way, the speaker could be trained to use the word "like" less frequently.

Surveillance Technology: Persuasion through Observation

While self-monitoring technology enables individuals to learn about themselves, surveillance technology enables them to learn about others. For the purposes of captology, surveillance technology is defined as any computing technology that *allows one party to monitor the behavior of another to modify behavior in a specific way.*[30]

Of all the types of persuasive technology tools in this chapter, surveillance technology is the most common in today's marketplace. There are applications for tracking how employees use the Internet, how teenagers drive, how phone support workers serve customers, and many more.

As early as 1993, one researcher reported that 26 million American workers were monitored through their computers.[31] Another figure from 1998 showed that two-thirds of major U.S. companies electronically monitor their work-

Principle of Surveillance

Applying computing technology to observe others' behavior increases the likelihood of achieving a desired outcome.

ers.[32] And in 2001, a survey released by the American Management Association reported that over 77% of major U.S. firms used some form of high-tech workplace surveillance, a number that they say had doubled since 1997.[33] One reason that surveillance technology is so common is that it works: Surveillance has long been an active research topic in the field of social psychology, and the overwhelming conclusion is that observation has powerful effects on how people behave. When people know they're being watched, they behave differently. According to the research, if others can observe a person's actions and can reward or punish the person for them, the person is likely to make his actions meet the observer's expectations.[34]

Figure 3.7

Hygiene Guard is a surveillance system that tracks employee hand washing.

Hygiene Guard[35] is one example of a surveillance technology. The system (Figure 3.7), which monitors hand washing, is installed in employee restrooms to make sure workers follow hygiene rules. The system uses sensor technology located in various places: on the employee's ID badge, in the restroom ceiling, and at the sink. It identifies each employee who enters the restroom. After the employee uses the toilet facilities, it verifies that the employee stands at the sink for 30 seconds. If not, the system records the infraction.

Another example of surveillance technology is AutoWatch, a computer system that enables parents to monitor the driving behavior of their children.[36] (Makers of this system suggest AutoWatch can also let you monitor how employees drive corporate vehicles.) According to company literature, AutoWatch is a "little black box" that records driving speed, starts and stops, and other data. Parents can then remove the device from the vehicle and download the information to a PC.

Surveillance Must Be Overt

At first glance, AutoWatch seems a reasonable idea: Parents should be able to monitor how their children drive. However, the product literature suggests that parents "conceal the AutoWatch unit under the dash or under the seat."[37] AutoWatch is a *covert* technology when installed this way. When used covertly,

AutoWatch is no longer a persuasive technology because its goal is not to motivate or influence; it's just secretly monitoring.

This brings up a key point: For surveillance technologies to effectively change behaviors, they must be *overt,* not covert. Delivery companies sometimes post a message on the back of their trucks: "How am I driving?" with a toll-free number to report problems. The fact that the truck drivers know others can report them for reckless driving probably motivates them to drive more safely.

Contrast this with a covert installation of AutoWatch. How will teens be motivated to avoid driving recklessly if they don't know their driving is being monitored by AutoWatch? When used covertly, AutoWatch is geared toward punishment, not persuasion. There are important ethical questions surrounding the use of covert technologies, but I will not address them here, since covert technologies by definition are not persuasive technologies.

Rewarding through Surveillance

While surveillance technologies may use the threat of punishment to change behavior, they also can be designed to motivate people through the promise of rewards. For example, parents could use the AutoWatch system to reward their teens for driving safely, perhaps providing teens with gas money for future driving.

In terms of workplace surveillance, several companies have created systems that track employee behavior and reward them for doing what their company wants done.[38] (Rather than calling these products "surveillance systems," companies may refer to them as "incentive systems" or "incentive management technology."[39])

An Illinois-based company called Cultureworx has created a product that can track employee behavior throughout the day. And it can reward employees who do things that meet company policies or help boost the bottom line. If a company wants employees in its call centers to use its customer relationship management (CRM) software, inputting customer information and results of each customer contact, the Cultureworx system can track employee performance along these lines. The harshness of tracking employees this way is softened somewhat because the surveillance system gives points that can be exchanged online for products from places like Eddie Bauer and Toys R Us. (However, it's not clear to what extent employees would embrace such a system simply because it offers rewards.)

Public Compliance without Private Acceptance

While surveillance can be effective in changing behavior, in many cases it leads to public compliance without private acceptance. Some theorists describe this as "compliance versus internalization."[40] People will behave in a prescribed way if they know they are being observed, but they will not continue the behavior when they are no longer being observed unless they have their own reasons for doing so.[41] In other words, without motivation to internalize the behavior, the conformity and compliance effects will weaken and often disappear when a person is no longer being observed.

The real power in surveillance technology lies in preventing infractions; surveillance should focus on deterrence, not punishment. Even so, using surveillance as a motivating tool is not the most noble approach to persuasion, even when it leverages the promise of rewards rather than the fear of punishment. The use of surveillance technology also raises serious ethical questions about maintaining the privacy and dignity of individuals. (We'll explore the ethical concerns in more detail in Chapter 9.)

Conditioning Technology: Reinforcing Target Behaviors

The last type of persuasive technology tool is what I call "conditioning technology." A conditioning technology is a *computerized system that uses principles of operant conditioning to change behaviors.*

B. F. Skinner was the leading proponent of operant conditioning,[42] which peaked in popularity four decades ago and now is controversial in some circles. In simple terms, operant conditioning (also called "behaviorism" and "instrumental learning") is a method that uses positive reinforcements—or rewards—to increase the instances of a behavior or to shape complex behaviors.[43] (Operant conditioning also may involve the use of punishments to decrease the instances of a behavior, but this approach is fraught with ethical problems and is not, in my view, an appropriate use of conditioning technology.[44] As a result, I will not discuss it further here.)

If you've ever tried to train a dog to do tricks, you've probably used operant conditioning. By rewarding your dog with praise, petting, or a snack after a successful performance, you've given positive reinforcement. When you praise

Figure 3.8

The Telecycle research prototype, a simple application of operant conditioning.

your child, send a thank-you note to a friend, or give someone a gift, you are subtly shaping their future behavior, whether you intend to or not. Operant conditioning is pervasive among human beings.[45]

Technology Applications of Operant Conditioning

Computers also can use operant conditioning to bring about behavior changes. In my classes at Stanford, my students and I explored various approaches to using high-tech conditioning technology. Two engineering students built a prototype of "Telecycle" (Figure 3.8), an exercise bike connected to a TV through a small computer.[46] In this system, as you pedal at a rate closer to the target speed, the image on the TV becomes clearer. If you slow down too much or stop pedaling, the TV picture becomes fuzzy, almost worthless. The students hypothesized that receiving a clearer picture would be reinforcing and produce the desired behavior change—exerting more effort on the exercise bike.

The Telecycle is a simple example of using reinforcement for a specific target behavior. More complex uses of operant conditioning can be found in many computer games.

Operant Conditioning in Computer Games

While game designers rarely talk about their designs in terms of behaviorism,[47] good game play and effective operant conditioning go hand in hand. From a designer's perspective, one mark of a good computer game is one that players want to keep playing. The bottom line is that game designers seek to change people's behaviors. Ideally, players become obsessed with the game, choosing it above other computer games or above other things they could be doing with their time.

Computer games provide reinforcements through sounds and visuals. The rewards also come in other ways: through points accumulated, progression to the next level, rankings of high scores, and more. Discussed in Chapter 1 as an example of microsuasion, Warcraft III is just one of thousands of computer games using reinforcement to keep players engaged with the game.

Computer games may be the purest example of technology using operant conditioning. They are effective platforms for administering reinforcements and punishments, with a bit of narrative and plot layered over the top.

Applying Periodic Reinforcement

To be most effective, positive reinforcement should immediately follow the performance of the target behavior. However, the reinforcement need not follow *every* performance of the behavior. In fact, to strengthen an existing behavior, reinforcers are most effective when they are unpredictable. Playing slot machines is a good example: Winning a payoff of quarters streaming into a metal tray is a reinforcer, but it is random. This type of unpredictable reward schedule makes the target behavior—in this case, gambling—very compelling, even addictive.

A good example of the use of periodic reinforcement can be found at TreeLoot.com (Figure 3.9). When you visit the site, you'll be asked to click on the image of a tree. After you click, you will get feedback from the system, depending on where you click. Sometimes you'll just get a message to click again. Other times, the system will tell you that you've won "Banana Bucks."

Although the TreeLoot experience is more complicated than what I've just described, the relevant point is that TreeLoot.com behaves much like a slot machine: it offers unpredictable rewards to reinforce a behavior. Some of my students have admitted to spending hours clicking over and over on the tree image in hopes of hitting it big. Like pigeons pecking a lever to get a food pellet, some of my students—and thousands of other people—keep clicking on the TreeLoot image. Operant conditioning is undeniably powerful.

Figure 3.9

TreeLoot.com uses periodic reinforcement to persuade visitors to keep playing at the site.

Shaping Complex Behaviors

As noted earlier, operant conditioning can be used not just to reinforce behavior but to shape complex behaviors. Shaping is a process of reinforcing behaviors that approximate the target behavior. You find this approach in animal training. Through shaping, dolphins can be trained to jump out of the water over a rope. At the beginning of the training, the dolphin receives a reward for swimming over a rope that is resting on the bottom of the tank. Then the rope is moved up a few feet in the water, and the dolphin gets rewarded for swimming over it, not under it. The process continues until the rope is out of the water.

Principle of Conditioning

> Computing technology can use positive reinforcement to shape complex behavior or transform existing behaviors into habits.

Technology could be designed to shape complex behaviors in a similar way. For example, conditioning technology might be used to foster collaboration among employees working in different locations. While there's no clear formula for collaboration, certain activities are likely to indicate collaboration is taking place: email to colleagues, sharing of documents, follow-up phone calls, and scheduling appointments, to name a few examples. It's possible that a computer system could be designed to shape such collaborative behavior by reinforcing the elements of collaboration.

Despite the widespread use of operant conditioning in everyday life, we have yet to see the full potential of using computer-based operant conditioning to affect human behavior (except in making computer games compelling or nearly addictive). My lab is currently researching what technology can do to reinforce behavior; we're studying sounds, images, and other digital experiences to develop an effective reportoire of "digital rewards." But we apply our new knowledge with caution. Like surveillance, this use of technology raises ethical questions, especially since operant conditioning can change our behaviors even when we don't consciously recognize the connection between the target behavior and the reinforcement given.

The Right Persuasive Tool(s) for the Job

The research on intrinsic and extrinsic motivation shows that the gentler the intervention to achieve the desired behavior change, the better the long-term outcome.[48] It's good to keep that research in mind when considering persuasive technology tools. For example, if a suggestion technology can produce the desired behavior, that approach should be used rather than surveillance technology. Not only will the gentler suggestion technology produce better results, it will do so without raising the ethical issues relating to surveillance.

In many cases, effective persuasion requires more than using a single tool or strategy. Some of the examples I've described in this chapter are combinations of persuasive technology tools: The heart rate monitor is a combination of self-monitoring and suggestion technologies; it monitors the heart rate, and it notifies the users when the rate wanders beyond the preset zone. The chemical scorecard at scorecard.org uses tailoring technology to provide targeted information and reduction technology to make it easy to take action—to send e-mail and faxes to government officials and offending companies. It even writes the letter for you, including relevant details.

As these examples illustrate, in many cases effective persuasion requires more than one tool or strategy. Whether you are designing, analyzing, or using persuasive technology, look for these natural synergies as different tool types come together to create a persuasive interactive experience.

Notes and References

For updates on the topics presented in this chapter, visit *www.persuasivetech.info*.

1. In 1946 the ENIAC (Electronic Numerical Integrator and Computer) was introduced. This was the world's first "fully electronic, general-purpose (programmable) digital computer" (*http://www.kurzweilai.net*). For a recent book on the ENIAC, see S. McCartney, *ENIAC: The Triumphs and Tragedies of the World's First Computer* (New York: Berkley Pub Group, 2001).

2. The now-famous 1943 comment by IBM chair Thomas Watson is widely cited.

3. In investigating the effectiveness of Amazon's one-click shopping method, Stacy Perman concluded that the technique does increase sales, although Amazon would not release any data to her. In the August 2000 issue of *Business 2.0* (see *http://www.business2.com/articles/mag/0,1640,6864|6925,00.html*), she writes:

   Amazon.com's patented one-click technology, which allows shoppers to place an order by clicking a single button, is simplicity itself. We asked Amazon what the feature has done for its business—whether it has increased sales, how many books are sold via one-click, and so on—but the company politely declined to give us any information. Here's what we know about one-click: Apart from the fact that everyone we know uses it, Amazon's big rival, Barnesandnoble.com, liked it a lot too and built a similar feature into its site. Amazon felt sufficiently threatened that it asked Barnesandnoble.com to cease and desist. So we're assuming that one-click has been a success for Amazon—but that it would rather keep just how successful it is several clicks away from the rest of us.

4. Various theories in both cognitive science and social psychology account for our natural inclinations to do a cost/benefit assessment. One of the most explicit is expectancy theory (or valence-instrumentality-expectancy theory), which posits that behavior results from expectations about what alternatives will maximize pleasure and minimize pain. A noted work in this domain is

    V. H. Vroom, *Work and Motivation* (New York: John Wiley and Sons, 1964; reprinted Malabar, FL: Krieger Publishing Company, 1982).

    Much of economics hinges on assessments of cost/benefit. For an overview, see J. Taylor, *Economics,* 3rd ed. (New York: Houghton Mifflin Company, 2001).

5. A. Bandura, *Self-Efficacy: The Exercise of Self-Control* (New York: W. H. Freeman, 1997).

6. A. Bandura, *Self-Efficacy: The Exercise of Self-Control* (New York: W. H. Freeman, 1997). For an online article by Bandura on self-efficacy, see *http://www.emory.edu/EDUCATION/ mfp/BanEncy.html.*

7. The stated goal of CapWiz can be found at *http://www.e-advocates.com/aboutus.html.*

8. To see the current volume of messages sent by CapWiz, click on the "current stats" link found at *http://capitoladvantage.com.*

9. S. Plous, *The Psychology of Judgment and Decision Making* (New York: McGraw-Hill, 1993).

10. The text from ediets.com was found at *http://www.ediets.com/dietprofile/dietprofile20.cfm.*

11. For a review of tailoring in the context of computer technology, see H. B. Jimison. Patient-specific interfaces to health and decision-making information, in R. L. Street, W. R. Gold, and T. Manning (eds.), *Health Promotion and Interaction Technology: Theoretical Applications and Future Directions* (Mahwah, NJ: Lawrence Earlbaum, 1997). See also:

    a. V. J. Strecher et al., The effects of computer-tailored smoking cessation message in family practice settings, *J. Fam Prac,* 39: (1994).

    b. C. S. Skinner, J. F. Strecher, and H. Hospers, Physician recommendations for mammogram; do tailored messages make a difference? *AM J Public Health,* 84: 43–49 (1994).

    c. M. K. Campbell et al., The impact of message tailoring on dietary behavior change for disease prevention in primary care settings, *Am J Public Health,* 84: 783–787 (1993).

    d. M. W. Kreuter and V. J. Strecher, Do tailored behavior change messages enhance the effectiveness of health risk appraisal? Results from a randomized trial, *Health Educ. Res.,* 11(1): 97–105 (1996).

    e. James O. Prochaska and John C. Norcross, *Changing for Good* (Avon Books, 1995).

12. See *http://www.scorecard.org.*

13. For example, see J. R. Beninger, Personalization of mass media and the growth of pseudo-community, *Communication Research,* 14(3): 352–371 (1987).

14. S. J. Ball-Rokeach, M. Rokeach, and J. Grube, *The Great American Values Test: Influencing Behavior and Belief through Television* (New York: Free Press, 1984). See also J. R. Beninger, Personalization of mass media and the growth of pseudo-community, *Communication Research*, 14(3): 352–371 (1987).

15. R. E. Petty and J. T. Cacioppo, *Attitude and Persuasion: Classical and Contemporary Approaches* (Dubuque, IA: Wm. C. Brown, 1981).

16. James Kinneavy and Catherine Eskin, Kairos in Aristotle's Rhetoric, *Written Communication*, 11(1): 131–142 (January 1994). See also Stephen P. Witte, Neil Nakadate, and Roger D. Cherry (eds.), *A Rhetoric of Doing: Essays on Written Discourse in Honor of James L. Kinneavy* (Carbondale, IL: Southern Illinois University Press, 1992).

17. For more on kairos, see *http://www.sagepub.co.uk/journals/details/issue/sample/a009710.pdf*.

18. You'll find more information about these trailers at *http://www.kustomsignals.com*.

19. For more details on the effects of moods on persuasion processes, see the following:

   a. Diane M. Mackie and Leila T. Worth, Feeling good, but not thinking straight: The impact of positive mood on persuasion, in J. Forgas (ed.), *Emotion and Social Judgments* (Oxford: Pergamon Press, 1991), 201–219.

   b. Richard E. Petty, Faith Gleicher, and Sara M. Baker, Multiple roles for affect in persuasion, in J. Forgas (ed.), *Emotion and Social Judgments* (Oxford: Pergamon Press, 1991), 181–200.

   c. N. Schwarz, H. Bless, and G. Bohner, Mood and persuasion: Affective states influence the processing of persuasive communications, *Advances in Experimental Social Psychology*, 24: 161–199 (1991).

   d. Joel B. Cohen and Charles S. Areni, Affect and consumer behavior, in T. Robertson and H. Kassarjian (eds.), *Handbook of Consumer Behavior* (Englewood Cliffs, NJ: Prentice Hall, 1991), pp. 188–240.

20. Unless the circumstances are unusual (such as belonging to a doomsday group whose predictions fail) or people feel personally threatened, what psychologists call "disconfirming information" will lead people to experience cognitive dissonance and seek new beliefs and actions that are more consistent. The classic work in this area is L. Festinger, *A Theory of Cognitive Dissonance* (Stanford, CA: Stanford University Press, 1957).

   For a more recent treatment of dissonance and consistency issues in persuasion, see Chapter 5 ("Motivational Approaches") in R. Petty and J. Cacioppo, *Attitudes and Persuasion: Classic and Contemporary Approaches* (Dubuque, IA: Wm. C. Brown Publishers, 1981).

   For studies of how self-worth mediates assimilation of disconfirming information, see Geoffrey L. Cohen, Joshua Aronson, and Claude M. Steele, When beliefs yield to evidence: Reducing biased evaluation by affirming the self, *Personality & Social Psychology Bulletin*, 26(9): 1151–1164 (2000).

21. For more on how the rule of reciprocity works as well as its role in compliance, see the following:

a. A. W. Gouldner, The norm of reciprocity: A preliminary statement, *American Sociological Review*, 25: 161–178 (1960).

b. M. S. Greenberg, A theory of indebtedness, in K. Gergen, M. S. Greenberg, and R. H. Willis (eds.), *Social Exchange: Advances in Theory and Research* (New York: Plenum, 1980), pp. 3–26.

c. M. S. Greenberg and D. R. Westcott, Indebtedness as a mediator of reactions to aid, in *New Directions in Helping*, Vol. 1, (Orlando, FL: Academic, 1983), pp. 85–112.

22. For more on how people comply with requests in order to affirm their self-concept after it has been threatened, see

a. Claude M. Steele, The psychology of self-affirmation: Sustaining the integrity of the self, in L. Berkowitz (ed.) et al., *Advances in Experimental Social Psychology, Vol. 21: Social Psychological Studies of the Self: Perspectives and Programs* (1988), 261–302.

b. Amy Kaplan and Joachim Krueger, Compliance after threat: Self-affirmation or self-presentation? *Current Research in Social Psychology*, Special Issue: 4(7): (1999).

c. For an online literature review by Kaplan, see *http://www.uiowa.edu/~grpproc/crisp/crisp.4.7.htm*.

23. For a relatively recent meta-analysis of "door in the face" research, see Daniel J. O'Keefe and Scott L. Hale, An odds-ratio-based meta-analysis of research on the door-in-the-face influence strategy, *Communication Reports*, Special Issue: 14(1): 31–38 (2001).

24. My Stanford students Daniel Berdichevsky and Kavita Sarin carried out early explorations into location-based persuasion.

25. Various theories support the idea that people are more likely to do things that are easy to do. See, for example, A. Bandura, *Self-Efficacy: The Exercise of Self-Control* (New York: W. H. Freeman, 1997).

26. L. Festinger, A theory of social comparison process, *Human Relations*, 7: 117–140 (1954).

27. The concept of intrinsic motivation—the natural desire to do something because it is inherently rewarding—is discussed in more detail in Chapter 8.

28. You can find out more about the HealthyJump jump rope at *http://tanitascale.com/healthyjump.html*.

29. The "Like's Gone" concept was created by captology students Marissa Treinen, Salvador Avila, and Tatiana Mejia.

30. Strictly speaking, surveillance technology is not interactive in the way I've described other interactive computing products to this point; these products focus on interactivity between the technology and the end user. However, I consider surveillance systems to be persuasive technology under my definition, as they do incorporate a limited kind of interactivity. Input comes from one person (the user) and output is sent to another person (the observer), who then closes the loop by interacting with (rewarding or punishing) the person observed.

31. K. Bell DeTienne, Big brother or friendly coach? Computer monitoring in the 21st century, *The Futurist*, pp. 33–37 (1993).

32. Jennifer Granick, Big Brother: Your boss, *Wired* (July 1998).

33. The American Management Association (AMA) conducts an annual survey of workplace testing and monitoring. For a summary of its recent results, showing the increased prevalence of workplace monitoring and surveillance since 1997, see *http://www.amanet.org/research/pdfs/ems_short2001.pdf.*

34. J. C. Turner, *Social Influence* (Pacific Grove, CA: Brooks/Cole, 1991).

35. Hygiene Guard is produced by Net/Tech International in New Jersey.

36. For more information on AutoWatch, see *http://drivehomesafe.com/control_teendriver_speeding_driverlicense2.htm.*

37. The user manual for AutoWatch suggests various ways to conceal this device. To see an online version of the manual, go to *http://www.obd2.com/pdffiles/Userawfw.pdf.*

38. For a long list of companies that provide incentive management solutions, see *http://www.workindex.com/extrefs.asp?SUBCATID=1714.*

39. For a brief article explaining incentive management in call centers, see *http://www.callcentermagazine.com/article/CCM20010627S0002.*

40. II. C. Kelman, Compliance, identification, and internalization: Three processes of attitude change, *Journal of Conflict Resolution*, 2: 51–60 (1958).

41. Can compliance lead to internalization? Yes, in some cases. At least four theories argue that behaviors can eventually change attitudes, even if the behaviors were initially motivated by extrinsic factors. These theories include cognitive dissonance, self-perception, self-presentation, and self-affirmation. For brief reviews, see D. R. Forsythe, *Our Social World* (Pacific Grove, CA: Brooks/Cole, 1995). While I won't describe each theory here, I should note that scholars don't agree whether these are competing or complementary theories. However, taken together, one thing seems clear: behaviors—even those motivated by compliance strategies—can eventually change attitudes.

42. B. F. Skinner, *About Behaviorism* (New York: Alfred A. Knopf, 1974).

43. Operant conditioning is more complex than I describe here. For a readable overview of operant conditioning (my lab's favorite introduction to the topic), see R. A. Powell, D. G. Symbaluk, and S. E. MacDonald, *Introduction to Learning and Behavior* (Belmont, CA: Wadsworth, 2002).

44. For an example of software that punishes, see B. Caldwell and J. Soat, The hidden persuader (booby-trapped software), *InformationWEEK*, 42(3): 47 (1990).

45. An intriguing (and readable) book on this topic is Karen Pryor, *Don't Shoot the Dog: The New Art of Teaching and Training* (New York: Bantam Doubleday Dell, 1999).

46. Ajit Chaudhari and Emily Clark were my students who created the Telecycle prototype.

47. People who create computer games rarely talk about the role operant conditioning plays in their products. For an article that outlines how operant conditioning is a key part of successful computer games, see John Hopson, Behavioral Game Design, *Gamasutra* (April 27, 2001), at *http://www.gamasutra.com/features/20010427/hopson_01.htm.*

48. M. R. Lepper and D. Greene, Over justification research and beyond: Toward a means-end analysis of intrinsic and extrinsic motivation, in M. R. Lepper and D. Greene (eds.), *The Hidden Costs of Reward: New Perspectives on the Psychology of Human Motivation* (Hillsdale, NJ: Erlbaum, 1978), pp. 109–148.

chapter **4**

Computers as Persuasive Media
Simulation

Computers can shape attitudes and behavior by providing compelling simulated experiences.

When it comes to shaping attitudes and behavior, experience makes a difference.[1] Those in the business of persuading understand and apply this principle. AOL gives out trial memberships on CD. Auto dealers encourage customers to take a test drive. Government programs send at-risk kids to visit correctional facilities to get a glimpse of prison life. The goal in these and other scenarios is to provide a compelling experience that will persuade people to change their attitudes or behaviors.

The experience principle can be applied to persuasive technologies as well. When computers are used as persuasive media—particularly when they are used to create simulations—they can have a powerful impact on shaping attitudes and behaviors in the real world.[2] This chapter will focus on computers as persuasive media—the second corner of the functional triad (Figure 4.1).

Computer simulations can create experiences that mimic experiences in the real world, or they can create hypothetical worlds that are experienced as "real." Simulations can be as simple as an Indy 500 race game on a handheld computer or as complex as virtual reality.[3] People often react to virtual experiences as though they were real-world experiences.[4] And it's this reaction that sets the stage for influence dynamics to play out.

Technology innovators have only begun to explore the persuasive possibilities of computer-simulated experiences. This is perhaps the most promising new path for computers as persuasive technologies.

This chapter will outline three classes of computer-based simulations and explore the current and potential use of simulations to change attitudes and

61

Figure 4.1

Computers as persuasive media.

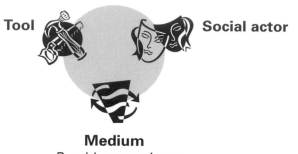

Tool

Social actor

Medium
Provides experience

A medium can be persuasive by

- Allowing people to explore cause-and-effect relationships
- Providing people with vicarious experiences that motivate
- Helping people rehearse a behavior

behavior. For each type of simulation, I'll present examples, highlight key advantages, and offer relevant principles for designing and understanding computer simulation.

Persuading through Computer Simulation

From the standpoint of persuasion, the technological elements of a simulation are less important than what the user actually experiences. Drawing on how people experience computer simulations, I propose three categories of simulation that are relevant to persuasive technologies:[5]

- Simulated cause-and-effect scenarios

- Simulated environments

- Simulated objects

Within each of these categories, theories from social science—especially psychology—offer insight into computers as persuasive sensory media. The pages that follow discuss each type of simulation in turn.

Cause-and-Effect Simulations:
Offering Exploration and Insight

Principle of Cause and Effect

> Simulations can persuade people to change their attitudes or behaviors by enabling them to observe immediately the link between cause and effect.

Computing technology has long allowed people to simulate dynamic systems—the weather, population growth, the economy, and so on. With these technologies, people can vary the inputs, or causes, and observe the outputs, or effects, almost immediately. Suppose city planners are concerned about their city's population boom. With a good simulation program (say, a professional version of SimCity) city officials can input various levels of growth and then observe how each level would affect other variables, such as traffic congestion or the demand for phone lines. Using cause-and-effect simulators, planners don't have to wait for city populations to grow before making the necessary arrangements. It's a powerful way to understand different scenarios.[6]

Cause-and-effect simulations can be powerful persuaders. The power comes from the ability to explore cause-and-effect relationships without having to wait a long time to see the results[7] and the ability to convey the effects in vivid and credible ways.[8] Because these simulations can clearly show cause-and-effect relationships, they enable users to gain insight into the likely consequences of their attitudes or behaviors.

Cause-and-effect simulations enable users to explore and experiment in a safe environment, free of real-world consequences.[9] In such an environment it is less threatening to try out new attitudes or behaviors that might then be transferred to the real world. In addition, people who are in exploration mode expect to find new things, to be enlightened, to be surprised. This frame of mind makes it easier to form new attitudes and adopt new behaviors[10] in a simulated environment—attitudes and behaviors that then might be transferred to the real world.

By compressing time, a computer simulation can immediately show the link between cause and effect, which can help to change attitudes or behavior. You may know intellectually that eating burgers and fries every day can lead to heart disease in the future, but the effects aren't apparent immediately in the real world. A cause-and-effect simulation could make this link clear and compelling, prompting you to change your eating habits.

It's also important to realize that cause-and-effect simulations can persuade in subtle ways because users may not recognize the biases built into simulations. When absorbed in a simulation, people can easily forget that the outcomes are determined by rules defined by human beings who may have injected their own biases into the simulation. The natural inclination is to accept the simulation as true and accurate.[11] (I'll say more about the issue of accuracy later in this chapter.) People usually don't scrutinize the content of a simulation, in part because their minds are busy processing other aspects of the experience.[12] Because of this, those who design simulated experiences can get across their message without seeming to preach.

▪▪▪▪▪

Cause-and-Effect Simulation: Sources of Persuasive Power

- Enables users to explore and experiment in a safe, nonthreatening environment

- Shows the link between cause and effect clearly and immediately

- Persuades in subtle ways, without seeming to preach

HIV Roulette: A Cause-and-Effect Simulator

One example of a persuasive cause-and-effect simulation is a kiosk called HIV Roulette.[13] Located in San Francisco's Exploratorium, this exhibit (Figure 4.2) seems unremarkable at first; it's just a simple kiosk. But those who take the time to sit down and "play" gain immediate insights into how their sexual behavior can affect their HIV status.

Here's how it works: First, the user views images of hypothetical people. The user then selects the gender and behavior of the group he or she wishes to simulate contact with, and their geographic location. Then the computer does a calculation—spins the roulette wheel, if you will—and reports whether the behavior is likely to result in contracting HIV or another sexually transmitted disease.

The report is based on real data, taking into account various factors, including the hypothetical partner's history of sexual behavior and intravenous drug use. Most people who play HIV Roulette quickly see that the risks involved in sexual behavior depend not only on the partner selected, but also on all the people in that person's sexual history.

HIV Roulette allows people to safely explore the health consequences of sexual activity. Most people play HIV Roulette in a predictable way:[14] At first, they are careful and cautious, choosing low-risk sexual partners. Then they begin

Figure 4.2

HIV Roulette is a kiosk that simulates the health risks of sexual contact.

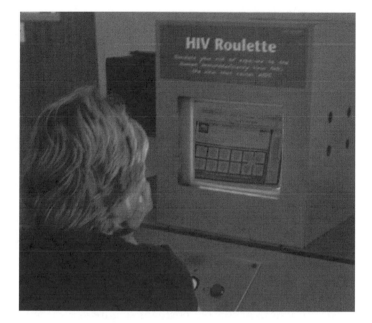

Figure 4.3

A report is generated at the end of each round of HIV Roulette.

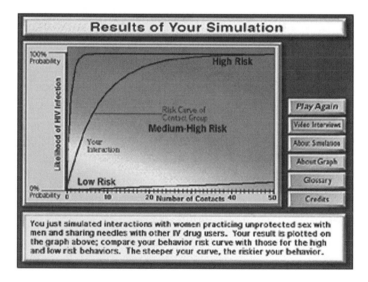

making risky sexual choices, just to see what happens, until the computer reports they have contracted HIV. Sometimes this takes longer than players expect; sometimes it happens sooner. By graphically showing the conse-

Figure 4.4

In the game Rockett's New School, users decide how the main character will respond to social situations.

quences of specific behavior (Figure 4.3), based on real data, the simulation attempts to persuade users to engage in safer sex. You see that just a single sexual encounter can expose you to literally hundreds of indirect sexual contacts, depending on the sexual history of each partner. Of course, you don't need a computer to calculate how quickly indirect sexual contacts add up. However, by having the HIV Roulette computer do the calculations for you and present the results graphically, the exponential risks due to indirect sexual partners become more readily apparent, more "in your face" and harder to ignore.

Rockett's New School: Learning Social Skills

Rockett's New School, a game targeted to preteen girls, is another example of a cause-and-effect simulation.[15] The objective of the game is to help the protagonist, an eighth-grade student named Rockett (Figure 4.4), navigate social situations at a new school. The story begins when Rockett arrives at her school for the first time. Periodically the narrative stops and the user must make a decision for Rockett—such as what she should say or what attitude she should adopt toward events. The user then vicariously experiences the effects of those decisions.

Although the product is marketed as a game, the rules that underlie the simulation make the experience more than mere diversion.[16] One goal of the product is to shape how players respond to social situations in their own lives.

The Rockett simulation has a bias if you make choices that reflect Rockett's self-confidence, generally Rockett fares well; people like her, and she feels good about what she's done. In contrast, if you make choices for Rockett that stem from fear or self-doubt, she doesn't fare as well. For example, after Rockett arrives at class on the first day, the teacher invites her to introduce herself. At this point you must decide what attitude Rockett will have. If you choose a timid approach, the narrative then unfolds with students responding with slight derision and Rockett feeling as though she's made a fool of herself. If you choose a confident attitude for Rockett, the teacher praises her and her classmates find their new classmate to be witty and interesting.

Some might say this program is being simplistic or downright misleading, that the world doesn't necessarily reward sincerity or outspokenness. But this is the bias the designers have chosen.[17] They have deliberately created this game to inspire girls to build qualities like confidence, adventurousness, and empathy.

Implications of Designer Bias

This brings up an important aspect of simulations: the possibility of built-in bias of the designers. Although simulations can be informative, engaging, and persuasive, nothing guarantees that they are accurate. The rules built into the system may not be based on the best knowledge of cause-and-effect relationships but rather on the bias of the designer.

SimCity, the popular game developed by Will Wright to show the impact of planning decisions on the growth of urban areas, has been a focal point for spirited debate about the issue of designer bias. Technology watcher Ester Dyson notes that SimCity has been the poster child of the simulation-as-subtle-propaganda debate. While people have asserted different types of political bias inherent in the game's simulation rules, one example stands out. Dyson writes: "When asked about the effects of raising taxes, a 14-year-old experienced with SimCity replied, 'Why, the citizens riot, of course.'"[18]

In the February 1990 issue of *Byte* (now defunct), columnist Jerry Pournelle wrote:

The simulation is pretty convincing—and that's the problem, because it's a simulation of the designer's theories, not of reality. Case in point: the designer prefers rail transportation to automobiles. It's costly, but it doesn't pollute. In fact, you can design a whole city with nothing but rail transport, not a single road in the place. In the real world, such a city would soon strangle in garbage. [M]y point is not to condemn these programs. Instead, I want to warn against their misuse. For all too many, computers retain an air of mystery, and there's a strong temptation to believe what the little machines tell us.[19]

Of course, "what the little machines tell us" depends on what the designers programmed into the simulation.

It's impossible to create a simulation that is truly objective, since the designer cannot know precisely how all variables would interact in the real world, so bias is inevitable. Consider the above examples of Rockett and SimCity. Although research and facts can help build the underlying rules to the simulation, for some types of simulations, especially those involving social issues, data is insufficient or conflicting. Much like the writing of history is an inevitably biased interpretation of the past, those who create simulations are likely to introduce bias of some sort into their work.

Should those who create simulations reveal their biases to the users? I believe they should, if the simulation was designed not just as entertainment but to help people make health, financial, and other choices about their lives.

However, revealing bias is not always desirable, practical, or effective. There is no standard way in simulations to let users know about the designer's biases— no type of initial information screen or "about this simulation" section. Certainly, designers could—and perhaps should—try to expose users to the assumptions underlying a simulation. But if the product is designed to sell or to promote an ideology, it's unlikely that creators will risk undermining their effectiveness by admitting to biases, however small. Yet you can also imagine how the creators of a simulation could boost their credibility by impressing the user with how accurate the facts are underlying the simulations. (One product called Great Cities does this by acknowledging its biases up front and allowing users to review and even change the rules and assumptions of the simulation.[20])

The other challenge surrounding disclosure of biases is that the creators themselves may not recognize their biases. We are often blind to our own biases and assumptions.

In my view, the most reasonable path is also one that will take time and effort: educating people—both researchers and end users—about how interactive simulations will inevitably have biases built into the rules underlying the experience. As interactive simulations become a greater part of our information and entertainment landscape, we would do well to add simulations to the list of things that require a critical eye and careful evaluation.

Environment Simulations: Creating Spaces for Persuasive Experiences

Principle of Virtual Rehearsal

Providing a motivating simulated environment in which to rehearse a behavior can enable people to change their attitudes or behavior in the real world.

Environment simulations—those that provide users with new surroundings—can be another form of persuasive technology. Sometimes the surroundings are immersive, as in high-end virtual reality applications. More often, the virtual environments are much simpler and use basic technology. Alcohol 101 is a desktop application that simulates a college party. Hewlett-Packard's MOPy is a screen saver that simulates a fish swimming in an aquarium. Life Fitness Rower simulates rowing while spectators cheer you on and other people compete against you. Even these simple systems can be engaging because immersion is a function of the mind, not of the technology.[21] In fact, in learning simulations, some argue that realism can detract from the learning experience.[22]

Like cause-and-effect scenarios, simulated environments provide a safe "place" to explore new behaviors and perspectives.[23] And unlike real environments, virtual environments are controllable;[24] users can start or stop the experience at any time, and when they return for additional virtual experiences, they can pick up where they left off.

Simulated environments can persuade through creating situations that reward and motivate people for a target behavior; allow users to practice a target behavior; control exposure to new or frightening situations; and facilitate role-playing, adopting another person's perspective.

Environment Simulation: Sources of Persuasive Power

- Can create situations that reward and motivate people for a target behavior

- Allows rehearsal—practicing a target behavior

- Can control exposure to new or frightening situations

- Facilitates role-playing—adopting another person's perspective

The health and fitness industry is among the leaders in using environment simulations to motivate and influence people.[25] These technologies leverage the fact that our environment plays a key role in shaping our behaviors and thoughts.[26]

LifeFitness VR Rowing Machine: Competing in a Virtual Environment

Exercising alone and without media can be boring or tedious, so it's not surprising that early innovators of exercise equipment sought ways to make the time pass more quickly and enjoyably, such as adding LED displays to show an exerciser's progress on an imaginary jogging track. Today, many types of exercise devices add simulation to make workouts more compelling. By simulating a new environment, fitness companies have found that they can increase their customers' motivation and enjoyment while changing their attitudes and behaviors related to exercise.

Principle of Virtual Rewards

Computer simulations that reward target behaviors in a virtual world, such as giving virtual rewards for exercising, can influence people to perform the target behavior more frequently and effectively in the real world.

One early example of using simulation to promote exercise is the Life-Fitness VR Rowing Machine (Figure 4.5). This stationary rowing device includes a screen that depicts you, the exerciser, rowing a boat on virtual water. As you row faster, your boat moves through the water faster. You row past scenery, distance markers, and landmarks. You can also race against a virtual competitor, who helps set a pace for you. For added motivation, some versions of the product depict a shark that chases you.

The LifeFitness VR Rowing Machine uses a number of persuasive strategies to motivate users to exercise more effectively. It provides feedback, competition, and rewards. In addition, the simulated environment distracts or "dissociates" users from focusing on the discomfort that comes with exercise.

The Tectrix VR Bike: Pedaling to Explore a Virtual Environment

The Tectrix[27] VR Bike (Figure 4.6) is another example of how an environment simulation can motivate and reward people for performing certain behaviors—in this case, exercising more effectively. As you work out on this device, you can explore a virtual world, navigating by plane or snowmobile and choosing whichever route you prefer.

Figure 4.5

The LifeFitness VR Rowing Machine provides a virtual environment to motivate users.

Figure 4.6

The Tectrix VR Bike simulates a journey by land, sea, or air.

When you pedal faster, you travel faster in your virtual world. You can snowmobile though the mountains or explore a tropical island by plane. As you do so, a fan embedded near the monitor blows on your face, adding a tactile dimension to the simulated environment. To turn or maneuver, you must lean from side to side in the bike seat. If you choose to go down the beach and under the sea, you get a view of life in the deep blue. In some versions of this product, your exercise bike becomes the input device for multiplayer competition in a virtual world. (My gym in Santa Rosa has two of these bikes, and I've seen that the competition mode is popular, especially with younger members.)

Although the VR bike has yet to become common in health clubs (perhaps because of the hefty price tag), research on the effects of these devices shows that they do succeed in changing users' attitudes and behaviors toward exercise.[28] In one study, 18 people rode the bikes using the virtual environment simulation, and 18 people rode the bikes without the simulation. During the 30-minute period of the study, people using the VR version of the bike had higher heart rates and burned more calories.

Despite the increased performance for those using the VR exercise equipment, when asked how much effort they exerted during the 30-minute exercise period, the two groups showed no significant differences in perceived exertion. In other words, even though the VR group worked harder in the exercise, they didn't feel like they worked harder;[29] the simulated environment led to greater physical exertion with less awareness of the effort. This finding matches other research demonstrating that people enjoy running more and that they run harder when exercising outside rather than on a treadmill.[30]

These studies confirm what we know through common sense and experience: the context for an activity makes a difference. The research also shows that a virtual environment can offer some of the same beneficial effects as the real world.

Managing Asthma in a Simulated Environment

Other health products have leveraged the power of simulation to achieve persuasive ends in maintaining chronic health conditions. One such product is Click Health's Bronkie the Bronchiasaurus (Figure 4.7), a Nintendo-based video game designed to help kids with chronic asthma to manage the condition.[31] In the United States, 15 million people have asthma (one-third of them under the age of 18). People who manage their asthma successfully enjoy much better health than those who don't.[32]

The game puts players into a new environment—a prehistoric dinosaur world—where they take on the role of Bronkie, a dinosaur who has asthma. In this Nintendo setting, players try to find and reassemble pieces of a wind machine, a device that will clear dust from the air. During the game, players must manage Bronkie's asthma or they cannot continue their quest.

To manage Bronkie's asthma, players have to perform asthma management tasks that are similar to those for human asthmatics. They must help Bronkie use an inhaler and avoid smoke and dust, among other things.

Figure 4.7

Bronkie the Bronchia-
saurus is a Nintendo
game with a persuasive
goal: getting kids to
manage their asthma
more effectively.

On the one hand, Bronkie is a game; it's fun to play. But on the other hand, this product is a vehicle for practicing self-care. This type of "influtainment" is a powerful strategy, especially for the target age group, kids aged 8 to 14.

Research on the Bronkie video game shows striking results. Asthmatic kids who play Bronkie for as little as 30 minutes report increased self-efficacy in caring for their chronic condition. They not only believe they can take successful action in managing their asthma, but they are more likely to do so than those with low self-efficacy.[33] The research showed that playing this video game not only had an immediate impact on participants in the study, but that the effects continued long after the session was over.

Although the study showed other positive outcomes as well (more knowledge, more sharing with friends about their condition, etc.), the key point of this example is that by practicing behaviors in a simulated environment, people can increase their self-efficacy in performing those behaviors. This in turn leads to increased likelihood of performing the behaviors in the real world.

The interactive nature of the game is important. One study compared the Bronkie video game with a videotape on the same topic. Kids who watched the videotape reported *decreased* self-efficacy, as opposed to *increased* self-efficacy for those who played the interactive video game.[34] The implication is that interactive experiences can boost self-efficacy more than passive experiences. Unlike the interactive Bronkie video game, the videotape doesn't allow for rehearsing behavior, apparently causing viewers to feel less assured about their ability to perform the behavior in the real world.

Using Simulation to Overcome Phobias

Not only can environment simulations lead to increased self-efficacy, they can also reduce fear (an attitude) and the behavior it spawns. While virtual reality has been lauded for training fighter pilots and medical doctors, a lesser-known use of this immersive technology is in helping people to overcome their phobias—specifically, to change their attitudes and behaviors related to their phobias.

About 10% of the general population has a phobia toward something, such as spiders, heights, or flying in planes. Virtual reality therapy technologies can help people change their phobic attitudes and reactions.[35]

Researchers at the University of Washington have created a virtual reality application designed to treat arachnophobia—fear of spiders (Figure 4.8). In undergoing this treatment, patients wear a head-mounted display, which immerses them in a virtual room. The therapist or the patient can control the patient's exposure to virtual spiders. The strategy is to help the patient become less anxious about spiders by increasing exposure to them in a safe, virtual world.[36]

Patients might start by seeing a small virtual spider far away. Later, they can work up to being at ease viewing larger spiders up close. In some cases, patients may pretend to touch the spider. Little by little, most patients feel less anxiety toward situations involving spiders.

Research at the University of Washington has shown that the reduction of fear in the virtual world transfers to the real world. In their first case study,[37] the results of which were later confirmed by a larger study,[38] the research team worked with a woman who had severe arachnophobia. Using a VR system called SpiderWorld for various one-hour sessions, this woman (called "Miss Muffett" in the study report) was progressively desensitized to spiders: little by little the woman would get closer to virtual spiders and have more interactions with them. The simulation was effective:

> In later sessions, after [Miss Muffett] had lost some of her fear of spiders, she was sometimes encouraged to pick up the virtual spider and/or web with her cyberhand and place it in orientations that were most anxiety provoking. Other times, the experimenter controlled the spider's movements (unexpected jumps, etc). Some virtual spiders were placed in a cupboard with a spider web. Other virtual spiders climbed or dropped from their thread from the ceiling to the virtual kitchen floor. Eventually, after getting used to them, Miss Muffet could tolerate holding and picking up the virtual spiders without panicking.[39]

Figure 4.8 Simulations have been successful in helping people overcome phobias, such as fear of spiders.

After this treatment, the woman who previously had an extreme fear of spiders decided to go camping in the woods, where she knew spiders would abound. The VR therapy had changed her attitude, then her behavior, and then parts of her life.

Similarly, researchers at other institutions, such as Georgia Tech, Emory University, and the California School of Professional Psychology in San Diego, have used simulation technology to treat people who are afraid of flying in planes. The simulator takes people through a series of flight-related experiences, from taxiing on the airport runway to flying in bad weather.[40] In a study by Barbara Rothbaum and colleagues published in 2002, after eight sessions of flight travel simulations, 90% of people who received virtual reality therapy reported flying during the year that followed, and did so with less anxiety.[41] This success rate is comparable to traditional (noncomputerized) exposure therapy.

Such persuasive technologies can be used for overcoming other phobias, from fear of heights to fear of public speaking. Compared to traditional forms of exposure therapy, virtual reality poses two key advantages: The stimuli (spiders, planes, etc.) are under the control of the therapist or patient, and the therapy can take place in a private and convenient setting as opposed to, say, an airplane.

In My Steps: Helping Doctors to Empathize with Cancer Patients

Technologies that simulate environments also can help to increase empathy by enabling users to view the world from another person's perspective.[42] The resulting attitude change can then lead to changes in behavior.

One such persuasive technology is In My Steps, a virtual reality system created by Ortho Biotech to increase doctors' empathy toward cancer patients by simulating the frustrations these patients face every day.[43]

The In My Steps system, which is built into a van, travels the country and allows doctors to spend 20 minutes in a virtual environment (Figure 4.9)—one that approximates the anemia-induced fatigue some of their patients feel 24 hours a day when undergoing chemotherapy. Wearing headgear and foot-operated pedals, the doctors go through routine activities, such as making breakfast and answering the door in the simulated environment of a patient's home. The doctors can move only at a limited rate, no matter how fast they operate the foot pedals. In the course of the simulation, they experience some of the frustration related to the physical limitations imposed by chemotherapy. For example, when they can't answer the door quickly enough, a van delivering needed medications drives away.

Figure 4.9

The In My Steps system helps physicians develop empathy for patients suffering from cancer-related fatigue.

(CNN)

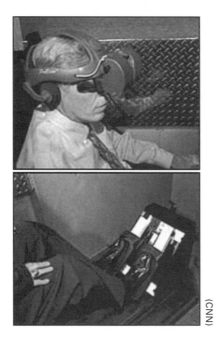

(CNN)

This simulated experience has been shown to be effective in helping doctors develop empathy for their patients, which in turn leads to changed behavior: about 60% of the doctors going through the simulation reported that they would change the way they treat cancer-related fatigue.[44]

From the standpoint of persuasion, for most simulated environments to be successful, users must take what they've learned in the virtual world and apply it in their real-world lives.[45] Otherwise, the simulation is just another gee-whiz technology experience, not a vehicle for changing attitudes or behavior. One way to increase the likelihood of transferring virtual behavior to the real world is to incorporate a virtual component into a real-world situation. That's the purpose of object simulations, our next topic of discussion.

Object Simulations: Providing Experiences in Everyday Contexts

Environment simulations create a virtual world into which people must mentally transport themselves. Object simulations do the opposite: these products go with users into a real-world setting. This approach enables users to experience more directly how their daily routines would be affected by what is being simulated.

Computer technologies that simulate objects can be powerfully persuasive because they fit into the context of a person's everyday life, they are less dependent on imagination or suspension of disbelief, and they make clear the likely impact of certain attitudes or behaviors.

■ ■ ■ ■ ■

Object Simulation: Sources of Persuasive Power

- Fits into the context of a person's everyday life

- Less dependent on imagination or suspension of disbelief

- Makes clear the impact on everyday life

Principle of Simulations in Real-World Contexts

Portable simulation technologies designed for use during everyday routines can highlight the impact of certain behaviors and motivate behavior or attitude change.

Designers who face hard-to-influence user groups should consider creating object simulations because of their unique persuasive powers. Two notable examples of object simulators both target teenagers: one deals with pregnancy, the other with drunk driving.

Baby Think It Over: An Infant Simulator

Perhaps the best-known object simulator used for persuasive purposes is the Baby Think It Over infant simulator. Used as part of many school programs, Baby Think It Over is a high-tech doll that looks like a human baby (Figure 4.10).[46] It's so realistic looking, in fact, that when I carry the device with me to lectures and seminars, many people initially think that I'm carrying a real baby. The doll has a simple computer embedded inside. Used as part of many school parenting programs, Baby Think It Over helps teenagers understand how much attention a baby requires. The point is to persuade teenagers to avoid becoming teen parents.

The doll contains an embedded computer that triggers a crying sound at random intervals. To stop the crying, the caregiver must pay immediate attention to the doll. The caregiver must insert a key into the back of the baby and hold it in place to stop the crying. Sometimes the care routine takes 2 or 3 minutes; other times the crying lasts for more than 15 minutes. If the key is not inserted and held properly, the embedded computer records the neglect, which later shows up on a tiny display locked inside. After a week or weekend of tending the infant simulator, students give the doll back to the teacher, who can unlock and view the display inside the doll.

The Baby Think It Over intervention program requires teens to take the infant simulator everywhere they go—to soccer practice, to parties, even to bed. When the infant simulator cries, demanding attention, the teen caregiver experiences firsthand how much a baby would impact his or her life.

Unlike reading books or listening to lectures, working with the infant simulator doesn't require teens to use much imagination to apply the new knowledge in their own lives. The teens get the point quickly. They show up at school sleepy after a night with interruptions from the crying. They may opt out of attending parties because they know their infant simulator will cry and perhaps embarrass them. At the end of the intervention period (usually a few days), teens are eager to return the infant simulator to their teachers and regain their normal, comparatively carefree lives.[47]

Figure 4.10

The Baby Think It Over
Infant Simulator is
designed to persuade
teens to avoid becoming
parents.

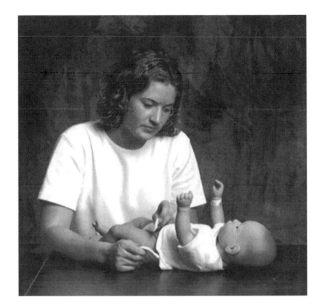

Studies have confirmed the effectiveness of infant simulators in changing teens' attitudes. In one study of 150 adolescents who participated in a Baby Think It Over program, 95% of the teens stated afterward that they felt they were not yet ready to accept the responsibility of parenting.[48] Perhaps nothing else—short of caring for a real baby—could have the same level of impact on how teens view the responsibilities of parenting. Simulated objects can be effective persuaders.

Drunk Driving Simulator

Another example of a persuasive object simulator is the Neon Drunk Driving Simulator (Figure 4.11), which is designed to prevent drunk driving among teenagers. DaimlerChrysler sponsors this specialized Dodge Neon automobile, which simulates what it's like to drive while under the influence of alcohol.[49] With a laptop computer and other special equipment installed, the Drunk Driving Simulator responds sluggishly and unpredictably to a driver's inputs. A handful of these cars tour the United States, making stops at high schools and giving teens a chance to experience how alcohol impairs their ability to drive safely.

Figure 4.11

The Neon Drunk Driving Simulator provides a sobering experience of the dangers of driving drunk.

The typical test drive goes as follows: Students first drive the car under normal conditions. They drive around a track, making turns and avoiding obstacles. On the second lap, the car is switched to "drunk" mode. Students then attempt to navigate the course as before, but with unpredictable steering and braking. They immediately feel the loss of control: they might hit orange pylons, which represent children, or miss turns that were easy to make on the previous lap. In this way, sober students can experience firsthand the plausible effects of drunk driving.

One study of more than 2,000 students who participated in a Drunk Driving Simulator program concluded that the technology has a significant impact on teens' attitudes toward getting in a car with a drunk driver.[50] In addition, the stories students tell after the experience—the genuine fear they felt—show that this simulated car has an impact.[51]

Here's what one of my own students had to say about his experience with the Drunk Driving Simulator in high school:

> They set up the program so everyone could watch the students drive and watch them fail. I remember seeing my friends try and fail. But part of me was thinking that it didn't really look so tough. I thought I'd be the one kid who could drive the car and manage to not knock over all the orange cones. And of course I got in the car and failed miserably. Even though I was highly motivated to succeed, I still managed to hit about half the cones. I think lots of people approached the simulation with the attitude that they were going to prove everybody wrong. And then when they failed, they had to stop and think a little.[52]

As the previous examples show, one key advantage of object simulators, compared with the other two simulation types discussed in this chapter, is that these devices are used in the context of real life. Users don't have to imagine how a virtual scenario might impact their lives; they can experience it firsthand through the object simulators. Object simulators are an excellent use of persuasive technology for abstract concepts such as parental responsibility, for promoting critical target behaviors (such as avoiding drunk driving), and for groups, such as teenagers, who are difficult to persuade.

As this chapter has shown, interactive technology can provide experiences that change people's attitudes and behaviors, through simulating cause-and-effect situations, virtual environments, and objects. The products can take many forms—Web experiences, stand-alone kiosks, mobile phones, and more. Although the forms of the technology may differ, the key principle is the same: when it comes to persuasion, experience makes a difference.

Notes and References

For updates on the topics presented in this chapter, visit *www.persuasivetech.info*.

1. E. Reed, *The Necessity of Experience* (New Haven, CT: Yale University Press, 1996).

2. For example, see the following:

   a. D. M. Towne, T. de Jong, and H. Spada (eds.), *Simulation-Based Experiential Learning* (Berlin: Springer-Verlag, 1993).

   b. Cognition and Technology Group at Vanderbilt, The Jasper experiment: An exploration of issues in learning and instructional design, *Educational Technology Research and Development,* 40 (1): 65–80 (1992).

   c. T. Manning, Interactive environments for promoting health, in R. S. Street, W. R. Gold, and T. Manning (eds.), *Health Promotion and Interactive Technology: Theoretical Applications and Future Directions* (Hillsdale, NJ: Lawrence Earlbaum, 1997), pp. 67–78.

3. There are various definitions of "virtual reality." According to M. W. Krueger: "The terms *virtual worlds, virtual cockpits,* and *virtual workstations* were used to describe specific projects. In 1989, Jaron Lanier, CEO of VPL, coined the term *virtual reality* to bring all of the virtual projects under a single rubric. The term therefore typically refers to three-dimensional realities implemented with stereo viewing goggles and reality gloves." M. W. Krueger, *Artificial Reality,* 2nd ed. (Reading, MA: Addison-Wesley, 1991), p. xiii.

4. You'll find a considerable body of evidence about people responding to interactive technologies as they respond to real-life experiences in Byron Reeves and Clifford Nass, *The Media Equation: How People Treat Computers, Television, and New Media Like Real People and Places* (Stanford, CA: Cambridge University Press, 1996).

5. Other taxonomies for simulations exist. For example, see the following:

   a. M. B. Gredler, A taxonomy of computer simulations, *Educational Technology,* 26: 7–12 (1986).

   b. In 1999, Kurt Schmucker wrote "A Taxonomy of Simulation Software" for Apple Computer. Available at *http://www.apple.com/education/LTReview/spring99/simulation/*.

   c. S. M. Alessi and S. R. Trollip, *Computer-Based Instruction, Methods and Development* (Englewood Cliffs, NJ: Prentice Hall, 1985).

   d. T. de Jong, Learning and instruction with computer simulations, *Education & Computing,* 6: 217–229 (1991).

    e. T. de Jong, Discovery learning with computer simulations of conceptual domains, IST memo 96–02, University of Twente, The Netherlands (1996).

6. See the following:

    a. D. A. Sisk, Simulation games as training tools, in Sandra M. Fowler and Monica G. Mumford (eds.), *Intercultural Sourcebook: Cross-cultural Training Methods*, vol. 1 (Yarmouth, ME: Intercultural Press, 1995).

    b. R. S. Street and Rimal, Health promotion and technology: A conceptual foundation, in R. S. Street, W. R. Gold, and T. Manning (eds.), *Health Promotion and Interactive Technology: Theoretical Applications and Future Directions* (Hillsdale, NJ: Lawrence Earlbaum, 1997), pp. 1–18.

7. T. de Jong, Learning and instruction with computer simulations, *Education & Computing*, 6: 217–229 (1991).

8. L. P. Rieber, Animation, incidental learning, and continuing motivation, *Journal of Educational Psychology*, 83: 318–328 (1991).

9. See the following:

    a. E. M. Raybourn, Computer game design: New directions for intercultural simulation game designers, *Developments in Business Simulation and Experiential Exercises*, vol. 24 (1997). See *www.unm.edu/~raybourn/games.html*.

    b. P. Pedersen, Simulations: A safe place to take risks in discussing cultural differences, *Simulation & Gaming*, 26 (2): 201–206 (1995).

    c. P. Carbonara, Game over, *Fast Company* (Dec. 1996).

10. See the following:

    a. D. A. Sisk, Simulation games as training tools, in Sandra M. Fowler and Monica G. Mumford (eds.), *Intercultural Sourcebook: Cross-Cultural Training Methods*, vol. 1 (Yarmouth, ME: Intercultural Press, 1995) pp. 81–92.

    b. T. M. Shlechter, Computer-based simulation systems and role-playing: An effective combination for fostering conditional knowledge, *Journal of Computer-Based Instruction*, 19(4): 110–114 (1992).

11. D. T. Gilbert, How mental systems believe, *American Psychologist*, 46(2): 107–109 (1991).

12. R. E. Petty and J. T. Cacioppo, *Communication and Persuasion: Central and Peripheral Routes to Attitude Change* (New York: Springer-Verlag, 1986).

13. See an online description at *http://www.exploratorium.edu/exhibit_services/exhibits/h/hivroulette.html*.

14. Personal conversation with Charles Carlson, director of Life Sciences, San Francisco Exploratorium.

15. The Purple Moon Web site has been taken down (due to an acquisition), but you can see what this site was like by visiting *http://web.archive.org/web/20000815075140/http://www.purple-moon.com*. For limited information and a couple of reviews about the

product Rockett's New School, see *http://www.cdaccess.com/html/shared/rocketts.htm.* This product can also be purchased from various online retailers.

16. Brenda Laurel, *The Utopian Entrepreneur* (Cambridge, MA: MIT Press, 2001).

17. Brenda Laurel, *The Utopian Entrepreneur* (Cambridge, MA: MIT Press, 2001).

18. One source for this is an article by Ester Dyson at *http://web.archive.org/web/20001121023100/ http://www.mg.co.za/pc/games/1999/03/11mar-simulation.htm.*

19. For an article by Ted Friedman ("Semiotics of SimCity") about simulations, including Jerry Pournelle's quote from the now-defunct *Byte* magazine about simulations having embedded values and messages, see *http://www.firstmonday.dk/issues/issue4_4/friedman/.*

20. The Great Cities simulation makes explicit the assumptions underlying the simulation. It even allows players to change the underlying assumptions. For more on the Great Cities simulation, contact the people at *http://arts4sv.org/.* (The software is not available directly through the Web; you need to send them email to purchase it). Also, Dan Gillmor wrote a column for the *San Jose Mercury News* about this product on October 20, 2000. To read this article online for free, see *http://www.arts4sv.org/pdf/2000–10-C3.pdf.*

21. R. T. Hays and M. J. Singer, *Simulation Fidelity in Training System Design* (New York: Springer-Verlag, 1989).

22. Some experts in simulations for learning and training argue that increased realism may detract from the learning experience. See, for example:

    a. P. Standen, Realism and imagination in educational multimedia simulations, in Clare McBeath and Roger Atkinson (eds.), *Proceedings of the 3rd International Interactive Multimedia Symposium,* Perth, Western Australia. January 21–25 1996, pp. 384–390. Standen is available online at *http://cleo.murdoch.edu.au/gen/aset/confs/iims/96/ry/ standen.html.*

    b. R. T. Hays and M. J. Singer, *Simulation Fidelity in Training System Design* (New York: Springer-Verlag, 1989).

23. See the following:

    a. E. M. Raybourn, Computer game design: New directions for intercultural simulation game designers, *Developments in Business Simulation and Experiential Exercises,* vol. 24 (1997). See *www.unm.edu/~raybourn/games.html.*

    b. P. Pedersen, Simulations: A safe place to take risks in discussing cultural differences, *Simulation & Gaming,* 26 (2): 201–206 (1995).

24. H. Brody, Kick that habit (the virtual way), *Technology Review,* (March/April): 29 (1999).

25. R. S. Street, W. R. Gold, and T. Manning (eds.), *Health Promotion and Interactive Technology: Theoretical Applications and Future Directions* (Hillsdale, NJ: Lawrence Earlbaum, 1997).

26. The significant impact of environment on behavior was one of the main tenants of B. F. Skinner and other behaviorists, though various other perspectives on human behavior

would also support this idea. In the area of health promotion, the impact of the environment on behavior has been clearly shown. See for example:

    a. N. Humpel, N. Owen, and E. Leslie, Environmental factors associated with adults' participation in physical activity: A review, *Am. J. Prev. Med.* 22(3): 188–199 (2002).

    b. D. Stokols, Establishing and maintaining healthy environments: Toward a social ecology of health promotion, *Am. Psych.,* 47(1): 6–22 (1992).

27. Tectrix was acquired by Cybex in 1998.

28. J. P. Porcari, M. S. Zedaker, and M. S. Maldari, Virtual motivation, *Fitness Management,* Dec: 48–51 (1998).

29. J. P. Porcari, M. S. Zedaker, and M. S. Maldari, Virtual motivation, *Fitness Management,* December, 1998, 48–51.

30. R. Ceci and P. Hassmen, Self-monitored exercise at three different PE intensities in treadmill vs. field running, *Medicine and Science in Sports and Exercise,* 23: 732–738 (1991).

31. For more on health-promoting video games, see *www.clickhealth.com.*

32. D. A. Lieberman, Three studies of an asthma education video game, in *Report to NIH: National Institute of Allergy and Infectious Diseases* (April 1995).

33. See the following:

    a. D. A. Lieberman, Three studies of an asthma education video game, in *Report to NIH: National Institute of Allergy and Infectious Diseases* (April 1995).

    b. D. A. Lieberman, Interactive video games for health promotion: Effects on knowledge, self-efficacy, social support, and health, in R. S. Street, W. R. Gold, and T. Manning (eds.). *Health Promotion and Interactive Technology: Theoretical Applications and Future Directions* (Hillsdale, NJ: Lawrence Earlbaum, 1997), pp. 103–120.

34. D. A. Lieberman, Three studies of an Asthma Education Video Game, in *Report to NIH: National Institute of Allergy and Infectious Diseases* (April 1995).

35. For a readable overview of VR therapy, you can see an article from researchers at the University of Washington: *http://www.hitl.washington.edu/research/exposure/.* Another academic center innovating in VR therapy is Georgia Tech. You can find a brief description of their work, a list of publications, and a list of researchers at *http://www.cc.gatech.edu/gvu/virtual/Phobia/phobia.html.*

    In addition, this type of therapy would be supported by psychology theories proposed by Albert Bandura. See A. Bandura, *Self Efficacy: The Exercise of Control* (New York: W.H. Freeman, 1997).

36. For more on overcoming fear of spiders using computing technology, see *www.hitl.washington.edu/projects/therapeutic.*

37. A. S. Carlin, H. Hoffman, and S. Weghorst, Virtual reality and tactile augmentation in the treatment of spider phobia: A case study, *Behavior Research and Therapy,* 35(2). 153–158 (1997).

38. H. G. Hoffman, A. Garcia-Palacios, C. Carlin, T. A. Furness III, and C. Botella-Arbona, Interfaces that heal: Coupling real and virtual objects to cure spider phobia, *International Journal of Human-Computer Interaction* (in press).

39. This quotation about "Miss Muffet" is from an article on the University of Washington research team's Web site at *http://www.hitl.washington.edu/research/exposure/*.

40. For more on overcoming the fear of flying, see a paper by the Georgia Tech researchers at *http://www.cs.northwestern.edu/~watsonb/school/docs/cga.pdf* and a press release at *www.cspp.edu/news/flying.htm*.

    To see how VR therapy for fear of flying has moved from the research lab into a commercial venture, visit *www.virtuallybetter.com*.

41. B. O. Rothbaum, L. Hodges, P. L. Anderson, L. Price, and S. Smith, 12-month follow-up of virtual reality exposure therapy for the fear of flying, *Journal of Consulting and Clinical Psychology*, 70: 428–432 (2002).

42. T. M. Shlechter, Computer-based simulation systems and role-playing: An effective combination for fostering conditional knowledge, *Journal of Computer-Based Instruction*, 19(4): 110–114 (1992).

43. Other companies have also aimed to make healthcare providers more empathetic toward cancer patients, such as a system by Medical Consumer Media. See C. Stubbs, Intersense smoothes out the rough spots in virtual reality, *Red Herring*, April: 34 (1999). See also *http://www.redherring.com/mag/issue65/news-one.html*.

44. For more information on In My Steps, visit the following sites:

    http://www.cnn.com/HEALTH/9809/25/virtual.reality.cancer/index.html

    http://www.procrit.com/cancer/cancer_04_05e.htm

    http://content.health.msn.com/content/article/1728.55144

    http://www.uicc.org/publ/pr/home/00022401.shtml

45. J. S. Brown, Process versus product: A perspective on tools for communal and informal electronic learning, *Journal of Education Computer Research*, 1: 179–201 (1985).

46. Manufactured by BTIO Educational Products Inc. See *www.btio.com*.

47. For peer-reviewed studies on Baby Think It Over, see the following:

    a. Jennifer W. Out, Baby Think It Over: Using role-play to prevent teen pregnancy, *Adolescence*, 36(143): 571–582 (2001).

    b. William Strachan and Kevin M. Gorey, Infant simulator lifespace intervention: Pilot investigation of an adolescent pregnancy prevention program, *Child & Adolescent Social Work Journal*, 14(3): 171–180 (1997).

48. For a synopsis of this Canadian study by Brenda Clark and other research on the effectiveness of the Baby Think It Over infant simulator, see *http://www.btio.com/cms.asp?SID=22* (click on "Studies" in the left-hand channel).

49. Advanced Animations created the Drunk Driving Simulator. See *http://www.advanced-animations.com.*

50. For a summary of the research, see *http://apha.confex.com/apha/128am/techprogram/paper_13286.htm.*

51. B. Machrone, Driving drunk, *PC Magazine,* July 1 (1998).

52. Based on personal conversation with Stanford student Matthew Yeh, January 26, 2002.

chapter **5**

Computers as
Persuasive Social Actors

*Shortly after midnight, a resident of a small town in southern California
called the police to report hearing a man inside a house nearby screaming
"I'm going to kill you! I'm going to kill you!" Officers arrived on the scene
and ordered the screaming man to come out of the house. The man stepped
outside, wearing shorts and a Polo shirt. The officers found no victim
inside the house. The man had been yelling at his computer.*[1]

No studies have shown exactly how computing products trigger social responses in humans, but as the opening anecdote demonstrates, at times people do respond to computers as though they were living beings. The most likely explanation is that social responses to certain types of computing systems are automatic and natural; human beings are hardwired to respond to cues in the environment, especially to things that seem alive in some way.[2] At some level we can't control these social responses; they are instinctive rather than rational. When people perceive social presence, they naturally respond in social ways—feeling empathy or anger, or following social rules such as taking turns. Social cues from computing products are important to understand because they trigger such automatic responses in people.

This chapter will explore the role of computing products as persuasive social actors—the third corner in the functional triad (Figure 5.1). These products persuade by giving a variety of social cues that elicit social responses from their human users.

89

Figure 5.1

Computers as
social actors.

Tool

Social actor
Creates relationship

A social actor can be persuasive by

- Rewarding people with positive feedback
- Modeling a target behavior or attitude
- Providing social support

Medium

Figure 5.2

Nintendo's Pocket
Pikachu was designed
to motivate users to be
physically active.

The Tamagotchi craze in the late 1990s was perhaps the first dramatic demonstration of how interacting directly with a computer could be a social experience.[3] People interacted with these virtual pets as though they were alive: They played with them, fed them, bathed them, and mourned them when they "died." Tamagotchi was soon followed by Nintendo's Pocket Pikachu (Figure 5.2) a digital pet designed to persuade. Like other digital pets, Pikachu required care and feeding, but with a twist: the device contained a pedometer that could register and record the owner's movements. For the digital creature to thrive, its owner had to be physically active on a consistent basis. The owner had to walk, run, or jump—anything to activate the pedometer. Pocket Pikachu is a simple example of a computing device functioning as a persuasive social actor.

Five Types of Social Cues

The fact that people respond socially to computer products has significant implications for persuasion. It opens the door for computers to apply a host of persuasion dynamics that are collectively described as *social influence*—the type of influence that arises from social situations.[4] These dynamics include normative influence (peer pressure) and social comparison ("keeping up with the Joneses") as well as less familiar dynamics such as group polarization and social facilitation.[5]

When perceived as social actors, computer products can leverage these principles of social influence to motivate and persuade.[6] My own research, discussed later in this chapter, confirms that people respond to computer systems as though the computers were social entities that used principles of motivation and influence.[7]

As shown in Table 5.1, I propose that five primary types of social cues cause people to make inferences about social presence in a computing product: *physical, psychological, language, social dynamics,* and *social roles.* The rest of this chapter will address these categories of social cues and explore their implications for persuasive technology.

Table 5.1 **Primary Types of Social Cues**

Cue	Examples
Physical	Face, eyes, body, movement
Psychological	Preferences, humor, personality, feelings, empathy, "I'm sorry"
Language	Interactive language use, spoken language, language recognition
Social dynamics	Turn taking, cooperation, praise for good work, answering questions, reciprocity
Social roles	Doctor, teammate, opponent, teacher, pet, guide

Persuasion through Physical Cues

One way a computing technology can convey social presence is through physical characteristics. A notable example is Baby Think It Over, described in Chapter 4. This infant simulator conveys a realistic social presence to persuade teenagers to avoid becoming teen parents.

Another example of how technology products can convey social presence comes from the world of gambling, in the form of Banana-Rama. This slot machine (Figure 5.3) has two onscreen characters—a cartoon orangutan and a monkey—whose goal is to persuade users to keep playing by providing a supportive and attentive audience, celebrating each time the gambler wins.

As the examples of Baby Think It Over and Banana-Rama suggest, computing products can convey physical cues through eyes, a mouth, movement, and other physical attributes. These physical cues can create opportunities to persuade.

Figure 5.3

The Banana-Rama slot machine interface has onscreen characters that influence gamblers to keep playing.

The Impact of Physical Attractiveness

Simply having physical characteristics is enough for a technology to convey social presence. But it seems reasonable to suggest that a more attractive technology (interface or hardware) will have greater persuasive power than an unattractive technology.

Physical attractiveness has a significant impact on social influence. Research confirms that it's easy to like, believe, and follow attractive people. All else being equal, attractive people are more persuasive than those who are unattractive.[8] People who work in sales, advertising, and other high-persuasion areas know this, and they do what they can to be attractive, or they hire attractive models to be their spokespeople.

Attractiveness even plays out in the courtroom. Mock juries treat attractive defendants with more leniency than unattractive defendants (unless attractiveness is relevant to the crime, such as in a swindling case).[9]

Psychologists do not agree on why attractiveness is so important in persuasion, but a plausible explanation is that attractiveness produces a "halo effect."

Principle of Attractiveness

> A computing technology that is visually attractive to target users is likely to be more persuasive as well.

If someone is physically attractive, people tend to assume they also have a host of admirable qualities, such as intelligence and honesty.[10]

Similarly, physically attractive computing products are potentially more persuasive than unattractive products. If an interface, device, or onscreen character is physically attractive (or cute, as the Banana-Rama characters are), it may benefit from the halo effect; users may assume the product is also intelligent, capable, reliable, and credible.[11]

Attractiveness issues are prominent in one of the most ambitious—and frustrating—efforts in computing: creating human-like faces that interact with people in real time. Over the past few decades, researchers have taken important steps forward in making these faces more technically competent, with better facial expressions, voices, and lip movements. However, because of the programming challenges involved, many of these interactive faces are not very attractive, as shown in Figure 5.4. If interactive faces are to be used for persuasive purposes, such as counseling, training, or advertising, they need to be visually pleasing to be most effective.[12]

Two studies performed at the School of Management at Boston University reinforce the power of attractiveness. In the initial study, in 1996, researchers had participants play a two-person social dilemma game, in which participants could cooperate with an onscreen character or could choose to serve their own selfish purposes.

In this initial study, the onscreen character (representative of the technology at the time) looked unattractive, even creepy, in my view. And it received rather low cooperation rates: just 32%.

A couple of years later, the researchers repeated the study. Thanks to technology developments, in this second study, the onscreen character looked less artificial and, I would argue, more attractive and less creepy. This new and improved character garnered cooperation rates of a whopping 92%—a figure

Figure 5.4

These interactive faces, created in the mid- to late 1990s, show that researchers have a long way to go in developing attractive, human-like interactive onscreen characters.

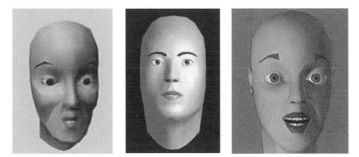

that in this study was statistically indistinguishable from cooperation rates for interacting with real human beings. The researchers concluded that "the mere appearance of a computer character is sufficient to change its social influence."[13]

Of course, people have different opinions about what is attractive. Evaluations vary from culture to culture, generation to generation, and individual to individual. (However, judging attractiveness is not entirely subjective; some elements of attractiveness, such as symmetry, are predictable).[14]

Because people have different views of what's attractive, designers need to understand the aesthetics of their target audiences when creating a persuasive technology product. The more visually attractive the product is to its target audience, the more likely it is to be persuasive. The designer might review the magazines the audience reads and music they listen to, observe the clothes they wear, determine what trends are popular with them, and search for other clues to what they might find attractive. With this information, the designer can create a product and test it with the target group.

Computing technology also can convey social presence without using physical characters. We confirmed this in laboratory experiments at Stanford. We designed interface elements that were simple dialog boxes—no onscreen characters, no computer voices, no artificial intelligence. Yet participants in the experiments responded to these simple computer interfaces as though they were responding to a human being. Among other things, they reported feeling better about themselves when they were praised by a computer and reciprocated favors from a computer. (These experiments are discussed in detail later in this chapter.)

Using Psychological Cues to Persuade

Psychological cues from a computing product can lead people to infer, often subconsciously, that the product has emotions,[15] preferences, motivations, and personality—in short, that the computer has a *psychology*. Psychological cues can be simple, as in text messages that convey empathy ("I'm sorry, but . . .") or onscreen icons that portray emotion, such as the smiling face of the early Macintosh computer. Or the cues can be more complex, such as those that convey personality. Such complex cues may become apparent only after the user interacts with technology for a period of time; for example, a computer that keeps crashing may convey a personality of being uncooperative or vengeful.

It's not only computer novices who infer these psychological qualities; my research with experienced engineers showed that even the tech savvy treat computing products as though the products had preferences and personalities.[16]

The Stanford Similarity Studies

In the area of psychological cues, one of the most powerful persuasion principles is similarity.[17] Simply stated, the principle of similarity suggests that, in most situations, people we think are similar to us (in personality, preferences, or in other attributes) can motivate and persuade us more easily than people who are not similar to us.[18] Even trivial types of similarity—such as having the same hometown or rooting for the same sports teams—can lead to more liking and more persuasion.[19] In general, the greater the similarity, the greater the potential to persuade.

In the mid-1990s at Stanford, my colleagues and I conducted two studies that showed how similarity between computers and the people who use them makes a difference when it comes to persuasion. One study examined similarity in personalities. The other investigated similarity in group affiliation—specifically, in belonging to the same team. Both studies were conducted in a controlled laboratory setting.

The Personality Study

In the first study, my colleagues and I investigated how people would respond to computers with personalities.[20] All participants would work on the same task, receiving information and suggestions from a computer to solve the Desert Survival Problem.[21] This is a hypothetical problem-solving situation in which you are told you have crash-landed in the desert in the southwestern part of the United States. You have various items that have survived the crash with you, such as a flashlight, a pair of sunglasses, a quart of water, salt tablets, and other items. You have to rank the items according to how important each one is to surviving in the desert situation. In our study, participants would have to work with computers to solve the problem.

To prepare for the research, we designed two types of computer "personalities": one computer was dominant, the other submissive. We focused on dominance and submissiveness because psychologists have identified these two traits as one of five key dimensions of personality.[22]

How do you create a dominant or submissive computer? For our study, we created a dominant computer interface by using bold, assertive typefaces for the text. Perhaps more important, we programmed the dominant computer to go first during the interaction and to make confident statements about what the user should do next. Finally, to really make sure people in the study would differentiate between the dominant and submissive computers, we added a "confidence scale" below each of these messages, indicating on a scale of 1 to 10 how confident the computer was about the suggestion it was offering. The dominant computer usually gave confidence ratings of 7, 8, and 9, while the submissive computer offered lower confidence ratings.

For example, if a participant was randomly assigned to interact with the dominant computer, he or she would read the following on the screen while working with the computer on the Desert Survival Task:

In the desert, the intense sunlight will clearly cause blindness by the second day. The sunglasses are absolutely important.

This assertion from the computer was in a bold font, with a high confidence rating.

In contrast, if a person was assigned to the submissive computer, he or she would read a similar statement, but it would be presented in this way:

In the desert, it seems that the intense sunlight could possibly cause blindness by the second day. Without adequate vision, don't you think that survival might become more difficult? The sunglasses might be important.

This statement was made in an italicized font, along with a low ranking on the confidence meter. To further reinforce the concept of submissiveness, the computer let the user make the first move in the survival task.

Another step in preparing for this study was to find dominant and submissive people to serve as study participants. We asked potential participants to fill out personality assessments. Based on the completed assessments, we selected 48 people who were on the extreme ends of the continuum—the most dominant and the most submissive personalities.

We found these participants by having almost 200 students take personality tests. Some, but not all, were engineers, but all participants had experience using computers. In the study, half of the participants were dominant types and half were submissive.

In conducting the study, we mixed and matched the dominant and submissive people with the dominant and submissive computers. In half the cases, participants worked with a computer that shared their personality type. In the other half, participants worked with a computer having the opposite personality.

The information provided by all the computers was essentially the same. Only the computer's style of interacting differed, as conveyed through text in dialog boxes: either the computer was dominant ("The intense sunlight will clearly cause blindness"), or it was submissive ("It seems that the intense sunlight could possibly cause blindness").

After we ran the experiment and analyzed the data, we found a clear result: participants preferred working with a computer they perceived to be similar to themselves in personality style. Dominant people preferred the dominant computer. Submissive people preferred the submissive computer.

Specifically, when working with a computer perceived to be similar in personality, users judged the computer to be more competent and the interaction to be more satisfying and beneficial. In this study we didn't measure persuasion directly, but we did measure key predictors of persuasion, including likability and credibility.

■ ■ ■ ■ ■

Research Highlights: The Personality Study

- Created dominant and submissive computer personalities

- Chose as participants people who were at extremes of dominant or submissive

- Mixed and matched computer personalities with user personalities

- Result: Participants preferred computers whose "personalities" matched their own.

The evidence from this study suggests that computers can motivate and persuade people more effectively when they share personality traits with them—at least in terms of dominance and submission. For designers of persuasive technology, the findings suggest that products may be more persuasive if they match the personality of target users or are similar in other ways.

The Affiliation Study

While running the personality study, we set out to conduct another study to examine the persuasive effects of other types of similarity between people and computers.[23] For this second study we investigated similarity in affiliation— specifically, the persuasive impact of being part of the same group or team. The study included 56 participants, mostly Stanford students along with a few people from the Silicon Valley community. All the participants were experienced computer users.

In this study, we gave participants the same Desert Survival Problem to solve. We assigned them to work on the problem either with a computer we said was their "teammate" or with a computer that we gave no label. To visually remind them of their relationships with the computers, we asked each participant to wear a colored wristband during the study. If the participant was working with a computer we had labeled as his or her teammate, the participant wore a blue wristband, which matched the color of the frame around the computer monitor. The other participants—the control group—wore green wristbands while working with the blue-framed computers. For both groups, the interaction with the computer was identical: the computer gave the same information, in the same style.

■ ■ ■ ■

Research Highlights: The Affiliation Study

- Participants were given a problem to solve and assigned to work on the problem either with a computer they were told was a "teammate" or a computer that was given no label.

- For all participants, the interaction with the computer was identical; the only difference was whether or not the participant believed the computer was a teammate.

- The results compared to responses of other participants: people who worked with a computer labeled as their teammate reported that the computer was more similar to them, that it was smarter, and that it offered better information. These participants also were more likely to choose the problem solutions recommended by the computers.

After completing the study, we examined the data and found significant differences between the conditions. When compared with other participants, people who worked with a computer labeled as their teammate reported that the computer was more similar to them, in terms of approach to the task, suggestions offered, interaction style, and similarity of rankings of items needed for survival. Even more interesting, participants who worked with a computer labeled as a teammate thought the computer was smarter and offered better information.

In addition, participants who worked on the task with a computer labeled as a teammate reported that the computer was friendlier and that it gave higher-quality information. Furthermore, people who perceived the computer to be similar to themselves reported that the computer performed better on the task.[24]

During the study we also measured people's behavior. We found that computers labeled as teammates were more effective in influencing people to choose problem solutions that the computer advocated. In other words, teammate computers were more effective in changing people's behavior.

All in all, the study showed that the perception of shared affiliation (in this case, being on the same "team") made computers seem smarter, more credible, and more likable—all attributes that are correlated with the ability to persuade.

Among people, similarity emerges in opinions and attitudes, personal traits, lifestyle, background, and membership.[25] Designers of persuasive technology should be aware of these forms of similarity and strive to build them into their products.

Principle of Similarity

> People are more readily persuaded by computing technology products that are similar to themselves in some way.

One company that has done a good job of this is Ripple Effects, Inc., which "helps schools, youth-serving organizations, and businesses change social behavior in ways that improve performance."[26] The company's Relate for Teens CD-ROM leverages the principle of similarity to make its product more persuasive to its target audience—troubled teens. It conveys similarity through the language it uses, the style of its art (which includes graffiti and dark colors), audio (all instructions are given by teen voices), and photos and video clips that feature other, similar teens. Researchers at Columbia University and New York University have shown that the product produces positive effects on teen behavior, including significant reductions in aggressive acts, increases in "prosocial" acts, and improvements in educational outcomes.[27]

As this example and the Stanford research suggests, designers can make their technology products more persuasive by making them similar to the target audience. The more that users can identify with the product, the more likely they will be persuaded to change their attitudes or behavior in ways the product suggests.

Ethical and Practical Considerations

The two studies just described suggest that people are more open to persuasion from computers that seem similar to themselves, in personality or affiliation. In addition to similarity, a range of other persuasion principles come into play when computers are perceived to have a psychology. Computers can motivate through conveying ostensible emotions, such as happiness, anger, or fear.[28] They can apply a form of social pressure.[29] They can negotiate with people and reach agreements. Computers can act supportively or convey a sense of caring.

Designing psychological cues into computing products can raise ethical and practical questions. Some researchers suggest that deliberately designing computers to project psychological cues is unethical and unhelpful.[30] They argue that psychological cues mislead users about the true nature of the machine (it's not *really* having a social interaction with the user). Other researchers maintain that designing computer products without attention to psychological cues is a bad idea because users will infer a psychology to the technology one way or another.[31]

While I argue that designers must be aware of the ethical implications of designing psychological cues into their products, I side with those who maintain that users will infer a psychology to computing products, whether or not the designers intended this. For this reason, I believe designers must embed appropriate psychological cues in their products. I also believe this can be done in an ethical manner.

The Oscilloscope Study

My belief that users infer a psychology to computing technology stems in part from research I conducted in the mid-1990s for a company I'll call Oscillotech, which made oscilloscopes. The purpose of the research was to determine how the engineers who used the scopes felt about them.

What I found surprised Oscillotech's management. The scopes' text messages, delivered on a single line at the bottom of the scopes' displays, were somewhat harsh and at times unfriendly, especially the error messages. I later found out that the engineers who wrote these messages, more than a decade earlier, didn't consider what impact the messages would make on the scope users; they didn't think people would read the messages and then infer a personality to the measuring device.

They were wrong. My research showed that Oscillotech's scopes made a much less favorable impression on users than did a competitor's scopes. This competitor had been gaining market share at the expense of Oscillotech. While many factors led to the competitor's success, one clear difference was the personality its scopes projected: the messages from the competitor's scopes were invariably warm, helpful, and friendly, but not obsequious or annoying.

What was more convincing was a controlled study I performed. To test the effects of simply changing the error messages in Oscillotech's scopes, I had a new set of messages—designed to portray the personality of a helpful senior engineer—burned into the Oscillotech scopes and tested users' reactions in a controlled experiment.

The result? On nearly every measure, people who used the new scope rated the device more favorably than people who used the previous version of the scope, with the unfriendly messages. Among other things, users reported that the "new" scope gave better information, was more accurate, and was more knowledgeable. In reality, the only difference between the two scopes was the personality of the message. This was the first time Oscillotech addressed the issue of the "personality" of the devices it produced.

This example illustrates the potential impact of psychological cues in computing products. While it is a benign example, the broader issue of using computer technology to convey a human-like psychology—especially as a means to persuade people—is a controversial area that has yet to be fully explored and that is the subject of much debate. (Chapter 9 will address some of the ethical issues that are part of the debate.)

Influencing through Language

Computing products also can use written or spoken language ("You've got mail!") to convey social presence and to persuade. Dialogue boxes are a common example of the persuasive use of language. Whether asking questions ("Do you want to continue the installation?"), offering congratulations for completing a task (Figure 5.5), or reminding the user to update software, dialog boxes can lead people to infer that the computing product is animate in some way.

E-commerce sites such as Amazon.com make extensive use of language to convey social presence and persuade users to buy more products. Amazon.com is a master of this art. When I log on, the site welcomes me by name,

Figure 5.5

Quicken rewards users with a celebratory message each time they reconcile their accounts.

offers recommendations, and lists a host of separate stores tailored to my preferences. Each page I click on addresses me by name and lists more recommendations. To keep me online, I'm asked if the site's recommendations are "on target" and to supply more information if they are not. The designers' goal, it's safe to say, is to persuade me and other users to maximize our online purchases.

Iwin.com, a leading site for online gaming and lotteries, uses language in a very different way. The site conveys a young, brash attitude in an attempt to persuade users to log in, amass iCoins (a type of online currency) by performing various activities on the site, and use that currency to play lotteries.

When you arrive at the homepage, you can answer a "Daily Poll" and gain 25 iCoins. One sample question was "Who's eaten more?" You can choose from two answers: "Pac Man" or "Dom DeLuise." Obviously this question is not serious, more of a teaser to get people to start clicking and playing. The submit button for the survey doesn't even say "submit." Instead, it reads "Hey big daddy" or something similarly hip (the message changes each time you visit the site).

If you keep playing games on the main page without logging in, you'll see this message in large type:

What's the deal? You don't call, you don't log in . . . Is it me?

And if you continue to play games without logging in, again you'll get a prompt with attitude:

Well, you could play without logging in, but you won't win anything. It's up to you.

Later, as you log out of your gaming session, the Web site says:

You're outta here! Thanks for playing!

The use of language on this Web site is very different from Amazon. Note how the creators of Iwin.com had the option to choose standard language to move people through the transactional elements (register, log in, log out, enter lotteries for prizes) of the online experience. Instead, they crafted the language to convey a strong online personality, one that has succeeded in acquiring and keeping users logging in and playing games.[32]

Persuading through Praise

One of the most powerful persuasive uses of language is to offer praise. Studies on the effect of praise in various situations have clearly shown its positive impact.[33] My own laboratory research concludes that, offered sincerely or not, praise affects people's attitudes and their behaviors. My goal in this particular line of research was to determine if praise from a computer would generate positive effects similar to praise from people. The short answer is "yes."[34]

My colleagues and I set up a laboratory experiment in which Stanford students who had significant experience using computers played a "20 Questions" game with computers. As they played this game, they could make a contribution to the computer's database. After they made a contribution, the computer would praise them via text in a dialog box (Figure 5.6). Half of the people in the study were previously told this feedback was a true evaluation of their contribution (this was the "sincere" condition). The other half were told that the positive feedback had nothing to do with their actual contribution (the "insincere" condition).

Figure 5.6

Dialog boxes were a key element in our research on the impact of positive feedback from computers.

Your question makes an interesting and useful distinction. Great job!

OK

In all, each study participant received 12 messages from the computer during the game. They saw text messages such as:

Very smart move. Your new addition will enhance this game in a variety of ways.

Your question makes an interesting and useful distinction. Great job!

Great! Your suggestions show both thoroughness and creativity.

Ten of the messages were pure praise. The other two were less upbeat: All the players received the following warning message after their fourth contribution to the game: "Be careful. Your last question may steer the game in the wrong direction." After their eighth contribution, players received this somewhat negative message: "Okay, but your question will have a negligible effect on overall search efficiency." Previous studies had shown that adding the non-praise messages to the mix increased the credibility of the 10 praise messages.

After participants finished playing the 20 Questions game with the computer, they responded to a questionnaire about their experience. The questionnaire had a few dozen questions about how they felt, their view of the computer, their view of the interaction, and their view of the computer's evaluations of their work.

In analyzing the data, we compared the two praise conditions (sincere and insincere) along with a third condition that offered no evaluation, just the text, "Begin next round." The findings were clear. Except for two questions that focused on the sincerity of the computer, participants responded to true praise and flattery identically—and these responses were positive.

In essence, after people received computer praise—sincere or not—they responded significantly more positively than did people who received no evaluation. Specifically, compared to the generic, "no evaluation" condition, the data show that people in both conditions who received praise

- Felt better about themselves

- Were in a better mood

- Felt more powerful

- Felt they had performed well

Principle of Praise

> By offering praise, via words, images, symbols, or sounds, computing technology can lead users to be more open to persuasion.

- Found the interaction engaging

- Were more willing to work with the computer again

- Liked the computer more

- Thought the computer had performed better

Although these aren't direct measures of persuasion, these positive reactions open the door to influence. These findings illustrate the importance of using language in ways that will set the stage for persuasive outcomes, rather than in ways that build barriers to influence. Language—even language used by a computing system—is never neutral. It can promote or hinder a designer's persuasion goals.

Social Dynamics

Most cultures have set patterns for how people interact with each other—rituals for meeting people, taking turns, forming lines, and many others. These rituals are *social dynamics*—unwritten rules for interacting with others. Those who don't follow the rules pay a social price; they risk being alienated.

Computing technology can apply social dynamics to convey social presence and to persuade. One example is Microsoft's Actimates characters, a line of interactive toys introduced in the late 1990s. The Microsoft team did a great deal of research into creating toys that would model social interactions.[35] The goal of the toys, of course, is to entertain kids, but it also seems that the toys are designed to use social rituals to persuade kids to interact with the characters.

Consider the Actimates character named DW (Figure 5.7). This interactive plush toy says things like "I love playing with you" and "Come closer. I want to tell you a secret." These messages cue common social dynamics and protocols.

By cueing social dynamics, DW affects how children feel and what they do. DW's expressions of friendship may lead children to respond with similar expressions or feelings. DW's invitation to hear her secret sets up a relationship of trust and support.

E-commerce sites also use social dynamics to help interactions succeed. They greet users, guide people to products they may like, confirm what's being

Figure 5.7

DW, an interactive plush toy developed by Microsoft, puts social dynamics into motion.

I just love playing with you.

Come closer. I want to tell you a secret.

Achoo! Oh, pardon me.

Let's have a tea party.

purchased, ask for any needed information, and thank people for making the transaction.[36] In short, they apply the same social dynamics users might encounter when shopping in a brick-and-mortar store.

An application of social dynamics can be found by users of Eudora, an email program. If you don't register the product immediately, every week or so the program will bring up a dialogue box, inviting you to register. The registration screen (also shown in the Introduction, as an example of how computers can be persistent) has some funny, informal text ("As a registered user of Eudora we won't nag you as often as we do. We'll also erect a giant statue in your image on the front lawn of our corporate headquarters"—with a note below: "Giant statue offer void on the planet Earth.")

All of this text is designed to persuade you to choose one of two buttons in the dialogue box (Figure 5.8):

Take me to the registration page!

or

Maybe later.

Figure 5.8

The dialogue box that Eudora uses to persuade users to register.

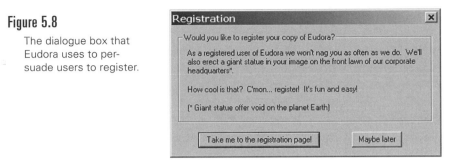

Eudora doesn't give users the option of clicking "no" (although you can avoid choosing either option above by simply clicking the "close" button). Instead, to get the dialogue box to vanish and get on with their task at hand, people most likely click on "Maybe later." By clicking on this box, the user has made an implicit commitment that *maybe* he or she will register later. This increases the likelihood that the user will feel compelled to register at some point.

The Eudora dialogue box seems simple-minded—even goofy. But it's actually quite clever. The goofy content and language serve a few purposes: elevating the mood of the user, making the request seem fun and easy, positioning the requestor as approachable and good-humored. Perhaps the main purpose of the goofiness is to serve as a distraction, just as people can use distractions effectively during negotiations.

The truth is that Eudora is making a very serious request. Getting people to eventually say yes is vital to the future of the product. And the dynamic that plays out with this dialogue box is not so different from the social dynamics that play out during serious human-human exchanges, such as asking for a raise. (If you can get the boss to say "maybe later" rather than "no" in response to your request for a raise, you're in a much more powerful position when you raise the issue again later, as the boss has made a subtle commitment to considering it.)

Other social dynamics can be set in motion when people interact with computing products. Users may succumb to "peer pressure" from computers. Or they may judge information as more accurate when it comes from multiple computing sources. These and many other social dynamics have yet to be tested, but based on early efforts by Amazon.com, Eudora, and others, the potential for using technology to leverage social dynamics appears to be strong.

The Reciprocity Study

One social dynamic that may have potential for persuasive technology is the rule of reciprocity. This unwritten social rule states that after you receive a favor, you must pay it back in some way. Anthropologists report that the reciprocity rule is followed in every human society.[37]

In my laboratory research, my colleagues and I set out to see if the rule of reciprocity could be applied to interactions between humans and computers. Specifically, we set up an experiment to see if people would reciprocate to a computer that had provided a favor for them.[38]

I recruited Stanford students and people living in the Silicon Valley area to be participants in the research. In total, 76 people were involved in the reciprocity study.

Each participant entered a room that had two identical computers. My research assistants and I gave each person a task that required finding specific types of information, using the computer. In this study, we again used the context of the Desert Survival Problem. The study participants were given a modified version of the challenge. They needed to rank seven items according to their survival value (a compress kit, cosmetic mirror, flashlight, salt tablets, sectional air map, topcoat, and vodka). To do this, they could use a computer to find information about each item.

Half the participants used a computer that was extremely helpful. We had preprogrammed the computer to provide information we knew would be useful: Months before the study, we tested lots of information about these items in pilot studies and selected the bits of information people had found most useful. We put this information into the computer program.

As a result, when study participants performed a search on any of the survival items, they received information that we had already confirmed would be helpful to them in ranking the items ("The beam from an ordinary flashlight can be seen as far as 15 miles away on a clear night."). The computer also claimed to be searching many databases to get the best information for the participants (this experiment took place just before the Web was popular, though the search we designed was much like searching on Google today).

The user could search for information on five of the seven items to be ranked. Users had to make separate requests for each search. The idea behind all of this was to set up a situation in which study participants would feel that the computer had done them a favor: it had searched many databases on the user's behalf and had come up with information that was useful.

Only half of the participants worked with computers that provided this high quality of help and information. The other half also went into the lab alone and were given the same task but used a computer that provided low-quality help. The computer looked identical and had the same interface. But when these participants asked the computer to find information on the items, the information that came back was not very helpful.

We again had pretested information and knew what would seem a plausible result of an information search, but because of our pilot tests we knew the information would *not* be useful to the participants ("Small Flashlight: Easy to find yellow Lumilite flashlight is there when you need it. Batteries included.").

In setting up the experiment this way, our goal was to have two sets of participants. One group would feel the computer had done a favor for them; the other group would feel the computer had not been helpful.

In a subsequent, seemingly unrelated task (it was related, but we hid this fact from participants), each participant was given the opportunity to help a computer create a color palette that matched human perception. The computer would show three colors, and the participants would rank the colors, light to dark. The participants could do as many, or as few, of these comparisons as they wished for the computer.

Because this was a controlled study, half of the participants worked with the same computer on the second task, the color perception task (the reciprocity condition), and half of the participants worked with a different computer (the control condition).

Those who worked with the same helpful computer on the second task—the color perception task—had an opportunity to reciprocate the help the computer had provided earlier. (During the experiment, we never mentioned anything about reciprocity to participants.) In contrast, those who worked with a different computer served as a control group.

After completing the study, we analyzed the data and found that people did indeed reciprocate to the computer that helped them. Participants who returned to work with the initially helpful computer performed more work for that computer on the second task. Specifically, participants in the reciprocity condition performed more color evaluations—almost double the number—than those who worked with a different, although identical, computer on the second task. In summary, the study showed that people observed a common social dynamic, the rule of reciprocity; they repaid a favor that a computer had done for them.

┌ ■ ■ ■ ■

Research Highlights: The Reciprocity Study

- Participants entered a room with two computers and were assigned a task of finding information, with the help of one of the computers.

- Half of the participants used the computer that was helpful in finding the information; the other half used the computer that was not helpful.

- In a subsequent task, participants were asked to help one of the computers to create a color palette. Half of the participants worked with the same computer they'd worked with on the initial task; half worked with the other computer.

- Result: Those participants who worked with the same helpful computer on both tasks performed almost twice as much work for their computers on the second task as did the other participants.

This reciprocity study included control conditions that rule out other possible explanations for the results. One such explanation is that getting good information during the first task made participants happy, so they did more work in the second task. This explanation is ruled out because half of those who received good information from a computer for the first task used a different but identical-looking computer on the second task, but only those who used the same computer for *both* tasks showed the reciprocity effect.

Principle of Reciprocity

> People will feel the need to reciprocate when computing technology has done a favor for them.

The other alternative explanation is that people who remained at the same workstation for the second task were more comfortable and familiar with the chair or the setup, leading to an increase in work on the second task. This explanation can be ruled out because participants who received bad information from the computer in the first task and used the same computer on the second task did less work, not more, indicating that people may have retaliated against the computer that failed to help them on the previous task. (The retaliation effect may be even more provocative than the reciprocity effect, though it is not very useful for designing persuasive computer products.) With the alternative explanations ruled out, the evidence suggests that the rule of reciprocity is such a powerful social dynamic that people followed it when working with a machine.

The implication for designers of persuasive technology is that the rule of reciprocity—an important social dynamic—can be applied to influence users. A simple example that leverages the rule of reciprocity is a shareware program that, after multiple uses, might query the user with a message such as "You have enjoyed playing this game ten times. Why not pay back the favor and register?"

Persuading by Adopting Social Roles

In the mid-1960s, MIT's Joseph Weizenbaum created ELIZA, a computer program that acted in the role of a psychotherapist. ELIZA was a relatively simple program, with less than 300 lines of code. It was designed to replicate the initial interview a therapist would have with a patient. A person could type in "I have a problem," and ELIZA would respond in text, "Can you elaborate on that?" The exchange would continue, with ELIZA continuing to portray the role of a therapist.

The impact of a computer adopting this human role surprised many, including Weizenbaum. Even though people knew intellectually that ELIZA was software, they sometimes treated the program as though it were a human therapist who could actually help them. The response was so compelling that Weizenbaum was distressed over the ethical implications and wrote a book on the subject.[39] Even though Weizenbaum was disturbed by the effects of his creation, the controversial domain of computerized psychotherapy continues today, with the computer playing the role of a therapist.[40]

Computers in Roles of Authority

Teacher, referee, judge, counselor, expert—all of these are authority roles humans play. Computers also can act in these roles, and when they do, they gain the automatic influence that comes with being in a position of authority, as the example of ELIZA suggests. In general, people expect authorities to lead them, make suggestions, and provide helpful information. They also assume authorities are intelligent and powerful. By playing a role of authority convincingly, computer products become more influential.

That's why Symantec's popular Norton Utilities program includes Norton Disk Doctor and WinDoctor. The doctor metaphor suggests smart, authoritative, and trustworthy—more persuasive than, say, "Disk Helper" or "Disk Assistant."

Figure 5.9

Broderbund created a fictional authority figure—a teacher—to persuade users of its typing program.

That's also why Broderbund used the image of a teacher when creating its popular software program Mavis Beacon Teaches Typing (Figure 5.9). Mavis Beacon is a marketing creation, not a real person. But her physical image, including prim hairdo, and her name suggest a kindly, competent high school typing teacher. By evoking the image of a teacher, Broderbund probably hoped that its software would gain the influence associated with that role.

Principle of Authority

> Computing technology that assumes roles of authority will have enhanced powers of persuasion.

Although the power of authority has received the most attention in formal persuasion studies, authority roles aren't the only social roles that influence people. Sometimes influence strategies that *don't* leverage power or status also can be effective. Consider the roles of "friend," "entertainer," and "opponent," each of which can cause people to change their attitudes or behavior.

Ask Jeeves is a search engine that takes on the role of a butler (Figure 5.10) to distinguish its product from competing search engines.[41] When you visit ask.com, you ask a simple question, and Jeeves the butler is at your service, searching his own database and the most common Web search engines.

It's likely that setting up the search engine in the role of a butler was a deliberate attempt to influence. In terms of attitude, the creators likely wanted peo-

Figure 5.10

The Ask Jeeves Web search engine adopts a social role of butler or servant.

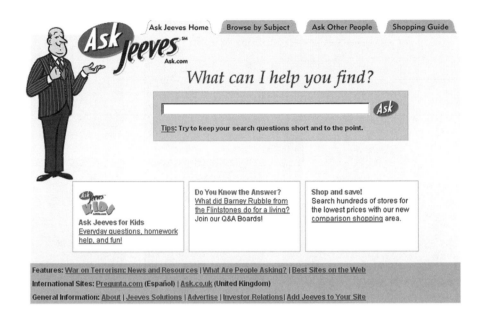

ple to feel the site would be easy to use, the service was helpful, and the site would treat them as special and important—all attributes associated with a butler or servant.

In terms of behavior, the Ask Jeeves creators probably hoped a butler-based Web site would influence users to return and use the site frequently, developing a kind of ongoing social relationship with the character, something the other search engines don't provide. If the popularity of Web sites is any indication, the Ask Jeeves strategy is working. The site consistently ranks—according to some accounts—in the top 20 Web sites in terms of unique visitors.[42]

Another example, the Personal Aerobics Trainer (PAT), takes the concept of persuasiveness one step further. PAT is a virtual interactive fitness trainer created by James Davis of MIT. The system lets users choose the type of coach they will find the most motivational (including the "Virtual Army Drill Sergeant" shown in Figure 5.11). The virtual coach uses computer vision technology to watch how the person is performing and offers positive feedback ("Good job!" and "Keep up the good work!") or negative feedback ("Get moving!").[43]

For computers that play social roles to be effective in motivating or persuading, it's important to choose the role model carefully or it will be counterproductive. Adult authority figures might work well for traditional business types,

Figure 5.11   The Personal Aerobics Trainer (PAT) is an interactive fitness trainer that lets users choose from a variety of coaches, including a virtual army drill sergeant.

but teenagers may not respond. One user may prefer the "Army Drill Sergeant," and another may find it demotivating. The implication for designers of persuasive technology that incorporates social role-playing: know your target audience. As the PAT system suggests, a target audience can have multiple user groups. Designers should provide a way for different groups of users to choose the social roles they prefer.

Social Cues: Handle with Care

Although people respond socially to computer products that convey social cues, to be effective in persuasion, designers must understand the appropriate use of those cues. In my view, when you turn up the volume on the "social" element of a persuasive technology product, you increase your bet: you either win bigger or lose bigger, and the outcome often depends on the user. If you succeed, you make a more powerful positive impact. If you fail, you make users irritated or angry.

With that in mind, when is it appropriate to make the social quality of the product more explicit? In general, I believe it's appropriate to enhance social cues in leisure, entertainment, and educational products (smart toys, video games, kids' learning applications). Users of such applications are more likely to indulge, accept, and perhaps even embrace an explicit cyber social actor— either embodied or not. The Actimates toys are a good example. In the case of Actimates, one purpose of the toys is to teach social dynamics, so designers can rightly focus on maximizing the use of social cues.

When is it not appropriate to enhance social cues? When the sole purpose of the technology product is to improve efficiency.

When I buy gas for my car, I choose a station with gas pumps that take credit cards directly. I don't want to deal with a cashier; I'm not looking for a social experience. I believe the analogy applies to interactive technologies, such as word processing programs or spreadsheets, that people use to perform a task more efficiently. For such tasks, it's best to minimize cues for social presence, as social interactions can slow things down. This is probably why Amazon.com and other e-commerce sites use social dynamics but do not have an embodied agent that chats people up. As in brick-and-mortar stores, when people buy things they are often getting work done; it's a job, not a social event. Enhancing social cues for such applications could prove to be distracting, annoying, or both.

The quality and repetition of the social cue should be of concern to designers as well. For example, dialogue boxes designed to motivate need to be crafted with care to avoid being annoyingly repetitious. When I created my experiment to study praise in dialogue boxes, I started out with dozens of possible ways to praise users and winnowed down the options, through user testing and other means, to 10 praise messages that would show up during the task. Users never got the same type of praise twice; they were praised many times, but the message was varied so it didn't feel repetitious.

Notes and References

For updates on the topics presented in this chapter, visit *www.persuasivetech.info.*

1. Based on the preliminary report of the Seal Beach, CA, Police Department (June 8, 2002) and the police log of the Long Beach (CA) *News-Enterprise* (June 12, 2002), p. 18.

2. B. Reeves and C. Nass, *The Media Equation: How People Treat Computers, Television, and New Media Like Real People and Places* (New York: Cambridge University Press, 1996).

3. In many ways the Tamagotchi's success was helpful for those of us working with Cliff Nass at Stanford University. Since the early 1990s we had been researching people's social responses to computers (see Reeves and Nass (1996) for a summary). Before the Tamagotchi craze, many people didn't fully understand our research—or they didn't understand why we would study computers in this way. However, after the Tamagotchi became widely known, our research made more sense to people; they had seen how the human-computer relationship could take on social qualities.

4. P. Zimbardo and M. Leippe, *The Psychology of Attitude Change and Social Influence* (New York: McGraw-Hill, 1991).

5. "Group polarization" is a phenomenon whereby people, when part of a group, tend to adopt a more extreme stance than they would if they were alone. "Social facilitation" is a phenomenon whereby the presence of others increases arousal. This helps a person to perform easy tasks but hurts performance on difficult tasks.

6. B. J. Fogg, *Charismatic Computers: Creating More Likable and Persuasive Interactive Technologies by Leveraging Principles from Social Psychology*, doctoral dissertation, Stanford University (1997).

7. For academic work on computers as persuasive social actors, see the following:

   a. B. J. Fogg, *Charismatic Computers: Creating More Likable and Persuasive Interactive Technologies by Leveraging Principles from Social Psychology*, doctoral dissertation, Stanford University (1997).

   b. B. J. Fogg and C. I. Nass, How users reciprocate to computers: An experiment that demonstrates behavior change, in *Extended Abstracts of the CHI97 Conference of the ACM/SIGCHI* (New York: ACM Press, 1997).

   c. B. J. Fogg and C. I. Nass, Silicon sycophants: The effects of computers that flatter, *International Journal of Human-Computer Studies*, 46: 551–561 (1997).

   d. C. I. Nass, B. J. Fogg, and Y. Moon, Can computers be teammates? Affiliation and social identity effects in human-computer interaction, *International Journal of Human-Computer Studies*, 45(6): 669–678 (1996).

8. For more information on the role of attractiveness in persuasion, see the following:

   a. E. Berscheid and E. Walster, Physical attractiveness, in L. Berkowitz (ed.), *Advances in Experimental Social Psychology*, Vol. 7, (New York: Academic, 1974), pp. 158–216.

   b. S. Chaiken, Communicator physical attractiveness and persuasion, *Journal of Personality and Social Psychology*, 37: 1387–1397 (1979).

9. H. Sigall and N. Osgrove, Beautiful but dangerous: Effects of offender attractiveness and nature of crime on juridic judgement, *Journal of Personality and Social Psychology*, 31: 410–414 (1975).

10. For more on the connection between attractiveness and other qualities, see the following:

   a. K. L. Dion, E. Bersheid, and E. Walster, What is beautiful is good, *Journal of Personality and Social Psychology*, 24: 285–290 (1972).

   b. A. H. Eagly, R. D. Ashmore, M. G. Makhijani, and L. C. Longo, What is beautiful is good, but . . . : A meta-analytic review of research on the physical attractiveness stereotype, *Psychological Bulleting*, 110: 109–128 (1991).

11. The principle of physical attractiveness probably applies to Web sites as well, although my research assistants and I could find no quantitative public studies on how attractiveness of Web sites affects persuasion—a good topic for future research.

12. These interactive faces typically have not been created for persuasive purposes—at least not yet. Researchers in this area usually focus on the significant challenge of simply getting the faces to look and act realistically, with an eye toward developing a new genre of human-computer interaction. In the commercial space, people working on interactive talking faces are testing the waters for various applications, ranging from using these interactive faces for delivering personalized news to providing automated customer support online.

13. S. Parise, S. Kiesler, L. Sproull, and K. Waters, Cooperating with life-like interface agents, *Computers in Human Behavior*, 15 (2): 123–142 (1999). Available online as an IBM technical report at *http://domino.watson.ibm.com/cambridge/research.nsf/2b4f81291401771785256976004a8d13/ce1725c578ff207d8525663c006b5401/$FILE/decfac48.htm*.

14. For more on the predictability of attractiveness, see the following:

   a. M. Cunningham, P. Druen, and A. Barbee, Evolutionary, social and personality variables in the evaluation of physical attractiveness, in J. Simpson and D. Kenrick (eds.), *Evolutionary Social Psychology* (Mahwah, NJ: Lawrence Erlbaum, 1997), 109–140.

   b. J. H. Langlois, L. A. Roggman, and L. Musselman, What is average and what is not average about attractive faces? *Psychological Science*, 5: 214–220 (1994).

15. When it comes to emotions and computers, Dr. Rosalind Picard's Affective Computing Research Group at MIT has been blazing new trails. For more information about the group's work, see *http://affect.media.mit.edu/*.

16. My research involving engineers and social responses to computer devices was performed for HP Labs in 1995.

17. H. Tajfel, *Social Identity and Intergroup Relations* (Cambridge, England: Cambridge University Press, 1982).

18. R. B. Cialdini, *Influence: Science and Practice*, 3rd ed. (New York: HarperCollins, 1993).

19. Persuasion scholar Robert Cialdini writes, "As trivial as . . . similarities may seem, they appear to work. . . . even small similarities can be effective in producing a positive response to another." Robert B. Cialdini, *Influence: Science & Practice* (Boston: Allyn and Bacon, 2000). See also H. Tajfel, *Human Groups and Social Categories* (Cambridge: Cambridge University Press, 1981).

See also H. Tajfel, *Social Identity and Intergroup Relations* (Cambridge, England: Cambridge University Press, 1982).

20. C. I. Nass, Y. Moon, B. J. Fogg, B. Reeves, and D. C. Dryer, Can computer personalities be human personalities? *International Journal of Human-Computer Studies,* 43: 223–239 (1995).

21. For each study, we adapted the desert survival task from J. C. Lafferty and P. M. Eady, *The Desert Survival Problem* (Plymouth, MI: Experimental Learning Methods, 1974).

22. J. M. Digman, Personality structure: An emergence of the five-factor model, *The Annual Review of Psychology,* 41: 417–440 (1990).

23. C. I. Nass, B. J. Fogg, and Y. Moon, Can computers be teammates? Affiliation and social identity effects in human-computer interaction, *International Journal of Human-Computer Studies,* 45(6): 669–678 (1996).

24. B. J. Fogg, *Charismatic Computers: Creating More Likable and Persuasive Interactive Technologies by Leveraging Principles from Social Psychology,* doctoral dissertation, Stanford University (1997).

25. Part of my list about similarity comes from

    S. Shavitt and T. C. Brock, *Persuasion: Psychological Insights and Perspectives* (Needham Heights, MA: Allyn and Bacon, 1994).

26. *http://www.rippleeffects.com.*

27. To read about the research, see *http://www.rippleeffects.com/research/studies.html.*

28. To get a sense of how computers can use emotions to motivate and persuade, see R. Picard, *Affective Computing* (Cambridge, MA: MIT Press, 1997). See also the readings on Dr. Picard's Web site: *http://affect.media.mit.edu/AC_readings.html.*

29. C. Marshall and T. O. Maguire, The computer as social pressure to produce conformity in a simple perceptual task, *AV Communication Review,* 19: 19–28 (1971).

30. For more about the advisability (pro and con) of incorporating social elements into computer systems, see the following:

    a. B. Shneiderman, *Designing the User Interface: Strategies for Effective Human-Computer Interaction* (Reading, MA: Addison Wesley Longman, 1998).

    b. B. Shneiderman and P. Maes, Direct manipulations vs. interface agents, *Interactions,* 4(6): 42–61 (1997).

31. For more about the advisability of incorporating social elements into computer systems, see the following:

    a. B. Reeves and C. Nass, *The Media Equation: How People Treat Computers, Television, and New Media Like Real People and Places* (New York: Cambridge University Press, 1996).

    b. B. Shneiderman and P. Maes, Direct manipulations vs. interface agents, *Interactions,* 4(6): 42–61 (1997).

32. As of this writing, the Web rankings and search directory top9.com ranks iwin.com as the #1 site in the sweepstakes and lottery category, and trafficranking.com ranks the site above americanexpress.com, nih.gov, hotjobs.com, and nfl.com.

33. For more on the effects of praise, see the following:

   a. E. Berscheid and E. H. Walster, *Interpersonal Attraction*, 2nd ed. (Reading, MA: Addison-Wesley, 1978).

   b. E. E. Jones, *Interpersonal Perception* (New York: W. H. Freeman, 1990).

   c. J. Pandey and P. Singh, Effects of Machiavellianism, other-enhancement, and power-position on affect, power feeling, and evaluation of the ingratiator, *Journal of Psychology*, 121: 287–300 (1987).

34. For more on investigations into praise from computers, see the following:

   a. B. J. Fogg, *Charismatic Computers: Creating More Likable and Persuasive Interactive Technologies by Leveraging Principles from Social Psychology*, doctoral dissertation, Stanford University (1997).

   b. B. J. Fogg and C. I. Nass, Silicon sycophants: The effects of computers that flatter, *International Journal of Human-Computer Studies*, 46: 551–561 (1997).

35. For more on designing interfaces for children, see the following:

   a. Erik Strommen and Kristin Alexander, Emotional interfaces for interactive aardvarks: Designing affect into social interfaces for children, *Proceeding of the CHI 99 Conference on Human Factors in Computing Systems: The CHI Is the Limit*, 528–535 (1999).

   b. Erik Strommen, When the interface is a talking dinosaur: Learning across media with ActiMates Barney, *Conference Proceedings on Human Factors in Computing Systems*, 228–295 (1998).

36. An online article in *Info World* (Online 'agents' evolve for customer service, Dec. 11, 2000, *http://www.itworld.com/AppDev/1248/IWD001211hnenabler/online*) notes that "The new breed of agent is highly customizable, allowing e-tailers to brand them as they wish. The 'agents' also aim to assist and reassure customers by emoting: If an agent can't answer a question, it expresses disappointment and tries again or it pushes the user toward another channel of service. If the customer expresses interest in a product, the agent can suggest related items. If a transaction is completed, the agent can thank the customer and urge him or her to come back soon."

37. A. W. Gouldner, The norm of reciprocity: A preliminary statement, *American Sociological Review*, 25: 161–178 (1960).

38. For more on investigations into computers and reciprocity, see

   B. J. Fogg, *Charismatic Computers: Creating More Likable and Persuasive Interactive Technologies by Leveraging Principles from Social Psychology*, doctoral dissertation, Stanford University 1997.

39. His book is entitled *Computer Power and Human Reason* (San Francisco: W. H. Freeman, 1976).

40. For a good introductory discussion of computerized therapy with pointers to other sources, see the Web page of John Suler, Ph.D., at *http://www.rider.edu/users/suler/psycyber/eliza.html.*

41. *www.ask.com.*

42. In March 2002, top9.com rated AskJeeves.com just above Google, Excite, and About.com. In May 2002, the Search Engine Watch ranked AskJeeves as the #3 search engine, behind Google and Yahoo (source: *http://searchenginewatch.com/sereport/02/05-ratings.html*). Although these and other reports differ, the main point remains the same: AskJeeves is a popular site.

43. For more information on PAT, see *http://www-white.media.mit.edu/~jdavis/Pat/.*

chapter **6**

Credibility and Computers

"Are computers credible?" That's a question I like to ask students in my Stanford classes. It invariably generates a lively debate.

There's no easy answer, but the question is an important one. When it comes to believing information sources—including computers—credibility matters. Credible sources have the ability to change opinions, attitudes, and behaviors, to motivate and persuade. In contrast, when credibility is low, the potential to influence also is low.[1]

Throughout most of the brief history of computing, people have held computers in high esteem[2]—a view that is reflected in popular culture. Over the past several decades, computers often have been portrayed as infallible side-kicks in the service of humanity, from Robby the Robot in *Forbidden Planet*, the 1956 movie classic, to B-9, the robot in the 1960s television program *Lost in Space*, to R2-D2 in *Star Wars*.[3]

In the consumer realm, computer-based information and services have been marketed as better, more reliable, and more credible sources than humans. Marketers assured the buying public that if a computer said it or produced it, then it's believable.

Due in part to the emergence of the Internet and the proliferation of less-than-credible Web sites, the cultural view of computers as highly credible sources has been seriously challenged. (Web credibility, which deserves special attention, is the subject of Chapter 7.) As consumers become more skeptical, it's important for designers of persuasive technology to understand the

121

components of credibility, the contexts in which credibility matters, and the forms and dynamics of credibility—the focus of this chapter.

What Is "Credibility"?

Credibility is a *perceived* quality that has two dimensions: trustworthiness and expertise.

Scenario 1: A man wearing a suit knocks at your door. His face is familiar, and he says, "You've won our sweepstakes!" He hands you a big check, and the TV cameras are rolling. Outside your house, three reporters compete for your attention.

Scenario 2: You receive a letter in the mail, sent using a bulk mail stamp. The letter inside says, "You've won our sweepstakes!" The letter has your name spelled incorrectly, and you notice the signature at the bottom is not an original.

Even though the overt message in both scenarios is exactly the same ("You've won our sweepstakes!"), the elements of Scenario 1—a personal contact, a famous face, media attention, and even the cliché oversized check—make the message believable. In contrast, under the second scenario, you'd probably trash the letter without giving it a second thought. It's not credible.

A Simple Definition

Simply put, "credibility" can be defined as *believability*. In fact, some languages use the same word for these two English terms.[4] The word *credible* comes from the Latin *credere,* to believe. In my research I've found that "believability" is a good synonym for "credibility" in virtually all cases.

The academic literature on credibility dates back five decades, arising primarily from the fields of psychology and communication. As a result of research in these areas, scholars agree that credibility is a *perceived quality*; it doesn't reside in an object, a person, or a piece of information.[5]

In some ways, credibility is like beauty: it's in the eye of the beholder. You can't touch, see, or hear credibility; it exists only when you make an evaluation of a person, object, or piece of information. But credibility isn't completely arbitrary. Much like agreement in evaluating beauty, people often agree when evaluating a source's credibility.

Figure 6.1

The two key dimensions of credibility.

Some studies suggest there may be a dozen or more elements that contribute to credibility evaluations.[6] However, most researchers and psychologists confirm that there are just two key dimensions of credibility: trustworthiness and expertise (Figure 6.1). People evaluate these two elements, then combine them to develop an overall assessment of credibility.[7]

Trustworthiness

Trustworthiness is a key factor in the credibility equation. The trustworthiness dimension of credibility captures the perceived goodness or morality of the source. Rhetoricians in ancient Greece used the term *ethos* to describe this concept. In the context of computers, a computer that is "trustworthy" is one that is perceived to be truthful, fair, and unbiased.

Principle of Trustworthiness

> Computing technology that is viewed as trustworthy (truthful, fair, and unbiased) will have increased powers of persuasion.

People in certain professions, such as judges, physicians, priests, and referees, are generally perceived to be trustworthy. These individuals have a professional duty to be truthful, unbiased, and fair. If it's perceived that they are not trustworthy, they lose credibility. (The controversy over judging of pairs figure skating at the 2002 Winter Olympics offers a good example. So does the Enron accounting debacle, which called the credibility of accountants into question.)

What leads to perceptions of trustworthiness? Research doesn't provide concrete guidelines, but a few key points seem clear. First and most obvious, the perception that a source is fair and unbiased will contribute to trustworthiness.[8] That's one reason we have independent audits, turn to the opinions of respected third parties, and conduct double-blind studies.

Next, sources that argue against their own interest are perceived as being credible.[9] If a UPS representative told you FedEx is faster (or vice versa), you would probably consider this a credible opinion, since the rep ostensibly would have nothing to gain (and something to lose) by telling you that a competitor is more efficient. In general, the apparent honesty of sources makes them highly credible and therefore more influential.

Finally, perceived similarity leads to perceived trustworthiness.[10] People tend to think other people (or other computers, as we discovered in the Stanford

Principle of Expertise

> Computing technology that is viewed as incorporating expertise (knowledge, experience, and competence) will have increased powers of persuasion.

Similarity Study) are more trustworthy when they are similar to themselves in background, language, opinions, or in other ways. As noted in Chapter 5, the similarities don't even have to be significant to be effective.

Expertise

The second dimension of credibility is expertise—the perceived knowledge, skill, and experience of the source. Many cues lead to perceptions of expertise. Among them are labels that proclaim one an expert (such as the title "professor" or "doctor"), appearance cues (such as a white lab coat), and documentation of accomplishments (such as an award for excellent performance). In general, a source that is considered an expert on a given topic will be viewed as more credible than one that is not.

Combinations of Trustworthiness and Expertise

> **The most credible sources are those perceived to have high levels of trustworthiness *and* expertise.**

Trustworthiness and expertise don't necessarily go hand in hand. A car mechanic may have the expertise to know exactly what's wrong with your car, but if he has a reputation for charging for unneeded repairs, he's not trustworthy and therefore is not perceived as credible.

Similarly, there can be trustworthiness without expertise. A friend might suggest you try acupuncture for your back pain, although she only read about it. Your friend's good intentions probably would not be enough to persuade you to pursue the ancient tradition because she lacks the credibility of an expert.

Given that both trustworthiness and expertise lead to credibility perceptions, the most credible sources are those that have high levels of trustworthiness and expertise—the car mechanic who is also your brother, the close friend who has spent years practicing Eastern medicine.

The same is true for computing products. The most credible computing products are those perceived to have *high levels of trustworthiness and high levels of expertise.*

If one dimension of credibility is strong while the other dimension is unknown, the computing product still may be perceived as credible, due to the "halo effect" described in Chapter 5 (if one virtue is evident, another virtue may be assumed, rightly or wrongly). However, if one dimension is known to be weak, credibility suffers, regardless of the other dimension. If a computerized hotel advisor contained more information than any other system in the world,

Credibility versus Trust

In the academic and professional literature, authors sometimes use the terms *credibility* and *trust* imprecisely and interchangeably. Although the two terms are related, *trust* and *credibility* are not synonyms. *Trust* indicates a positive belief about the perceived reliability of, dependability of, and confidence in a person, object, or process.[11] If you were planning to bungee jump off a bridge, you'd need to have *trust* in your bungee cord. Credibility wouldn't apply.

People often use the word *trust* in certain phrases when they really are referring to credibility (e.g., "trust in the information" and "trust in the advice"[12]). When you read about "trust" and computers, keep in mind that the author may be referring either to *dependability* or to *credibility*.

One way to avoid confusion: when you see the word *trust* applied to technology, replace it with the word *dependability* and then replace it with the word *believability* and see which meaning works in that context. In my lab, we have an even better solution: we simply never use the word *trust*. We've settled on words that have more precise meanings to us, such as *entrustable, dependable,* and *credible*.

you'd rightfully assume the system is an expert. However, if you learned that the system was controlled by a single hotel chain—an indication of possible bias— you might question the trustworthiness of any hotel suggestion the system offers.

When Credibility Matters in Human-Computer Interaction

In some cases, it doesn't matter whether or not a computing device is perceived as being credible.[13] In many situations, though, credibility does matter; it helps to determine whether or not the technology has the potential to persuade. I propose that there are seven contexts in which credibility is essential in human-computer interactions.

■ ■ ■ ■

Credibility Matters When Computers

1. Instruct or advise users

2. Report measurements

3. Provide information and analysis

4. Report on work performed

5. Report about their own state

6. Run simulations

7. Render virtual environments

If a computing technology operating in one of these seven contexts is not perceived as credible, it likely will not be persuasive. Suppose a computer system reports measurements, such as air quality in a "take the bus" initiative or body fat percentage in a weight control system. If the measurements are credible, the system will be more likely to influence. If they are not credible, they're not likely to persuade people to take the bus or motivate them to lose weight.

These seven contexts, discussed below, are not mutually exclusive. A complex computing product, such as an aviation navigation system, may incorporate elements from various categories—presenting information about weather conditions, measuring airspeed, rendering a visual simulation, and reporting the state of the onboard computer system.

Instructing or Advising

Credibility matters when computers give advice or provide instructions to users. If the instruction or advice is poor or biased, the computer will lose credibility. For instance, several search engines have been criticized for sorting systems that are driven by advertising revenues rather than relevancy.[14] Their credibility has been called into question.

In some cases, it's clear that a computer is giving instructions or advice, such as when an in-car navigation system gives advice about which route to take. If the directions are faulty, the system will lose credibility.[15]

But it's not always obvious when a computing product is giving instructions or advice. Think of default buttons on dialog boxes. The fact that one option is automatically selected as the default suggests that certain paths are more likely or profitable. This is a subtle form of advice. If the default options are poorly chosen, the computer program could lose credibility because the dialogue boxes, in essence, offer bad advice.

In some cases, the loss of credibility can threaten the marketability of a product. Chauncey Wilson, a colleague who is director of the Design and Usability Testing Center of Bentley College in Waltham, Massachusetts, tells the story of working on a team to develop a new software product. An early alpha version of the product went out with a dialog box that asked users if they wanted to delete tables from a critical database. The project team started getting calls from some early adopters who reported that tables were mysteriously vanishing. The team tracked the problem to a poorly chosen default option. When asking users if they wanted to delete a table, the system offered "Yes" as the default. From past experience with other software, users had become accustomed to choosing the default option as a safe choice. The fix took only a few minutes, but this minor coding mistake cost the product credibility with early adopters, who then were somewhat reluctant to use the beta version.

Reporting Measurements

Imagine how users would respond to the following:

- A GPS device that reported the user was somewhere in Arizona when she clearly was in Oregon.

- A heart rate monitor that indicated the user's heart was beating 10 times per minute.

- A UV ray monitor that reported a person's sun exposure to be very low, even as she could feel and see that she was getting a severe sunburn.

- A Web-based typing tutor that reports a typist's speed as more than 500 words per minute.

As these examples make clear, credibility is key when computing products report measurements. If reported measurements are questionable or obviously inaccurate, the products will lose credibility. If the product were designed to influence or motivate, it likely would fail because of the inaccurate measurements it had reported.

Providing Information and Analysis

A friend of mine is an avid golfer. If she has a round of golf scheduled for a Monday afternoon and the weather looks questionable Monday morning, she'll turn to an online weather service she's bookmarked to get hourly updates on local weather conditions. But over time, she's lost faith in the system, which too often shows a sun icon when the sky is dark with clouds, or rain when the sun is peeking through. She likes the hourly updates, but she no longer views them as entirely credible.

Credibility matters when computers provide data or information to users. Whether a technology product provides investment information, reports on local weather conditions, or does comparison to find the lowest airfare for your next business trip, if the information is not accurate, the product will not be credible.

If a computing product offers dynamic information, tailored to users in real time, not only is the credibility of the information at stake, so is the method used to tailor the information. Amazon.com and a host of successful e-commerce sites analyze users' purchase histories and draw on those analyses to suggest other products that users may want to buy. The credibility of such systems depends on how the information is analyzed to develop recommendations. Such systems are far from perfect. (Amazon recently recommended that a friend purchase a lightweight gardening book because she had previously purchased *The Botany of Desire*—a philosophical treatise on how plants might view humans.)

Another example is MyGoals.com. The site offers to help users set and achieve their goals, from remodeling their home to finding a new job. The system coaches users in setting specific goals and milestones, drawing on information from experts in relevant domains. This expert knowledge is accessible on demand, and the success of the site hinges on users believing that the information provided is credible. While the system uses automated reminders and other interactive features, the aspect that relates to credibility is the expert knowledge stored in the MyGoals.com system.

Reporting on Work Performed

A colleague of mine uses a popular antivirus software. He's diligent about downloading updated virus definitions twice a month. In downloading the updates, the system asks which files he wants to update, including program files as well as virus definitions. He checks only definitions, then clicks. The downloading and updating begins.

When the system has finished updating and installing his virus definitions, it gives him the following message: "You chose not to install any 1 of the available update(s)." This message apparently refers to other updated files available, not the definitions files. But the message always makes my colleague worry that somehow the definitions didn't get downloaded. He checks the date of the virus definition list installed, just to be sure. It always seems to be correct, reflecting the most recent update. But the confusing message makes my colleague question the credibility of the program.

As this anecdote illustrates, if the report on work performed does not match the actual outcome, the credibility of a product may be questioned. In some cases, the product's survival may be jeopardized, as the following example shows.

In the late 1990s, a now defunct company was a leader in creating lasers for eye surgeries to improve vision. The company's sophisticated, expensive laser surgery machine lost credibility because it would, at times, print out incorrect reports about the procedure it had just performed. (This mistake was limited to a special set of circumstances: if the patient was undergoing a double toric optical correction, the device would report whatever was done on the first eye for both eyes, rather than giving the real report for each eye.) Although the machine would carry out the surgical procedure (fortunately) according to the surgeon's specifications, the report the machine gave about the surgery it had just performed would be incorrect.[16]

Although this reporting error did not change the clinical outcome for the patients, it's understandable that ophthalmologists would not want to risk their reputation or their patients' vision by using a product that was known to be flawed. Ultimately, the manufacturer took the product off the market. Clearly, credibility matters when computers report on work performed.

Reporting on Their Own State

Similarly, credibility is at issue when computers report on their own state: how much disk space they have left, how long their batteries will last, how long a process will take. You would assume that a computer should be able to report about itself accurately, but as many frustrated PC users will testify, this is not

always the case. If a computer indicates that no printer is attached when one is, or that it must shut down a program to conserve space when you have only one program running, you may question how much the computer knows about itself—or anything else, for that matter. Any future reporting from the computer will be less believable.

For example, Figure 6.2 shows the message a user received when trying to edit a large file in Microsoft Notepad. In this example, the user was able to open the file but received the error message upon trying to edit it. The message itself is false. The problem is not the size of the computer's memory—you would get the same message if you deleted all other applications—but the fact that Notepad can't deal with files larger than 32,000 bytes.[17]

Running Simulations

Credibility also is important when computers run simulations, a topic discussed in Chapter 4. Computers can simulate everything from chemical processes and the progress of a disease in a population to aircraft navigation, nuclear disasters, and the effects of global warming. For simulations to be persuasive, they must be credible.

If users perceive that a computer simulation designed to convey a real-world experience doesn't closely match reality, the application won't be credible. An expert surgeon using a computer simulation to teach surgical procedures would notice where a silicon-based simulation doesn't match flesh-and-blood reality. If the technology diverged too far from the real experience, the computer product will lose credibility in the eyes of the surgeon.

Rendering Virtual Environments

Virtual environments must be credible as well if they are to persuade. A credible virtual environment is one that matches the user's expectations or experiences. Often this means making the virtual environment model the real world as closely as possible—at least for issues that matter. In some cases, though, virtual environments don't need to match the physical world; they simply need to model what they propose to model. Like good fiction or art, a virtual world for a fantasy arcade game can be highly credible if the world is internally consistent. It may not match anything in the real world, but if the virtual world seems to follow a consistent set of rules, the digital reality may appear credible to users. If it is inconsistent, it will not be credible.

Four Types of Credibility

Within each of the seven contexts of credibility outlined above, different types of credibility may come into play. Although psychologists have outlined the main factors that contribute to credibility—perceptions of trustworthiness and expertise—no research has identified various types of credibility. This is surprising, considering that credibility plays such a large role in everyday life as well as in computing products. For other common dynamics, such as "friendship," there are various flavors: best friends, old friends, acquaintances, and more.

I will attempt to fill this research gap by proposing a taxonomy of credibility. I believe that four types of credibility—presumed, reputed, surface, and earned—are relevant to computing products. The overall assessment of computer credibility may hinge on a single type, but the assessment can draw on elements of all four categories simultaneously (Table 6.1).

Table 6.1 Credibility of Computing Products

Type of credibility	Basis for believability
Presumed	General assumptions in the mind of the perceiver
Surface	Simple inspection or initial firsthand experience
Reputed	Third-party endorsements, reports, or referrals
Earned	Firsthand experience that extends over time

Presumed Credibility

"Presumed credibility" can be defined as the extent to which a person believes someone or something because of *general assumptions in the person's mind.* People usually assume that their friends tell the truth, so they presume their friends are credible. People typically assume that physicians are good sources of medical information, so they are credible. In contrast, many people assume car salespeople may not always tell the truth; they lack credibility. Of course, the negative view of car salespeople is a stereotype, but that's the essence of presumed credibility: assumptions and stereotypes contribute to credibility perceptions.

Principle of Presumed Credibility

People approach computing technology with a preconceived notion about credibility, based on general assumptions about what is and is not believable.

When it comes to computing technology, at least until recently, people have tended to assume that computers are credible.[18] Computers have been described in the academic literature as

- "Magical"[19]

- Having an "'aura' of objectivity"[20]

- Having a "scientific mystique"[21]

- Having "superior wisdom"[22]

- "Faultless"[23]

In short, researchers have proposed that people generally are in "awe" of computers and that people "assign more credibility" to computers than to humans.[24] This provides an advantage to designers of persuasive technology, as people may be predisposed to believe that these products are credible.

As noted earlier, with the emergence of the Internet and the widely varying credibility of Web sites, this traditional view of computers may be changing. In the future, designers of persuasive technology may have to work harder to persuade users that their products are credible.

Surface Credibility

"Surface credibility" is derived from simple inspection. People make credibility judgments of this type almost every day, forming an initial judgment about credibility based on first impressions of surface traits, from a person's looks to his or her dress. The same holds true for computing products. A desktop software application may appear credible because of its visual design. The solid feel of a handheld device can make people perceive it as credible. A Web site that reports it was updated today will have more credibility than one that was updated last year. Users assess the credibility of computing products based on a quick inspection of such surface traits.

In some contexts, the surface credibility of a computing product is critical because it may be the only chance to win over a user. Think about how people surf the Web. Because there are so many Web pages to choose from, and there may not be clear guidelines on which pages are "best," it's likely that Web surfers seeking information will quickly leave sites that lack surface credibility. They may not even be aware of what caused their negative view of the site's surface credibility. Was it the visual design? The tone of the text? The domain name? Many factors can enter into these instant credibility assessments.

A study at my Stanford research lab has demonstrated the key role that surface credibility can play. As part of the lab's research in 2002 on Web credibility (a topic discussed in more detail in Chapter 7), we asked 112 people to evaluate the credibility of 10 health-related Web sites.[25] We were mainly seeking people's qualitative assessments of what made these health Web sites credible or lacking in credibility.

Among the sites we chose for this particular study, participants ranked NIH.gov as the most credible site and Thrive Online as the least credible (Figure 6.3). Some of their comments about the sites reflect how surface credibility works.

After viewing the Thrive Online site, participants generally had negative comments, some of which related to surface credibility:

- "Pop-health look and feel, like one of those covers at the Safeway magazine rack"

- "Too cartoony"

- "Has ads right at top so makes me think it's not committed to the topic"

- "Seems kind of flashy"

- "Too many ads"

- "Online greeting cards don't seem very health-oriented"

- "A lite health site"

Figure 6.3

Study participants perceived thriveonline.com to have the lowest level of surface credibility among 10 health sites and NIH.gov to have the highest.

In contrast to Thrive Online, NIH.gov received positive comments relating to surface credibility, including

- "Very professional looking"

- "Laid out in a very matter-of-fact manner"

- "It looks like it's intended for doctors and researchers"

- "Addresses important issues"

- "Lack of marketing copy makes it more credible"

- "Gov[ernment] affiliation makes it credible"

- "Site owners don't have ulterior motives for presenting the information"

Principle of Surface Credibility

People make initial assessments of the credibility of computing technology based on firsthand inspection of surface traits like layout and density of ads.

The cues that shape perceptions of surface credibility are not the same for everyone. They differ according to user, culture, situation, or target application.

After renting a car in San Diego, I went over to the kiosk that provides computerized directions. The kiosk seemed outdated to me, lacking the latest interface elements and the latest hardware. I hesitated before using it; I almost chose another source of information: the rental agency employees. For other customers, the kiosk may have appeared new and therefore more credible. (Notice how presumed credibility also comes into play. My assumption: Old computing products are less credible than new ones. In another setting—say, in a developing country—I may have viewed the kiosk as the best available technology and therefore highly credible.) Fortunately, the kiosk I used in San Diego gave me just the right information I needed to drive to my destination. But I was a bit skeptical, I'll admit.

My research at Stanford has shown that computing products are likely to be perceived as credible when they are aesthetically pleasing to users, confirm their positive expectations, or show signs of being powerful. But a comprehensive formula for surface credibility has yet to be developed.[26]

Reputed Credibility

Reputed credibility can be defined as the extent to which a person believes someone or something because of what third parties—people, media, or institutions—have reported. These third-party reports may come in the form of endorsements, reports, awards, or referrals. Reputed credibility plays a big role in human interactions. Prestigious awards, endorsements, or official titles granted by third parties make people appear more credible.

Principle of Reputed Credibility

> Third-party endorsements, especially from respected sources, boost perceptions of credibility of computing technology.

The reputed credibility effect also holds true for computing products. If an objective third party publishes a positive report on a product, the product gains credibility.

On the Web, reputed credibility is common. A link from one Web site to another may be perceived as an endorsement, which can increase perceived credibility. In addition, a site's credibility can be bolstered if the site receives an award, especially if it's a recognized award such as a Webby.[27]

In the future, we will likely see computer agents[28] that endorse one another.[29] For instance, a computer agent that searches online for travel deals that match my interests and budget may refer me to another agent, one that can give restaurant suggestions for the locations where I'm planning to travel. The restaurant agent, in this case, benefits from enhanced credibility because of the endorsement. Agent endorsement may become an important and influential form of reputed credibility, especially if the agent who makes the recommendation has a good track record.

Earned Credibility

If your tax accountant has shown herself to be competent and fair over many years, she will have a high level of credibility with you. This *earned credibility* is perhaps the most powerful form of credibility. It derives from people's interactions with others over an extended period of time.

Earned credibility can apply to interactions with computing products as well. If an ATM reported an unexpectedly low balance in a man's bank account, he may change his weekend vacation plans rather than question the credibility of the machine, especially if he has a long history of getting accurate information from the device. If a runner used a heart rate monitor for two years, and its measures always matched her own manual count of her heartbeats, the monitor would have a high level of earned credibility in her eyes. She would believe almost any measure it offered, within reason.

Earned credibility strengthens over time. But sometimes the opposite also is true: extended firsthand experience can lead to a decline in credibility. A trav-

Principle of Earned Credibility

> Credibility can be strengthened over time if computing technology performs consistently in accordance with the user's expectations.

eler using an information kiosk may eventually discover that it provides information only for restaurants that have paid a fee. This pay-for-listing arrangement may only become apparent over time, as the person becomes more familiar with the service. In that case, the credibility of the service may decline rather than increase with extended use.

Earned credibility is the gold standard, both in human-human interactions and in human-computer interactions. It is the most solid form of credibility, leading to an attitude that may not be easily changed (although in some cases, one misstep can instantly destroy credibility, as in the example of the laser surgery machine described earlier). Creating products that will earn rather than lose credibility over time should be a primary goal of designers of persuasive technologies.

The four types of computer credibility are not mutually exclusive; they represent different perspectives in viewing elements of computer credibility. And they can overlap. For example, presumed credibility, which is based on assumptions, also plays a role in surface credibility, which is based in part on making quick judgments, which in turn can be based on underlying assumptions about credibility.

Dynamics of Computer Credibility

> Credibility perceptions can strengthen or weaken over time, but once lost, credibility may be hard to regain.

Credibility perceptions are not fixed; they can strengthen or weaken over time. How is credibility gained over time? How is it lost? And how can it be regained? A small body of research examines these questions and provides some limited answers. Specifically, research confirms what seems obvious: computers gain credibility when they provide information that users find correct, and they lose credibility when they provide information that users find incorrect.[30]

If the treadmill at your gym reports that your heart rate is just 60 beats per minute when you're puffing and panting after running two miles, you'd be less inclined to believe other information from the machine: maybe you didn't really cover two miles, perhaps you didn't run at 8 miles/hour after all. If you believe one piece of information is in error, you will be less likely to believe other information the machine offers.

Another factor that matters in perceptions of credibility is the magnitude of errors, and that depends on the context of use. In some contexts, computer users are more forgiving than in others.

In a study of automobile navigation systems, error rates as high as 30% did not cause users to dismiss an onboard automobile navigation system.[31] Stated differently, even when the system gave incorrect directions 30% of the time, people still consulted the system for help in arriving at their destinations, probably because they didn't have a better alternative. In this context, getting correct information 70% of the time is better than not having any information at all.

In other situations, a small error from a computing product may have devastating effects on perceptions of credibility. Again, my earlier example of the defective reporting of a laser surgery machine illustrates this point.

As these examples suggest, it's not the size but the significance of the error that has the greatest impact on credibility. Most studies show that small but significant errors from computers have disproportionately large effects on perceptions of credibility.[32] But even simple, seemingly insignificant mistakes, such as typographical errors in a dialogue box or a Web page, can damage credibility.

Principle of (Near) Perfection

> Computing technology will be more persuasive if it never (or rarely) commits what users perceive as errors.

Once a computing product loses credibility, it may be possible to regain some credibility by one of two means. First, the product can win back credibility by providing accurate information over an extended period of time.[33] A blood pressure monitor that gives an inaccurate reading at one point may regain credibility if the next 20 readings seem accurate.

The other pathway to regaining some credibility is to make the same error repeatedly (if it is not a critical error). In such cases, users may learn to anticipate and compensate for the error,[34] and the computer wins credibility points just for being consistent. Every time I use the word "bungee," my spellchecker says it's not part of the dictionary. But I've come to expect this now, and the spellchecker doesn't lose any additional credibility for suggesting I've spelled the word incorrectly. (I also could add the correct spelling to the program's "custom dictionary," which would further compensate for the spellchecker's error.)

Although there are two paths to regaining credibility, in many cases the point is moot. Once people perceive that a computing product lacks credibility, they may stop using it, which provides no opportunity for the product to regain credibility through either path.[35] If a laser surgery system makes an error, it's doubtful that an ophthalmologist would give it a second chance.

Errors in Credibility Evaluations

In a perfect world, humans would never make errors in assessing credibility—but they do. These mistakes fall into two categories: gullibility and incredulity (Table 6.2).

Table 6.2   **Errors in Credibility Evaluations**

	User perceives product as credible	*User perceives product as not credible*
Product is credible	Appropriate acceptance	**Incredulity error**
Product is not credible	**Gullibility error**	Appropriate rejection

If a body-fat measuring device reports that your body fat is 4%, it's probably not accurate unless you are a world-class athlete spending most of your time training. If you accept the 4% figure as factual, you're probably committing the gullibility error. People commit this error when they perceive a computing product to be credible, even though it is not.

At the opposite extreme is the "incredulity error."[36] People—often experienced computer users—commit this error when they reject information from a computer, even though the computer's output is accurate. Sometimes when I seek the lowest fares on the Internet, I don't believe what I find at the first travel Web site I consult. I go to another travel Web site and check again. Almost always, I find the same fares for the dates I want to travel. For some reason, I don't completely believe the first site, even though I find out later it gave me the best information possible.

The gullibility error has received a great deal of attention. Those in education—especially librarians—have set out to teach information seekers to use credibility cues, such as the authority of content authors and frequency of site updating, when searching for online information.[37]

The incredulity error has not been given equal attention. People seldom advocate being *less* skeptical of computer technology. As a result, the burden for boosting the credibility of computing products seems to rest with the creators of these products.

To minimize the incredulity error, designers should strive not to give users any additional reasons, beyond their preconceived notions, to reject the information their products provide. They can do this in several ways, such as highlighting the aspects of their products that relate to trustworthiness and expertise—the key components of credibility—and focusing on the credibility perceptions they can impact. For example, while designers don't have much control over presumed credibility, they may be able to affect surface and earned credibility.

Appropriate Credibility Perceptions

A key challenge for developers of computing products, then, is to reduce incredulity errors without increasing gullibility errors. The goal is to create computing products that convey appropriate levels of credibility—that is, products that make their performance levels clear. This may be too lofty a goal, since companies that create computing products are unlikely to disparage what they bring to market. It doesn't make good business sense to undermine your own product.

Or does it?

In some cases a computing product that exposes its own shortcomings may be a winner in the long run. You've probably been in situations where people have done something similar: a taxi driver who says he can't quite remember how to get to your destination, a sales representative who confides that she makes a bigger commission if she closes your deal today, or a professor who says she's not sure about the answer. In all three cases, the overall credibility of the person is likely to go up in your estimation. Paradoxically, admitting a small shortcoming gives a person greater credibility.[38]

No research has been done to determine if this same dynamic applies to computers, but I suspect it does (as long as the "shortcoming" isn't a fundamental flaw in the software). Consider a fitness device that calculates the number of calories burned in a single workout session. Today such devices give an exact number, such as 149 calories. Those with a grasp of physiology know this precise number is almost certain to be incorrect. What if the device instead suggested a plausible range of calories burned, such as "140 to 160 calories"? This would show that the product is designed to report information as accurately as possible. As a result, it may appear more credible than a machine that reports an exact figure that is likely to be false.

The Future of Computer Credibility

The credibility of computing products should be a growing concern for designers. Thanks in part to notable cases of misinformation on the Web, such as the case of the 20-year-old hacker who changed the quotes in Yahoo's news stories,[39] people seem less inclined to believe information from computing products. Computers are losing their aura, their mystique, their presumed credibility. But this might be a good thing. Ideally, computing products of the future will be perceived to have *appropriate* levels of credibility, and they will be, in the end, appropriately persuasive.

As computers become ubiquitous, the question "Are computers credible?" will become even more difficult to address. Increasingly, computing technology will be too diverse for a single answer. As our ability to evaluate credibility matures, we'll examine computer credibility according to specific functions and contexts.

A reasonable approach is to design for and evaluate computer credibility in each of the seven contexts outlined in this chapter—tutoring, reporting measurements, and so on. It also will be useful to distinguish among the four categories of credibility—presumed, reputed, surface, and earned. As designers begin to understand and differentiate among these contexts and categories, they will be taking a big step forward in designing credible computing products.

Notes and References

For updates on the topics presented in this chapter, visit *www.persuasivetech.info.*

1. C. Hovland and W. Weiss, The influence of source credibility on communication effectiveness, *Public Opinion Quarterly,* 15, 635–650 (1951).

2. For more information on how people have viewed computers, see the following:

   a. T. B. Sheridan, T. Vamos, and S. Aida, Adapting automation to man, culture and society, *Automatica,* 19(6): 605–612 (1983).

   b. L. W. Andrews and T. B. Gutkin, The effects of human versus computer authorship on consumers' perceptions of psychological reports, *Computers in Human Behavior,* 7: 311–317 (1991).

3. For more on the subject, see J. J. Djikstra, W. B. G. Liebrand, and E. Timminga, Persuasiveness of expert systems, *Behaviour and Information Technology,* 17(3): 155–163 (1998). Of

course, computers also have been depicted as evil—most notably, the computer HAL in *2001: A Space Odyssey*—but even those portrayals suggested computers are credible.

4. In Spanish, for example, the word *creíble* means both "believable" and "credible."

5. C. I. Hovland, I. L. Janis, and H. H. Kelley, *Communication and Persuasion* (New Haven, CT: Yale University Press, 1953).

6. P. Meyer, Defining and measuring credibility of newspapers: Developing an index, *Journalism Quarterly*, 65: 567–574 (1988). See also C. Gaziano and K. McGrath, Measuring the concept of credibility, *Journalism Quarterly*, 63: 451–462 (1986).

7. C. S. Self, Credibility, in M. Salwen and D. Stacks (eds.), *An Integrated Approach to Communication Theory and Research* (Mahway, NJ: Lawrence Erlbaum, 1996).

8. For more on how being fair and unbiased contributes to perceived credibility, see C. S. Self, Credibility, in M. Salwen and D. Stacks (eds.), *An Integrated Approach to Communication Theory and Research* (Mahway, NJ: Lawrence Erlbaum, 1996).

9. E. Walster, E. Aronson, and D. Abrahams, On increasing the persuasiveness of a low prestige communicator, *Journal of Experimental Social Psychology*, 2: 325–342 (1966).

10. For a discussion on the effects of similarity on trustworthiness and, consequently, on credibility, see J. B. Stiff, *Persuasive Communication* (New York: Guilford Press, 1994).

11. For more about how to define "trust" see the following:

    a. J. K. Rempel, J. G. Holmes, and M. P. Zanna, Trust in close relationships, *Journal of Personality and Social Psychology*, 49 (1): 95–112 (1985).

    b. J. B. Rotter, Interpersonal trust, trustworthiness, and gullibility, *American Psychologist*, 35 (1): 1–7 (1980).

12. For examples of phrases that are synonymous with the idea of credibility, see the following:

    a. B. H. Kantowitz, R. J. Hanowski, and S. C. Kantowitz, Driver acceptance of unreliable traffic information in familiar and unfamiliar settings, *Human Factors*, 39 (2): 164–176 (1997).

    b. B. M. Muir and N. Moray, Trust in automation: Part II, Experimental studies of trust and human intervention in a process control simulation, *Ergonomics*, 39(3): 429–460 (1996).

13. Exceptions include when users are not aware of the computer (e.g., an automobile fuel-injection system); don't recognize the possibility of computer bias or incompetence (e.g., using a pocket calculator); don't have an investment in the interaction (e.g., surfing the Web to pass the time); and when the computer acts only as a transmittal device (e.g., videoconferencing).

14. See for example, "Google unveils new program for pay-per-click text ads," *The Wall Street Journal*, February 20, 2002.

15. For a study on user reactions to a navigation system that provided incorrect directions, see R. J. Hanowski, S. C. Kantowitz, and B. H. Kantowitz, Driver acceptance of unreliable route guidance information, *Proceedings of the Human Factors Society 38th Annual Meeting* (1994), pp. 1062–1066.

16. I learned about the problem with this machine from my brother, an ophthalmologist, and confirmed the problem by talking with a specialist at the company that acquired the manufacturer (after the product had been taken off the market).

17. From the "Interface Hall of Shame" section of the Isys Information Architects site. See *http://www.iarchitect.com/mshame.htm.*

18. For researchers' conclusions about presumed credibility, see the following:

    a. B. M. Muir and N. Moray, Trust in automation: Part II, Experimental studies of trust and human intervention in a process control simulation, *Ergonomics*, 39(3): 429–460 (1996).

    b. Y. Waern and R. Ramberg, People's perception of human and computer advice, *Computers in Human Behavior*, 12(1): 17–27 (1996).

19. J. A. Bauhs and N. J. Cooke, Is knowing more really better? Effects of system development information in human-expert system interactions, *CHI 94 Companion* (New York: ACM, 1994), pp. 99–100.

20. L. W. Andrews and T. B. Gutkin, The effects of human versus computer authorship on consumers' perceptions of psychological reports, *Computers in Human Behavior*, 7: 311–317 (1991).

21. L. W. Andrews and T. B. Gutkin, The effects of human versus computer authorship on consumers' perceptions of psychological reports, *Computers in Human Behavior*, 7: 311–317 (1991).

22. T. B. Sheridan, T. Vamos, and S. Aida, Adapting automation to man, culture and society, *Automatica*, 19(6): 605–612 (1983).

23. T. B. Sheridan, T. Vamos, and S. Aida, Adapting automation to man, culture and society, *Automatica*, 19(6): 605–612 (1983).

24. L. W. Andrews and T. B. Gutkin, The effects of human versus computer authorship on consumers' perceptions of psychological reports, *Computers in Human Behavior*, 7: 311–317 (1991).

25. Our Web credibility study is described in more detail in Chapter 7.

26. I believe the closest thing to a formula for surface credibility stems from my Stanford lab's work. See, for example, B. J. Fogg and H. Tseng, The elements of computer credibility, *Proceedings of ACM CHI 99 Conference on Human Factors in Computing Systems* (New York: ACM Press, 1999), vol. 1, pp. 80–87, *http://www.acm.org/pubs/articles/proceedings/chi/302979/p80-fogg/p80-fogg.pdf.*

27. Webby awards are presented annually by the International Academy of Digital Arts and Sciences to acknowledge "the best of the Web both in quality and in quantity." I am a judge for Web sites in the Science category. For more information, visit *www.webby-awards.com*.

28. I use "agent" in the same sense that Kurweil defines the term: "An intelligent agent (or simply an agent) is a program that gathers information or performs some other service independently and on a regular schedule." Source: KurzweilAI.net.

29. Nikos Karacapilidis and Paylos Moraïtis, Intelligent agents for an artificial market system, *Proceedings of the Fifth International Conference on Autonomous Agents* (New York: ACM Press, 2001), pp. 592–599 (see *http://doi.acm.org/10.1145/375735.376460*). See also C. Wagner and E. Turban, Are intelligent e-commerce agents partners or predators? *Communications of the ACM*, 54(5): (2002).

30. To read more about how computers gain or lose credibility, see the following:

    a. B. H. Kantowitz, R. J. Hanowski, and S. C. Kantowitz, Driver acceptance of unreliable traffic information in familiar and unfamiliar settings, *Human Factors*, 39(2): 164–176 (1997).

    b. J. Lee, The dynamics of trust in a supervisory control simulation, *Proceedings of the Human Factors Society 35th Annual Meeting* (1991), pp. 1228–1232.

    c. B. M. Muir and N. Moray, Trust in automation: Part II, Experimental studies of trust and human intervention in a process control simulation, *Ergonomics*, 39(3): 429–460 (1996).

31. B. H. Kantowitz, R. J. Hanowski, and S. C. Kantowitz, Driver acceptance of unreliable traffic information in familiar and unfamiliar settings, *Human Factors*, 39(2): 164–176 (1997).

32. For more on the disproportionate credibility cost of small errors, see the following:

    a. B. H. Kantowitz, R. J. Hanowski, and S. C. Kantowitz, Driver acceptance of unreliable traffic information in familiar and unfamiliar settings, *Human Factors*, 39(2): 164–176 (1997).

    b. J. Lee, The dynamics of trust in a supervisory control simulation, *Proceedings of the Human Factors Society 35th Annual Meeting* (1991), pp. 1228–1232.

    c. B. M. Muir and N. Moray, Trust in automation: Part II, Experimental studies of trust and human intervention in a process control simulation, *Ergonomics*, 39(3): 429–460 (1996).

33. B. H. Kantowitz, R. J. Hanowski, and S. C. Kantowitz, S.C., Driver acceptance of unreliable traffic information in familiar and unfamiliar settings, *Human Factors*, 39(2): 164–176 (1997).

34. B. M. Muir and N. Moray, Trust in automation: Part II, Experimental studies of trust and human intervention in a process control simulation, *Ergonomics*, 39(3): 429–460 (1996).

35. B. M. Muir and N. Moray, Trust in automation: Part II, Experimental studies of trust and human intervention in a process control simulation, *Ergonomics*, 39(3): 429–460 (1996).

36. For concepts related to the incredulity error, see the following:

    a. J. Lee, The dynamics of trust in a supervisory control simulation, *Proceedings of the Human Factors Society 35th Annual Meeting* (1991), pp. 1228–1232.

    b. T. B. Sheridan, T. Vamos, and S. Aida, Adapting automation to man, culture and society, *Automatica*, 19(6): 605–612 (1983).

37. To see an example of how librarians have taken an active role in helping people determine the credibility of online information, see *http://www.vuw.ac.nz/~agsmith/evaln/evaln.htm*.

38. The classic psychology study on how credibility increases when people reveal information that works against them, such as revealing a weakness or a bias, is E. Walster, E. Aronson, and D. Abrahams, On increasing the persuasiveness of a low prestige communicator, *Journal of Experimental Social Psychology*, 2: 325–342 (1996).

    A more recent publication explains how the credibility-boosting dynamic works: When premessage expectations are disconfirmed (as in the case of a person or a software product admitting a bias or a shortcoming), the receiver of the message (in this case, the user) perceives the sender (in this case, the software) as unbiased (discussed in Stiff 1994, p. 96), which is a key contributor to credibility. For more discussion on this concept, see J. B. Stiff, *Persuasive Communication* (New York: Guilford, 1994).

    More related to technology and credibility, a study about hate speech on Web sites showed that Web sites that reveal their biases appear more rational, even if their views are extreme. See M. McDonald, Cyberhate: Extending persuasive techniques of low credibility sources to the World Wide Web, in D. Schumann and E. Thorson (eds.), *Advertising and the World Wide Web* (Mahwah, NJ: Lawrence Earlbaum, 1999), pp. 149–157.

39. *http://www.usatoday.com/life/cyber/tech/2001/09/28/week.htm*.

chapter 7

Credibility and the World Wide Web

Credibility is a key factor in a Web site's ability to persuade.

If you look at the most frequently visited Web sites, you'll see that many sites seek to persuade users in some way. MSN and other leading portal sites such as AOL and Yahoo try to convince users to do their Web searching, shopping, and chatting with friends on their sites or those of their affiliates. They also hope that users will register with them—create a personalized homepage, such as My MSN, My AOL, or My Yahoo—giving the site operators information about users and providing a way to contact them directly in the future. These portals succeed only when they are successful at persuasion.

Even sites that focus mainly on providing information and content, such as about.com or cnet.com, attempt to persuade. Their goal is to convince users that visiting their site is the best way to get what they need, be it news, an mp3 file, or the latest games. Technical support sites try to persuade users to solve their problems online rather than calling the company. Even personal Web sites have persuasion as part of their objective. People want those visiting their site to think of them in the best light, as competent professionals or interesting human beings. As I see it, if someone didn't want to influence others in some way, he or she would not take the time or energy to set up a Web site.

The Importance of Web Credibility

While many factors contribute to a Web site's power to influence, one key factor is credibility. Without credibility, sites are not likely to persuade users to change their attitudes or behaviors—to embrace the site's cause, register personal information, make purchases, click on ads, complete surveys, or bookmark the site for return visits. For this reason, it's important to understand and design for Web credibility.

What makes a Web site credible? What elements cause people to believe what they find on the site? Web credibility—what it is, how it is won, and how to understand it better—is the focus of this chapter.

Variability of Web Credibility

The Web can be a highly credible source of information, depending on the person or organization behind a given Web site (the site "operator"). The Web also can be one of the least credible information sources. Many pages on the Web reflect incompetence, and some are pure hoaxes. You've probably been to Web sites that not only lacked expertise, but seem designed to deceive. Because few barriers prevent people from publishing on the Web, you'll find deceptive coverage of current events, health information that is factually incorrect, and ads that promise the impossible.

One notable example of bogus information online was designed to teach investors about online fraud and persuade people to be more skeptical about what they find online. At mcwhortle.com, Web surfers read that "McWhortle Enterprises is an established and well-known manufacturer of biological defense mechanisms." As surfers browse this site, they see an "About Us" page, along with a doctored photograph of the company headquarters in Washington, D.C., contact information, and testimonials. The company site claims to have technology to produce a portable biohazard alert detector and seeks outside funding. As Web surfers investigate more and click on the link that says, "When you are ready to invest, click here," the ruse is made known, with the heading "Watch out! If you responded to an investment idea like this . . . You could get scammed!" and a message below indicating that the site was posted by various government agencies, including the Securities and Exchange Commission and the Federal Trade Commission.[1] The SEC has said it will create hundreds of hoax Web sites of this type to increase investor awareness.

Some deceptive Web sites have been created with malicious intent, such as the fraudulent sites paypai.com, created to fool users into thinking it was the PayPal site, and wwwbankofamerica.com, which posed as the giant bank. Both sites attempted to elicit personal information from visitors for fraudulent purposes.[2]

Other deceptive sites are set up simply to amuse browsers who happen by,[3] such as the site for the Oklahoma Association of Wine Producers,[4] the Christian Women's Wrestling site,[5] and the site for the End of the Internet ("Thank you for visiting the End of the Internet. There are no more links. You must now turn off your computer and go do something productive.").[6]

Especially if they are new to the Web, people's general perception of this medium's credibility can plummet after they are deceived a few times or find factual errors.[7] If you spend a reasonable amount of time surfing the Web, you'll get a sense of the broad range of credibility online. With time and experience, most users learn how to separate the good from the bad, the believable from the unbelievable.

Two Sides of Web Credibility

Web credibility has two sides, one that relates mostly to Web surfers and one that relates to Web designers (Figure 7.1). On the one side, credibility is important to those who use the Web. People need to evaluate if Web sources are credible or not. This issue of "information quality" has been embraced by librarians and teachers.[8] To better assess the credibility of an online source, librarians

Figure 7.1

Web credibility from two points of view.

Credibility goals

Web surfers	**Web designers**
Determine what information is credible	Create highly credible sites

and others advocate that Web surfers examine who the author is, how timely the content is, and how the content compares with similar content from trusted sources, such as experts in the field. Fortunately, many good guidelines already exist to help students and researchers evaluate the information they find online.[9]

The other aspect of Web credibility relates primarily to Web site designers. The main issue for designers is how to create Web sites that convey appropriate[10] levels of credibility, as discussed in Chapter 6.

Although designing for Web credibility is an important issue for designers, in 1998 there was almost no information or research related to the subject.[11] To help fill the gap, my colleagues and I began conducting research projects to gain a better understanding of the factors that go into Web credibility. Our hope was that our research, described in this chapter, would be a key resource for people interested in Web credibility issues.[12] The chapter lays a foundation for deeper understanding by providing ways to think about Web credibility, sharing results from quantitative research, and offering general principles about designing for credibility.

The Stanford Web Credibility Studies

Over the past four years, my Stanford Persuasive Technology Lab has conducted a number of research studies related to Web credibility, involving over 6,000 participants. After conducting a few smaller experiments and surveys, in the fall of 1999, 10 graduate students[13] and I launched a large-scale research project to investigate Web credibility.[14]

We were intrigued by the results of the 1999 study[15] and decided to take another "snapshot" in 2002,[16] to see how perceptions had changed in the intervening years. We plan to repeat the study every two or three years, to give us not only a snapshot of Web credibility at single points in time but a better understanding of how the Web and user perceptions of Web credibility are changing over time.

The 2002 study was nearly identical in content and methodology. However, because the Web is a dynamic medium, some changes were necessary for the newer study. While trying to keep changes to a minimum, we discarded a few questions that seemed outdated, reworded a few questions, and added some questions to probe new issues in the shifting landscape of Web use and tech-

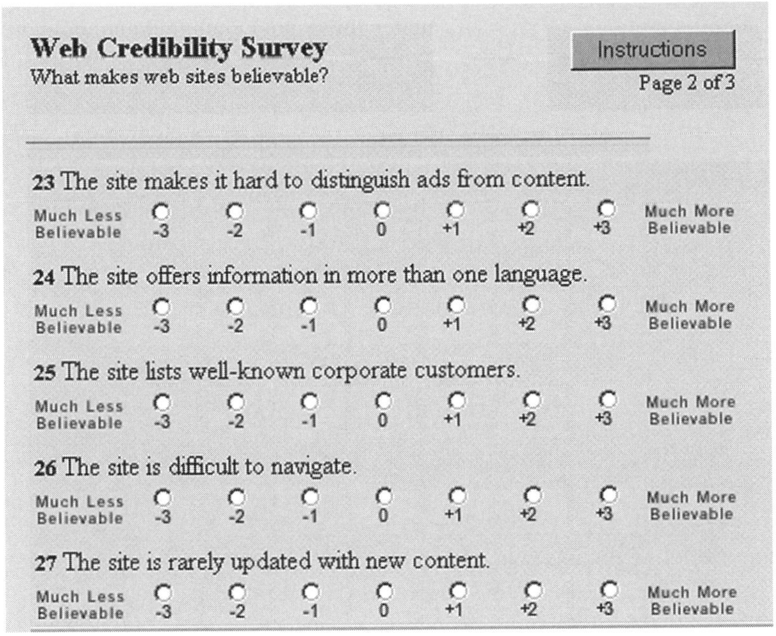

Figure 7.2

Excerpt from online
Web credibility survey.
In 1999, 1,410 partici-
pants completed the
survey; in 2002, we
had 1,481 participants.

nology. In 1999 we asked people about their credibility perceptions of 51 items; in 2002 we asked about 55 items.

Developing the questions for each survey was a rather involved and careful process. In 1999, after the graduate students and I reviewed the few existing pieces of literature on Web credibility and surfed many Web sites, taking notes, our team identified more than 300 elements that could affect the way users perceived the credibility of a given Web site. Because this set contained too many elements to manage in a single study, through an iterative process involving lots of discussion, we selected a subset—the items we found most important or interesting.[17]

We ran three pilot studies to refine our methodology and questions. Only after refining the questions and methodology did we launch our first large-scale online survey, in 1999.[18]

We made sure the experience of participating in the research was similar in both studies. After reading an introductory passage, the participants read through roughly 50 randomized items describing a Web site element. They were asked to rate each element on a scale of −3 to +3 to show how that element would affect their perception of the credibility of the site's information. We asked participants to draw upon their cumulative experience with the Web to make their evaluations. Figure 7.2 lists some of the survey questions used in both studies.

In 1999, more than 1,400 people participated in the survey; roughly the same number participated in 2002.[19] We used similar recruiting methods both times, and we were fortunate in how things shaped up: as you'll see in Table 7.1, the demographics for the studies are similar.

Table 7.1 **Demographics of Study Participants**

	1999 study (1,409 participants)	*2002 study (1,649 participants)*
Age (mean)	32.6 years old	35.5 years old
Gender	44% female, 56% male	45% female, 55% male
Country	41% U.S., 55% Finland, 4% elsewhere	33% U.S., 57% Finland, 10% elsewhere
Education level (median)	"College graduate"	"College graduate"
Annual income (median)	$40,000–$50,000	$40,000–$50,000
Years on the Internet (median)	"4 to 5 years"	">5 years"
Average number of hours/week spent online (mean)	13.5 hours/week	14.4 hours/week
Average number of purchases online (median)	"1 to 5 purchases"	">5 purchases"

A Few Words about Our Findings

The overall results from our two large studies are summarized on the continuum in Figure 7.3. This graphic illustrates the results of over 3,000 people responding to more than 50 items. As you examine the figure, you'll see how each item fared overall in 1999 (the scores in black boxes). Possible scores range from +3 to –3, matching the response scale we used in the study; in other words, if the average response to an item in 1999 was +1.5, Figure 7.3 lists the item at +1.5 on the continuum.

The graphic also shows how the data changed in the 2002 study. For each item that was worded identically in both studies, you'll find a small arrow and a value indicating how much the mean score for that particular item increased or decreased in the 2002 study. (As noted at the bottom of Figure 7.3, items that were reworded or dropped in 2002 are indicated with a * or "NA," respectively). As Figure 7.3 shows, the highest mean score in the studies was +2.2; the lowest was –2.1. All the other credibility items in the study fall between these points; they are placed along the continuum, top to bottom.

In reviewing the continuum, I find it interesting to see what items landed at the top (those that had the greatest positive impact on credibility), at the bottom (those that had the greatest negative impact), and which fell in the middle (items that had no impact on Web credibility).

It's also worth noting that items on the continuum must be at least 0.3 apart to be considered truly different in terms of their practical (versus statistical) significance. For example, looking at the 1999 data, there's no *practical* significant difference between listing "the organization's physical address" (+2.0) and listing a "contact phone number" (+1.9). However, there is a practical significant difference between a site that lists a physical address and a site that recognizes that you have been there before (+0.7).[20]

Next, it's important to note that the items listed in Figure 7.3 represent the exact wording used in our surveys. To be sure, people will differ in how they interpret each item; this is an inevitable weakness of any survey. This was one reason for conducting our pilot tests before launching the 1999 study—to weed out bad questions and refine other questions in order to reduce ambiguity. (For the most part we succeeded, as evidenced by the fact that the averages on each item for U.S. and Finnish respondents closely matched, despite the differences in native language. If the questions were ambiguous, you would expect to see more evidence of interpretation differences.)

My research team and I believe the results of these studies are robust, since the findings of the pilot studies[21] and our two large-scale studies were similar. The convergence in results we've seen, despite the differences in methodology, sample, and time, give us confidence in our findings.

Even though we've seen similar findings appear in our various studies, our work so far represents early investigations into the elements of Web credibility.

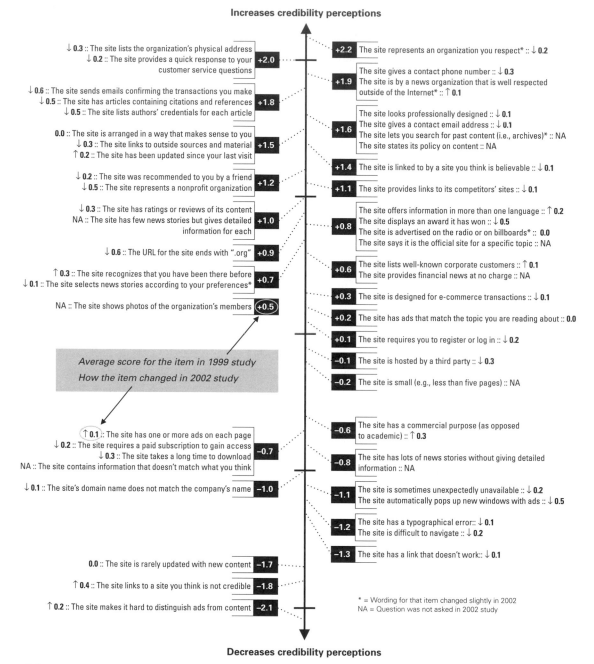

Increases credibility perceptions

↓ **0.3** :: The site lists the organization's physical address
↓ **0.2** :: The site provides a quick response to your customer service questions — **+2.0**

+2.2 The site represents an organization you respect* :: ↓ **0.2**

↓ **0.6** :: The site sends emails confirming the transactions you make
↓ **0.5** :: The site has articles containing citations and references
↓ **0.5** :: The site lists authors' credentials for each article — **+1.8**

+1.9 The site gives a contact phone number :: ↓ **0.3**
The site is by a news organization that is well respected outside of the Internet* :: ↑ **0.1**

0.0 :: The site is arranged in a way that makes sense to you
↓ **0.3** :: The site links to outside sources and material
↑ **0.2** :: The site has been updated since your last visit — **+1.5**

+1.6 The site looks professionally designed :: ↓ **0.1**
The site gives a contact email address :: ↓ **0.1**
The site lets you search for past content (i.e., archives)* :: NA
The site states its policy on content :: NA

↓ **0.2** :: The site was recommended to you by a friend
↓ **0.5** :: The site represents a nonprofit organization — **+1.2**

+1.4 The site is linked to by a site you think is believable :: ↓ **0.1**

+1.1 The site provides links to its competitors' sites :: ↓ **0.1**

↓ **0.3** :: The site has ratings or reviews of its content
NA :: The site has few news stories but gives detailed information for each — **+1.0**

+0.8 The site offers information in more than one language :: ↑ **0.2**
The site displays an award it has won :: ↓ **0.5**
The site is advertised on the radio or on billboards* :: **0.0**
The site says it is the official site for a specific topic :: NA

↓ **0.6** :: The URL for the site ends with ".org" — **+0.9**

+0.6 The site lists well-known corporate customers :: ↑ **0.1**
The site provides financial news at no charge :: NA

↑ **0.3** :: The site recognizes that you have been there before
↓ **0.1** :: The site selects news stories according to your preferences* — **+0.7**

+0.3 The site is designed for e-commerce transactions :: ↓ **0.1**

NA :: The site shows photos of the organization's members — (**+0.5**)

+0.2 The site has ads that match the topic you are reading about :: **0.0**

+0.1 The site requires you to register or log in :: ↓ **0.2**

–0.1 The site is hosted by a third party :: ↓ **0.3**

–0.2 The site is small (e.g., less than five pages) :: NA

Average score for the item in 1999 study
How the item changed in 2002 study

–0.6 The site has a commercial purpose (as opposed to academic) :: ↑ **0.3**

↑ **0.1** :: The site has one or more ads on each page
↓ **0.2** :: The site requires a paid subscription to gain access
↓ **0.3** :: The site takes a long time to download
NA :: The site contains information that doesn't match what you think — **–0.7**

–0.8 The site has lots of news stories without giving detailed information :: NA

↓ **0.1** :: The site's domain name does not match the company's name — **–1.0**

–1.1 The site is sometimes unexpectedly unavailable :: ↓ **0.2**
The site automatically pops up new windows with ads :: ↓ **0.5**

–1.2 The site has a typographical error :: ↓ **0.1**
The site is difficult to navigate :: ↓ **0.2**

–1.3 The site has a link that doesn't work :: ↓ **0.1**

0.0 :: The site is rarely updated with new content — **–1.7**

↑ **0.4** :: The site links to a site you think is not credible — **–1.8**

↑ **0.2** :: The site makes it hard to distinguish ads from content — **–2.1**

* = Wording for that item changed slightly in 2002
NA = Question was not asked in 2002 study

Decreases credibility perceptions

Figure 7.3 Summary of Stanford Web Credibility Survey results: 1999 and 2002.

This is not the final word. Our intention was to cover a lot of territory and, along the way, raise new issues and questions to explore in future credibility research. In other words, the results in Figure 7.3 and in the rest of this chapter provide a starting point for discussion, speculation, confirmation, and critique.

We consider these studies successful if they do any of the following:

- Contradict one of your hunches about what makes Web sites credible

- Generate a discussion (or argument) about Web credibility

- Lead you to form new hypotheses about Web credibility

- Motivate you to investigate Web credibility

- Change the way you perceive Web sites

- Change how you design Web sites

The remainder of this chapter will describe and integrate the findings of two Web credibility studies with the credibility frameworks outlined in Chapter 6. After laying out the results, I will describe a new framework for Web credibility, one that divides Web elements into three categories: Web site operator, content, and design.

By using the survey method of research to take snapshots of Web credibility perceptions in 1999 and in 2002, we hoped to assess how people felt about the Web at those times and, perhaps, identify trends that were starting to form. Frankly, it's too early to identify trends with confidence, but as you examine the data and combine it with your own experience, you can begin to form your own hypotheses about what makes Web sites credible and what is changing as the Web evolves along with the people who use it.

Interpreting the Data

In this chapter I present high-level findings from both the 1999 and the 2002 Web credibility surveys. When a study has a large number of responses, as these surveys have, even small differences in means (average scores) can end up being statistically significant. But these small differences may not be large enough to have much *practical* significance. One of our challenges in interpreting the data, therefore, was to determine which data have practical as well as statistical significance. These are the items I will highlight in this chapter.

(Readers who would like a fuller explanation of how we decided which items have practical significance may consult the endnotes.[22])

Trustworthiness and Expertise on the Web

Web credibility, like the general concept of credibility outlined in Chapter 6, is made up of two dimensions: trustworthiness and expertise (Figure 7.4). When a Web site conveys both qualities, people will find it credible. When it lacks one of these qualities, credibility will suffer. In essence, when people perceive a site to be unbiased (or biased in a way that fits the user's worldview) and knowledgeable—factors underlying trustworthiness and expertise—they also will view it as credible. This is the same general formula introduced in Chapter 6.

Trustworthiness and Web Credibility

Principle of "Real-World Feel"

> A Web site will have more credibility if it highlights the people or organization behind the content and services it provides.

People rely on perceptions of trustworthiness in evaluating Web credibility. Table 7.2 shows the trustworthiness-related elements from the Stanford studies that were reported to boost credibility the most. As Table 7.2 shows, elements that allow people to contact a Web site source increase perceptions of Web credibility. And the more direct the contact, the better. Listing an organization's physical address boosts credibility dramatically. Listing a phone number also has a major impact. These two elements rank significantly higher than listing an email address.[23] Why? The study data do not provide an exact answer, but it seems these elements may show more clearly that real people are behind the Web site—people who can be reached for questions, comments, or complaints. A site that opens itself

Figure 7.4

The two dimensions of Web credibility.

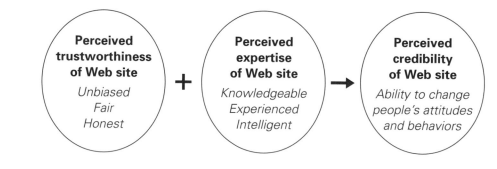

Principle of Easy Verifiability

Credibility perceptions will be enhanced if a Web site makes it easy for users to check outside sources to verify the accuracy of site content.

to direct contact from Web users shows confidence that its information and services are fair, unbiased, and honest.

Table 7.2 also illustrates that Web credibility increases when a site allows people to verify the information presented, including articles with citations and references, as well as links to outside sources. Providing a means for outside verification also shows confidence, as people can easily determine if the information is biased, by checking references or clicking to see what other sources have to say.

Table 7.2   Trustworthiness Elements That Increase Web Credibility

	1999	2002
The site lists the organization's physical address.	+2.0	+1.7
The site gives a contact phone number.	+1.9	+1.6
The site has articles containing citations and references.	+1.8	+1.3
The site gives a contact email address.	+1.6	+1.5
The site links to outside materials and sources.	+1.5	+1.2

Elements that Increase Credibility: Significant Changes in 2002 Results

When comparing the results of the 1999 and 2002 studies, three of the items in Table 7.2, when taken together, may have practical significance. These items (in boldface text) have to do with contact information: physical and email addresses and phone number. These items had a greater impact on credibility in 1999 than in 2002. It may be that by the time of the 2002 study, people came to view these contact elements as expected; they were less impressed than in 1999 if a site posted this information.

The score of one item in Table 7.2, regarding articles containing citations and references, dropped significantly between 1999 and 2002. A partial explanation is that country of origin made a large difference. Between 1999 and 2002, the average scores of Finnish participants on this item declined much more significantly than those of U.S. participants (these details are not shown in the table). It's important to note that in both studies, citations and references made a significant positive impact on credibility evaluations. What's not yet clear is why the Finns became much less impressed with citations and references in the years between 1999 and 2002, compared to the U.S. participants. Future research (or a deeper exploration of differences in culture, including Internet culture) may provide a clearer answer.

Table 7.2 shows elements related to trustworthiness that boost Web credibility. Our research also uncovered a number of elements related to trustworthiness that decrease credibility perceptions. These are listed in Table 7.3.

Table 7.3 **Trustworthiness Elements That Decrease Web Credibility**

	1999	2002
The site makes it hard to distinguish ads from content.	−2.1	−1.9
The site links to a site you think is not credible.	−1.8	−1.4
The site automatically pops up new windows with ads.	−1.1	−1.6
The site's domain name does not match the company's name.	−1.0	−1.1

As Table 7.3 shows, credibility suffers most when Web sites make it difficult to distinguish between ads and content. This takes a toll on perceived trustworthiness, probably because people feel the site is designed to fool them into clicking on the ads or at least viewing ads as part of the site's information. People know that advertisements are prone to bias. When there is no clear distinction between the two, people may view the entire site as biased.

Table 7.3 also illustrates that Web sites are judged by the company they keep. A Web site's credibility suffers when it links to another site that is perceived to lack credibility, as a link may imply an endorsement.

The next trustworthiness element has to do with advertisements. Our studies showed that ads that pop up in new browser windows hurt a site's credibility. This makes sense; people usually go to Web sites with goals in mind, and they expect the site to help them accomplish those goals. Pop-up ads are a distraction and a clear sign the site is not designed to help users as much as possible. Pop-up ads make people feel used, perhaps even betrayed. (This is not to say that all ads hurt the credibility of a Web site. In some cases they can increase credibility perceptions, if they match the content of the page and come from reputable sources.[24])

The last element that hurts credibility is using a domain name that doesn't match the company name. Last year I set out on the Web to reserve a campsite at Sunset State Beach near Santa Cruz. This is a park I've enjoyed before, supported by tax dollars and run by camp rangers. I was somewhat puzzled when I found out the Web site that handles these reservations for the state beach is "ReserveAmerica.com," not a park Web site or .gov site. It made me wonder if I was really working with the right people and if the information I was getting on camp site availability and price was accurate.

When it comes to companies, the same concept applies. If you're seeking information about ocean kayaks from a company called Wave Rider International and its Web site is PaddleAwayNow.com, you're likely to wonder why it doesn't have a URL similar to its company name. Has the company been acquired? Is it going out of business?

It's likely that respondents in our studies sensed something suspicious about a company that didn't operate under its own name. There may be other explanations as well. But one thing seems clear: to sustain credibility, a company should use a domain name that matches its company name as closely as possible. Credibility increases when people can identify the site operator, its values, and its motives.[25] Hidden identities or motivations make people wary.

Elements that Decrease Credibility: Significant Changes in 2002 Results

The items in Table 7.3 show some significant differences between the 1999 and the 2002 studies (highlighted in boldface). The most notable change is the increased damage that pop-up ads have on perceived credibility. It's likely that, as these types of ads have become more common, people are becoming more annoyed with them, viewing Web site operators that allow pop-up ads on their site as unconcerned about what attracted people to their site in the first place. Pop-up ads are a distraction, and the data suggest that they are doing significantly more damage to credibility in 2002 than they were in 1999.

Another significant difference between the years has to do with sites linking to other sites that are not credible. This is another change in results for which we have no satisfying explanation. Perhaps people are beginning to judge Web site credibility more by the merits of the particular site than the company the site keeps. Despite the change in scores between the two studies, the overall message for designers remains the same: to create a highly credible Web site, do not link to sites that are not credible.

Expertise and Web Site Credibility

Trustworthiness is only part of the Web credibility equation. In the Stanford Web Credibility studies, about half the elements that ranked highest in promoting Web credibility dealt with issues of expertise, including expertise in running a Web site efficiently and reliably, as indicated by the elements shown in Table 7.4.

Table 7.4 **Expertise Elements That Increase Web Site Credibility**

	1999	*2002*
The site provides a quick response to your customer service questions.	+2.2	+1.8
The site sends email confirming transactions you make.	+1.8	+1.2
The site lists authors' credentials for each article.	+1.8	+1.3
The site lets you search for past content (i.e., archives).	+1.6	NA
The site looks professionally designed.	+1.6	+1.5
The site has been updated since your last visit.	+1.5	+1.7

The top two elements of expertise—responding to customer service questions and confirming transactions via email—imply that the Web technology functions properly and, perhaps more important, that the site operator is expert at being responsive to customers. Listing the authors' credentials for each article is another form of expertise in the form of knowledge. Although not always done on Web sites, the simple act of listing credential information can boost credibility considerably.[26]

Technical and design expertise also emerge as elements that strongly enhance Web credibility. Having a search feature suggests the site operator is adept with the technical elements of Web design. This demonstration

Principle of Fulfillment

A Web site will have increased credibility when it fulfills users' positive expectations.

of technical expertise may create a halo effect, making the entire Web site seem more credible.

The visual design of the site is equally important; a professional-looking design boosts perceptions of Web credibility. Finally, updating content demonstrates that the site operator has been able to coordinate the many things that must happen to keep the site updated—another indication of expertise.

Elements that Increase Credibility: Significant Changes in 2002 Results

Table 7.4 shows significant practical differences in average scores of three items (shown in boldface) between 1999 and 2002.[27] The first two items—quick response in customer service and sending email confirmations—seem to go hand in hand. While these attributes still boost credibility perceptions significantly in 2002, they don't have as great an impact as they did in 1999. It seems reasonable to speculate that by 2002, many more site operators had figured out how to run effective and responsive sites. It became common, even expected, to receive confirmation emails when buying products and services online. Also, by 2002 people may have been less impressed by companies that responded quickly to customer questions, as this, too, has become a standard expectation. Again, in pointing out these slight drops in credibility scores between the two years, it must be noted that providing responsive service is one of the best ways to boost the credibility of a Web site.

The final item in Table 7.4 that shows a significant difference between years deals with how people viewed sites that listed author credentials. Here, too, the scores of Finnish participants declined far more than those of U.S. participants between 1999 and 2002 (these detailed findings are not shown in the table). The fact that major differences in scores between the United States and Finland occurred in two items suggests an opportunity for further research into cultural differences.

Web sites also can demonstrate a lack of expertise, causing people to doubt their credibility. Table 7.5 shows four items from the Stanford studies that relate to lapses in expertise and that result in reduced credibility. According to our studies, people viewed sites with outdated content as lacking in credibility. Ensuring that a site has the latest information takes dedication and skill. Sources that don't update their sites are probably viewed as not serious about the sites or simply negligent, both of which hurt expertise perceptions.

Table 7.5   **Expertise Elements That Decrease Web Credibility**

	1999	*2002*
The site is rarely updated with new content.	–1.7	–1.7
The site has a link that doesn't work.	–1.3	–1.4
The site has a typographical error.	–1.2	–1.3
The site is sometimes unexpectedly unavailable.	–1.1	–1.3

Some forms of Web content are more time-sensitive than others. In an online experiment my lab is currently running, we're investigating how sensitive different types of Web content are to being out of date. In planning a vacation to the Philippines (the task in our study), we hypothesize that a Web site will lose credibility if the travel advisory posted is from 1997 compared to a travel advisory from five days ago. In contrast, we are hypothesizing that information about the cuisine of the Philippines dated 1997 will have significantly less impact on the perceived credibility of the site.[28]

Even minor problems with a Web site can have a major impact on users' perceptions of the site's expertise and, therefore, its credibility. Participants in our studies reported that Web sites lose a great deal of credibility when a link doesn't work or when the site has a typographical error.[29]

Technical difficulties also affect the perceived credibility of a Web site. People expect the Web to be available around the clock except, in some cases, for scheduled and announced maintenance periods. When a site goes down (as some notable sites have in the past few years), people view this as a credibility issue, even though the fault may have nothing to do with the site operator.[30]

Elements that Decrease Credibility: No Significant Changes in 2002

None of the items in Table 7.5 differed from 1999 to 2002 to a degree that is practically significant. Why? Perhaps these items have been minimum expectations for Web sites since 1999, and these expectations had not changed by 2002. People still perceive sites to have less credibility when they are not updated, when a link doesn't work, and so on.

In summary, these study results show that when it comes to Web credibility, expertise matters. Demonstrations of expertise win credibility points, while a lack of expertise has the opposite effect.

The Four Types of Web Credibility

The four types of computer credibility described in Chapter 6—presumed, reputed, surface, and earned—also apply to users' experiences on the Web. Table 7.6 reviews each type of credibility and lists a Web-related example for each.

Table 7.6 **The Four Types of Web Credibility**

	Presumed	*Reputed*	*Surface*	*Earned*
Type of credibility	*Based on general assumptions in the user's mind*	*Based on third-party endorse-ments, reports, or referrals*	*Based on simple inspection, first impressions*	*Based on first-hand experience that extends over time*
Web example	A domain name that ends with ".org"	A site that won an award from *PC Magazine*	A site that looks professionally designed	A site that has consistently pro-vided accurate information over the past year

Presumed Credibility on the Web

Presumed credibility describes the extent to which a person believes some-thing because of general assumptions. These assumptions help people evalu-ate—rightly or wrongly—the credibility of Web sites.

Many elements from the Stanford Web Credibility Studies relate to pre-sumed credibility. The four key elements that boost presumed credibility are shown in Table 7.7. (Our studies had no items that decreased presumed credi-bility to any practically significant extent.) First, the results show that sites are seen as more credible if they "represent a nonprofit organization" or have a

URL that ends with ".org," which many people associate with nonprofit organizations.[31]

Table 7.7   **Key Elements That Increase Presumed Web Credibility**

	1999	*2002*
The site represents a nonprofit organization.	+1.2	+0.7
The URL for the site ends with ".org."	+0.9	+0.3
The site provides links to its competitors' sites.	+1.1	+1.0
The site says it is the official site for a specific topic.	+0.8	NA

Many people assume that, because nonprofit organizations are not seeking commercial gain, they are more likely to be trustworthy. This assumption is not always based in fact, but it does have an effect when it comes to perceived Web credibility.

Why the significant difference in scores for these two elements between 1999 and 2002? Clearly, nonprofits have lost some of their luster on the Web. The reason may have to do with people realizing that most anyone can set up a site that appears to be a nonprofit organization. As people gain more experience with the Web, they also are developing a healthy skepticism—things are not always what they appear to be, even with nonprofits. (Despite this decline in scores, it's important to note that Web sites for nonprofits and those ending with ".org" still are evaluated positively in regard to credibility.)

Another key finding: A site is more credible if it "links to its competitors' sites." The likely assumption behind this finding is that companies that give users all the facts, including those not under their control, are being totally honest. By helping people access information—even information that may not be in the source's best interest—the source will be viewed as highly trustworthy.[32]

The last key element that contributes to presumed credibility is having a site that "says it is the official site for a specific topic."[33] The assumption is that official sites have more expertise on a given topic than a site that isn't official. Official sites also may be assumed to be more trustworthy because if they were not fair or honest, they would lose their official status. (Of course, Web users still need to determine if the site that declares itself to be the "official" site is telling the truth.)

Reputed Credibility on the Web

People's perceptions of Web credibility often center on reputed credibility, a form of credibility that's based on the endorsement or recommendation of a third party. On the Web, reputed credibility shows up in the form of awards, seals of approval, links, and endorsements from friends, among others. The key elements that affect reputed credibility are shown in Table 7.8. (As with presumed credibility, no item in our studies decreased reputed credibility to any practically significant extent.)

Table 7.8   **Key Elements That Increase Reputed Web Credibility**

	1999	2002
The site displays an award it has won.	+0.8	+0.3
The site is linked to by a site you think is believable.	+1.4	+1.3
The site was recommended to you by a friend	+1.2	+1.0

Awards

The Web has spawned many endorsements in the form of awards (Figure 7.5). Some sites prominently list the awards they have won—site of the day, a top Web site, teacher approved. Posting awards is a good strategy to play up reputed credibility. Our study results show that they are a key element in enhancing perceptions of Web credibility, but perhaps not as much as we expected. It may be that the people in our sample were experienced enough to know that some awards on the Web are meaningless. This explanation seems especially true when you look at the change from 1999 to 2002. In 2002, participants reported that having received an award boosts perceived credibility of a Web site very little, if at all. Research in future years will help show if this decline was a fleeting result or something more permanent.

Seals of Approval

Seals of approval (Figure 7.6) are similar to awards. A handful of companies have set out to tame the lawless World Wide Web—or at least to offer users a sense of security. The lack of regulation on the Web has created a market for

Figure 7.5

Awards posted on Web sites can boost credibility, even though some people recognize that Web awards can be "pointless."

Figure 7.6

Various organizations have leveraged the fact that users seek third-party endorsements on the Web.

third-party endorsements. Similar to UL Lab endorsements or Good House-keeping seals of approval, Web-related endorsements can convey credibility.

Consider TRUSTe, a nonprofit consumer advocacy group. The trademarked motto for TRUSTe cuts to the heart of credibility: "Building a Web you can believe in." VeriSign—"the sign of trust on the net"—also aims to give a sense of security to people who make Web transactions. In the health arena, the Health on the Net Foundation has created a set of guidelines for health sites. Sites that display the HON code logo are supposed to follow the policies of the foundation.

Organizations such as TRUSTe, VeriSign, and the Health on the Net Foundation have found they can fill a void. Consumer Reports is currently moving into this space with its Consumer Webwatch Project, for which I serve as an adviser.[34] Web site operators seek these third-party endorsements, and Web users rely on them to determine the trustworthiness of Web sites.

Links from Credible Sources

Links from other Web sites to a given site also can convey credibility. The results from our studies confirm the impact of these incoming links. The studies showed that Web sites gain a great deal of credibility when "linked to by a site you think is believable." This effect is intuitive: If you were running a Web site on health information, a single link from a prestigious site such as the Mayo Clinic could dramatically boost your site's credibility. Through the link from their site, you received an implied endorsement from a prestigious organization.

Word-of-Mouth Referrals

Finally, our study data show that the classic word-of-mouth strategy boosts perceptions of Web credibility. Sites that are "recommended to you by a friend" are perceived as more credible. This is not surprising; in general, you would expect your friends to be trustworthy, looking out for your best interest.

The power of word-of-mouth referrals is not new, but it can take on new forms online. Some Web sites make it easy for you to send an article to a friend. Other sites, such as the community site Yahoo Groups, ask you to compose a personal message to a friend when you invite him or her into your virtual group. These are all referrals, which boost perceptions of site credibility.

The Web offers other types of reputed credibility, such as experts who endorse a site, magazines that favorably review a site's functionality or content, and search engines that list the site early in the list of matches. Although not part of our studies, these all likely have an impact on the perceived credibility of Web sites.

Surface Credibility on the Web

Presumed and reputed credibility can exist without people experiencing Web sites firsthand; however, the other types of credibility—surface and earned—require direct experience. Of the two, surface credibility is the most common, while earned credibility is the most robust.

Often people use the Web in ways that don't allow for earned credibility to develop. They surf around, hopping from page to page and site to site, making quick evaluations of Web credibility by browsing through sites. For casual Web surfing, surface credibility matters most and earned credibility matters little, since people are not processing information deeply and are not engaging with a site over an extended period of time.

Design Matters

What conveys the surface experience of a Web site, and how does this affect perceptions of credibility? Tables 7.9 and 7.10 show the key elements.

Table 7.9   **Key Elements That Increase Surface Web Credibility**

	1999	2002
The site looks professionally designed.	+1.6	+1.5
The site has been updated since your last visit.	+1.5	+1.7

Table 7.10   **Key Elements That Decrease Surface Web Credibility**

	1999	2002
The site makes it hard to distinguish ads from content.	−2.1	−1.9
The site automatically pops up new windows with ads.	−1.1	−1.6
The site takes a long time to download.	−0.7	−1.0
The site requires a paid subscription to gain access.	−0.7	−0.9
The site has one or more ads on each page.	−0.7	−0.6

One key element in surface credibility is visual design. People can quickly take in the design of a site—the colors, the layout, the images, and other design elements. The Stanford Web Credibility Studies show that site design matters a great deal in assessing surface credibility. Sites that look "professionally designed" boost credibility substantially. People apparently use these limited impressions to make an initial assessment of a site's credibility.

When evaluating credibility, Web surfers also consider how easy a site is to access. Sites that require "a long time to download" take a credibility hit. Also, according to the data in our studies, sites that require "a paid subscription to gain access" lose some credibility.[35]

Advertising is another element that affects surface credibility perceptions. People surfing the Web may not read a Web site's content in detail, but they are likely to get a sense of the advertising on the site. As noted earlier, a site loses a great deal of credibility by making it "hard to distinguish ads from content" or by "automatically pop[ping] up new windows with ads." As stated earlier, pop-up ads are more common in 2002 and, therefore, more annoying. It only takes a quick glance to sense the ad density on a page, making this a surface credibility issue. Participants in our research studies reported that sites having "one or more ads on each page" lose credibility.

Enhancing Surface Credibility

Because people can't absorb all Web site elements at once, Web designers must emphasize those elements that boost surface credibility most. Which elements to emphasize depends on the Web site's purpose. For example, if a site deals with news, it's important to quickly show that the site's information is current. Our studies show that sites gain credibility when they have been "updated since your last visit." To boost surface credibility, a news Web site could highlight the frequency of its updates.

Another example: If a site deals with health, it's important to convey the expert sources behind the information. In a recent pilot study asking people to compare the credibility of health Web sites, researchers in my Stanford lab found that participants responded quite positively to InteliHealth.com (Figure 7.7). In reading their comments, we found that one element made InteliHealth seem highly credible: the use of the Harvard Medical School name. Every page of the InteliHealth site contains in the upper left corner a prominent blue oval that says "Featuring Harvard Medical School's Consumer Health Information" along with an image of the Harvard crest. This is great example of bringing to the surface elements that are likely to boost credibility. The designers at InteliHealth did not hide the Harvard affiliation in a footnote or an "about us" page; the message is featured on each page, taking up valuable screen space but doing an important thing for a health site: clearly establishing credibility.

Designing for surface credibility is a balancing act. On the one hand, a site must fill users' needs for information or services quickly—or at least make a quick promise to fill those needs. A portion of the homepage must be devoted to this. On the other hand, the site must use the homepage to convey surface credibility—by showing a photo of the organization's headquarters building; listing clients, partners, or experts associated with the site; or including other content that instantly conveys expertise or trustworthiness. Both of these requirements must be met within the limitations of a browser window.

Figure 7.7

By making the Harvard name prominent, Inteli-Health gains surface credibility.

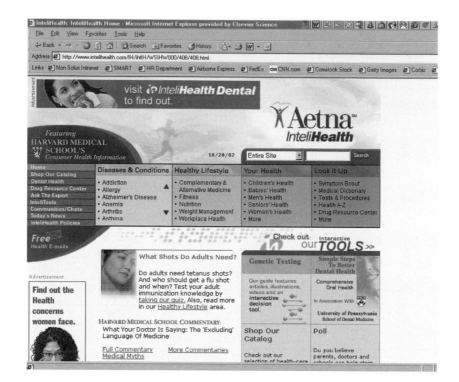

Earned Credibility on the Web

> **Earned credibility is the most difficult to achieve but the most likely to change attitudes or behaviors.**

The last type of Web credibility is the gold standard: earned credibility. Especially on the Web, where people surf quickly from site to site, earned credibility is the most difficult type to gain, but it is also the type of credibility that is most likely to lead to attitude and behavior changes. Conveying the three other types of Web credibility is useful primarily so that the site will eventually gain earned credibility. When earned credibility is high, people are likely to spend more time at the site, visit it more often, make repeated purchases (if it is an e-commerce site), tell others about it, and be open to persuasion techniques the site uses. Earned credibility is all about establishing an ongoing relationship between a Web user and the Web site or operator. According to our research, a solid, ongoing Web relationship is based on three key attributes of a site: interactions are easy, the site's information is personalized, and service is responsive (Tables 7.11 and 7.12).

Table 7.11 **Key Elements That Increase Earned Web Credibility**

	1999	*2002*
The site provides a quick response to your customer service questions.	+2.0	+1.8
The site sends emails confirming transactions you make.	+1.8	+1.8
The site is arranged in a way that makes sense to you.	+1.5	+1.5
The site recognizes you have been there before.	+0.7	+0.4
The site selects news stories according to your preferences.	+0.7	+0.6
The site has ads that match the topic you are reading about.	+0.2	+0.2

Table 7.12 **Key Element that Decreases Earned Web Credibility**

	1999	*2002*
The site is difficult to navigate.	–1.2	–1.4

The Interaction Is Easy

Principle of Ease-of-Use

A Web site wins credibility points by being easy to use.

Earned credibility grows from Web interactions that are easy. Our survey results show that Web sites gain credibility when "the site is arranged in a way that makes sense to you." At the opposite end of the spectrum, a site loses credibility when it "is difficult to navigate."

Likability is a stepping stone to credibility. A person who likes someone tends to think the other person is credible as well.[36] The same is true for human-computer relationships.[37] If a person finds a Web site easy to use, he or she likely will think the site is also credible.

The Information Is Personalized

In our studies, we found that a Web site was perceived to be more credible when it offers personalized information—specifically, when it "recognizes you have been there" and when it selects "news stories according to your preferences." Even ads on the Web become slight bonuses when they are personalized; the study data show that a site gains credibility when the "ads match the topic you are reading about."

Principle of Personalization

> Web sites that offer personalized content and services get a boost in credibility.

Personalization seems to enhance credibility in two ways. First, when a Web site has the capability to tailor content, people will view the site as smarter, boosting expertise perceptions. Next, tailored experiences can make people think the Web site understands their preferences and is working to help them achieve their goals. Unless the tailoring is done poorly (e.g., raising concerns about privacy by clumsily showing how much the Web site really knows about you[38]), users are likely to perceive the site—and the people behind it—as trustworthy. For instance, people who use sites such as my.yahoo.com or myschwab.com may view the personalized versions of these Web sites as more trustworthy.

The Service Is Responsive to Customer Issues

Finally, Web sites can earn credibility when people find them responsive. Our studies show significant increases in credibility for a Web site that "provides a quick response to your customer service questions." Participants also evaluated a Web site to be much more credible when it "sends emails confirming transactions you make." It may be that, in the period between the 1999 study and the 2002 study, people had become more comfortable with online transactions and that the email confirmation was less needed—or more expected.

Principle of Responsiveness

> The more responsive to users, the greater the perceived credibility of a Web site.

Earned credibility should be a key goal for creators of persuasive Web sites. The study data highlight some specific design issues for achieving this: make Web sites easy to use, personalized, and responsive. These three factors will do more than perhaps anything else to boost credibility perceptions that make a difference.

The Web Credibility Framework

What exactly is the Web? Is it an information system, a place for community gatherings, a space for accessing and using software applications, a huge shopping mall, or a next-generation broadcast medium? The answer seems to change over time. This dynamism has made the Web difficult to study rigorously because what exists today may not exist—or may not be relevant—tomorrow. By the time you plan, execute, and document a careful study, the Web playing field can shift, making your study a historical artifact rather than a useful research step forward.

Table 7.13   Web Credibility Framework

Category	Subcategory	Elements that boost credibility (examples)
Operator The organization or person offering the site	*Organization or Person*	■ Operator is a respected organization. ■ Operator is a nonprofit organization. ■ Site shows photos of the organization's members. ■ Site posts appropriate rules regarding content contribution or other issues related to use of the site.
Content What the site provides users in terms of information and functionality	*Information* The text, images, and sounds that have meaning for users (e.g., reviews of products, a journal article, a graphic showing the weather forecast)	■ Content is regularly updated. ■ Information is available in more than one language. ■ Site lists authors' credentials for each article.
	Functionality The work the site can do for the user (e.g., make travel reservations, translate from English to Spanish, calculate mortgages)	■ Users can search past content (i.e., archives). ■ Pages are tailored to individual users. ■ The site links to outside materials and sources.

(continued)

Table 7.13 **Web Creativity Framework** (*Continued*)

Category	Subcategory	Elements that boost credibility (examples)
Design How the site is put together—specifically, the integration of four key design elements: information, technical, aesthetic, and interaction	*Information design* The structure of information on each page and throughout the site	■ Site is arranged in a way that makes sense to users. ■ Ads are clearly differentiated from content.
	Technical design How the site works from a technical standpoint	■ Search feature is powered by Google or another respected search engine. ■ The site is rarely "down." ■ Links from all pages work properly.
	Aesthetic design Issues of taste—how things look, feel, or sound	■ Site looks professionally designed. ■ Photographs of people (content contributors or employees) are high quality.
	Interaction Design The overall, moment-by-moment experience of users as they go through the steps to accomplish their goals	■ Site matches users' expectations about what they should do at each step to accomplish their goals at the site.

To promote research and robust understanding of Web credibility, I've created a framework that outlines categories of Web site variables. Within this "Web Credibility Framework" (Table 7.13), a Web site can be described by three categories: the operator of the site, the content of the site, and the site's design. These categories are helpful in sorting out the many issues relating to Web credibility. For example, if you're a designer, you'll find that only certain issues are under your control, while other issues, such as content, may not be.

The main purpose of the framework is to provide an orderly way of thinking about the many elements of a Web site, which in turn provides a systematic way to think about researching or designing for Web credibility. When my Stanford team set out to study Web credibility, we used this framework to ensure that we were covering a wide variety of elements, since our goal was to create a foundation for focused research and design efforts.

The Web Credibility Grid

The Web Credibility Framework can be extended to another level when it is combined with the four types of credibility described in Chapter 6—presumed, reputed, surface, and earned. These two perspectives can be integrated to create a grid (Table 7.14) that captures many elements of a Web experience.

The Web Credibility Grid illustrates that the study of Web credibility has many facets, from brand perception of a company to the technical details of a Web site. Some elements that contribute to Web credibility are under the direct control of Web designers; others are not. As a result, increasing the credibility of a company's Web site requires a concerted effort from many parts of the organization.

Table 7.14 Web Credibility Grid

	Presumed credibility	*Reputed credibility*	*Surface credibility*	*Earned credibility*
	Based on general assumptions in the user's mind	Based on third-party endorse-ments, reports, or referrals	Based on simple inspection, first impressions	Based on firsthand experience that extends over time
Examples				
Site operator Person or organization	The source is a nonprofit organization.	The person writ-ing the Web article is a recognized expert.	Users are familiar with the source's brand outside the Web.	The source always sends quick an-swers to site users' questions.
Site content Information, functionality	The site has ads from reputable companies.	The content has been endorsed by a respected out-side agency (e.g., the Health on the Net Foundation).	The site appears to have lots of rel-evant information.	The site's content has always been accurate and unbiased.
Site design Information, technical, aesthetic, interaction	The site has a search feature on the top page.	The site won an award for techni-cal achievement.	The site has a pleasing visual design.	The site is easy to navigate.

Designers can use the grid to identify the cells they have control over, then focus on designing to boost credibility in those areas, such as making the site easy to navigate. Marketing and legal departments could use it to ensure credibility of content. Public relations personnel may focus on enhancing perceptions of the company's overall brand. Fulfillment or customer service personnel could concentrate on strengthening earned credibility by delivering fast responses. The grid provides a way for the entire organization to gain a better understanding of how its parts must work together to create and maintain a credible Web site.

The Future of Web Credibility Research and Design

Because academia and industry lack a deep understanding of Web credibility, many research and design explorations are waiting to be performed, with rich insights waiting to emerge. Like the study of persuasive technologies, the study of Web credibility is mostly uncharted territory, offering opportunities for those interested in creating new knowledge.

Web credibility can be difficult to study, not only because there are so many facets to a Web site but because of a host of factors external to the Web. One external factor is users—how they process information, how they value individual components of credibility, and their differing goals when using the Web, as well as contexts in which they do so. All of these factors can vary significantly from one person to the next, and all influence credibility perceptions.

The study of Web credibility also faces the "moving target" problem.[39] For Web credibility researchers, there are three significant moving targets: the Web user base, user experience levels, and Web technology itself. As these variables change and evolve, research done in the past may no longer apply or may not be as useful.

In addition to the challenge of individual differences, researchers must be aware that an individual user may have different goals at different times when using the Web, and these goals impact credibility perceptions. At one time, the user may seek specific information on the Web, such as mutual fund performance figures. At other times, they may be using the Web to catch up on the news. In both cases, site credibility matters a great deal. At other times a user might go to the Web just to pass the time, in which case credibility is not likely to matter much.

All of these factors complicate research efforts. Nonetheless, in assessing credibility, users will focus on the same basic factors: trustworthiness and expertise. In addition, the different types of credibility—presumed, reputed, surface, and earned—are likely to remain constant. For researchers, these constants will help to guide future research efforts. For designers, the need to create credible computing products won't change; in fact, it is likely to grow as people become more experienced users.

People will spend more time on a site they find credible; they'll subscribe to its services, buy its products, use its chat rooms, tell their friends about it. When a site is designed with credibility in mind, it will be well positioned to change users' attitudes or behaviors. Credibility makes persuasion possible.

Notes and References

For updates on the topics presented in this chapter, visit *www.persuasivetech.info.*

1. For more about the fake Web site whortle.com, see an article online by the Associated Press at *http://www.businesstoday.com/business/technology/ap_fake01302002.htm* or the SEC's press release at *http://www.sec.gov/news/headlines/scamsites.htm.*

2. For more information about these and other Internet scams, visit the Identity Theft Resource Center at *http://www.idtheftcenter.org/html/scam-alerts.htm.*

3. One site has gathered a few dozen examples of Web site hoaxes. See *http://www.museum-ofhoaxes.com/hoaxsites.html.*

4. The hoax Web site for the Oklahoma Association of Wine Producers is at *http://Web.fvdes.com/Web_Eval_TL/OKWine2/okawp.html.*

5. The farcical Christian Women's Wrestling (CWW) site can be found at *http://www.jesus21.com/poppydixon/sports/cww.html.*

6. The humor page claiming to be last page of the Internet is at *http://www.shibumi.org/eoti/index.htm.*

7. For one of the early editorials pointing out that the Web is facing a credibility crisis, see R.Kilgore, Publishers must set rules to preserve credibility, *Advertising Age,* 69 (48): 31 (1998).

8. For a librarian's view of evaluating Web information, see the site from Hope Tillman, director of Libraries at Babson College: *http://www.tiac.net/users/hope/findqual.html.*

9. Some excellent guidelines exist for evaluating Web information quality. For example, see *http://wwwlibrary.csustan.edu/lboyer/webeval/webeval.htm.* Also see the work of Kaaren

Struthers at *http://leo.stcloudstate.edu/research/credibility1.html*. Finally, visit the Librarians' Index to the Internet at *http://www.lii.org/*.

10. While most Web designers seek to design sites with maximum levels of credibility, a more admirable goal would be to design sites that convey appropriate levels of credibility—that is, sites that accurately convey their performance levels, the quality of their content, and so on.

11. As my lab team was researching Web credibility in 1998, Cheskin Research was researching a related, but not identical, area: trust in ecommerce. See eCommerce Trust Study, a joint research project by Cheskin Research and Studio Archetype/Sapient. (January 1999). Available online at *http://cheskin.com/think/trust/assets/images/etrust.pdf*.

    They followed up this study with a study with an international scope: Trust in the Wired Americas (July 2000). Online at *http://cheskin.com/think/studies/trustIIrpt.pdf*.

12. You can find the latest Stanford research on Web credibility at *www.webcredibility.org*.

13. The Stanford students who joined me in researching Web credibility in 1999 were Preeti Swani, Akshay Rangnekar, Marissa Treinen, Nicholas Fang, John Shon, M.D., Othman Laraki, Chris Varma, Alex Osipovich, Jonathan Marshall, and Jyoti Paul.

14. Conducted during December 1999, this Web credibility research project was supported by Timo Saari and Mauri Mattsson of Alma Media and Peter Dodd of Nortel Networks. For more information on this and other research we've done in this area, visit *www.webcredibility.org*.

15. My lab published a different analysis of our 1999 data previously. See B. J. Fogg, J. Marshall, O. Laraki, A. Osipovich, C. Varma, N. Fang, J. Paul, A. Rangnekar, J. Shon, P. Swani, and M. Treinen, What makes a web site credible? A report on a large quantitative study, *Proceedings of ACM CHI 2001 Conference on Human Factors in Computing Systems* (New York: ACM Press, 2001). *http://www.acm.org/pubs/articles/proceedings/chi/365024/p61-fogg/p61-fogg.pdf*.

16. We performed the 2002 research with the collaboration of Makovsky & Company, a New York–based communications agency. Mike Sockol was the person at Makovsky who worked with us to implement the study.

17. This process was based on our Web credibility teams' opinions. We went through the variables one by one and decided if having data about that item would be important or interesting. For example, to us it seemed the effects of advertising on the Web would be an important area to investigate and document. In contrast, the effects of animated gifs—simple eye candy—did not seem worthy of our time and effort. And we ruled out some elements because a survey as a research method would not be able to shed much light. For example, we ruled out asking people what they thought about Web sites with black backgrounds.

18. Each research method has its own set of weaknesses, including surveys. Surveys don't always capture how people actually feel or behave. However, we chose the survey method because it was the most efficient means of gathering a significant amount of data to begin

building a foundation for future research, including controlled laboratory and contextual field studies with behavioral measures.

19. Although we have a large sample, we cannot say this sample is representative of all Web users in 1999 or in 2002. We found no defensible way to obtain a true random sample of Web users. However, the fact that we found similar results in the pilots and among participants from both the United States and Finland gave us more confidence in our results. As with any research, readers must interpret findings with care, determining how well the results apply to their own situations.

20. For a description of how our team arrived at the 0.3 figure, see endnote 22.

21. We had more questions in the pilot studies, sometimes as many as 90 questions, and we recruited a different sample: in one pilot, the sample was HCI specialists; in another, it was our friends and family whom we could convince to test the survey.

    The purpose of the pilot studies was to refine the questions (finding confusing items and making them clearer, narrowing the question set down to a manageable number, which we decided was about 50), and make sure the backend part of the Web site was capturing data correctly. Even though the pilot studies weren't designed to give us data we'd publish, we still did the statistics to see what we would find.

    The items that affected credibility a great deal were roughly the same in all the studies, notwithstanding the different samples and size of the surveys.

22. Because we have such a large number of respondents, even small differences in means (such as 1.1 versus 1.0) are statistically significant. However, as I point out in the text, statistical significance is one thing; practical significance is another.

    Using statistics and rational thinking as our guides, in analyzing the data for practical significance, my team and I decided to drawn the line at 0.3. This means that, within a given study, if any two means are more than 0.3 points apart (when including the entire data set for the year), those two items do indeed have practical impacts on perceived credibility.

    Comparing items between the 1999 and 2002 studies, we chose to be more conservative, since the samples—although close—are not identical. Also, because the survey took place at a different time in history, there may be other factors, such as a news story about corruption in the United Way, that had a temporary impact on how people think about charity groups, including their presence on the Web. In the end, we chose the more conservative figure of 0.4 (when using the entire data set) to be the necessary difference between mean scores to be an interesting (practical) difference.

    Therefore, in the discussion of the data in this chapter, I point out the differences between data sets that are at 0.4 or higher and suggest reasons for this change. Of course, there is no way to prove that my explanations are accurate, but I think you'll find my comments to be reasonable. There are a couple items for which I cannot explain the difference. As a lab, we've looked over these items from various angles, and we're still scratching our heads. But that's how research usually proceeds: questions remain unanswered—some of which may be resolved in future studies.

23. As mentioned in the previous endnote, we determined that any two means that are at least 0.3 apart have a significantly different (in practical terms, not just statistical terms) impact on people's perceptions of Web credibility.

24. In 1999, I advised a Stanford honors thesis that showed, contrary to our expectations, that ads on Web pages increased the credibility of the Web page. We didn't expect this. But after reexamining the data and the pages, we realized that the banner ads from reputable companies—in this case, including Yahoo and Visa—could endow Web sites with credibility, making an impression on users: if Visa cares enough about this Web site to advertise, it must be a credible site. Thesis information: N. Kim, *World Wide Web Credibility: What Effect Do Advertisements and Typos Have on the Perceived Credibility of Web Page Information?* Senior honors thesis, Stanford University (1999).

25. Making the motives and policies of Web sites transparent is a major focus for Consumers Union Consumer Webwatch Project, for which I serve as an adviser. See *www.consumerwebwatch.org* for more.

26. Almost all guidelines for evaluating the credibility of Web information advocate checking on the author's credentials. However, I can find no other quantitative evidence, besides my lab's research, that shows that listing credentials will boost credibility. Perhaps other researchers have found this question too obvious to merit a controlled study.

27. In 2002, we dropped the item regarding searching archives because it seemed this feature was no longer prominent on the Web. Instead, we replaced this item with the following: "The site has search capabilities" (mean in 2002: +1.2).

28. When this study is complete, the results will be posted online at *www.webcredibility.org.*

29. In 1999, I advised a Stanford honors thesis investigating Web credibility. The results from this controlled laboratory study also showed that simple typos have clear negative effects on Web credibility. The more important the information (e.g., life-depending information), the stronger the negative effect. Thesis information: N. Kim, *World Wide Web Credibility: What Effect Do Advertisements and Typos Have on the Perceived Credibility of Web Page Information?* Senior honors thesis, Stanford University (1999).

30. In recent years hackers have brought down Web sites for titans like Yahoo, the *New York Times,* and eBay. This can be costly, in terms of lost dollars and lost credibility. For example, when eBay went down for 22 hours in 1999, not only did it cost the company $3.9 million in credits given to users and a 9% drop in share price, media reports suggested that the downtime also cost eBay credibility among its users. See the following:

    http://special.northernlight.com/ecommerce/always_there.htm

    http://www.gilian.com/webassets.pdf

    http://www.webtechniques.com/archives/2000/03/plat/

31. You don't need to be a nonprofit organization to register a domain name with an ".org" ending. Anyone can purchase these domain names, but many people don't know this.

32. E. Walster, E. Aronson, and D. Abrahams, On increasing the persuasiveness of a low prestige communicator, *Journal of Experimental Social Psychology,* 2: 325–342 (1966).

See also S. Chaiken and D. Maheswaran, Heuristic processing can bias systematic processing: Effects of source credibility, argument ambiguity, and task importance on attitude judgment, *Journal of Personality and Social Psychology,* 66: 460–473 (1994).

33. We deleted this topic in the 2002 survey because we felt it applied to a small number of sites.

34. See *www.consumerwebwatch.org.*

35. This finding surprised us in 1999. We expected people to think more highly of paid sites. Perhaps participants simply responded negatively to the idea of paying for anything.

36. For more on the connection between liking and credibility, see Charles Self, Credibility, in M. Salwen and D. Stacks (eds.), *An Integrated Approach to Communication Theory and Research* (Mahway, NJ: Erlbaum, 1996).

37. I discuss issues of likability and persuasion in my dissertation, *Charismatic Computers: Creating More Likable and Persuasive Interactive Technologies by Leveraging Principles from Social Psychology,* Stanford University (1997).

38. You can see how much a site may know about some personal details by visiting snoop. anonymizer.com. When I did this, the site displayed the following information about me—information that other sites could capture as well:

    Your IP Address Is: 171.64.23.189

    Your Machine Name Is: bjfogg.Stanford.EDU

    Your Browser Is: Microsoft Internet Explorer

39. The metaphor goes something like this: Even if you aim for the center of a target, you'll miss because the target is moving in ways no one can fully predict.

chapter 8

Increasing Persuasion through Mobility and Connectivity

Intervening at the Right Time and Place

Networking and mobile technologies create new potential to persuade at the right time and place.

As noted in the discussion of suggestion technology in Chapter 3, when it comes to influencing attitudes and behaviors, timing and context are critical. New computing capabilities, most notably networking and mobile technologies, create additional potential for persuading people at the optimal time and place. For example, networked and mobile technology could allow commercial offers to be made at the moment people have a need and can act on the offers, or safe driving could be promoted while the driver is on the road, as part of an in-car system.

Intervening at the right time and place via networked, mobile technology increases the chances of getting results. As you read the following hypothetical examples of Study Buddy and HydroTech, think about how connectivity and mobility enhance the products' ability to motivate and persuade.

The Study Buddy

Someday in the future, a first-year student named Pamela sits in a college library and removes an electronic device from her purse. It's just smaller than a deck of cards, easily carried around, and serves as Pamela's mobile phone, information portal, entertainment platform, and personal organizer. She takes

183

this device almost everywhere and feels a bit lost without it. Because she's serious about school, Pamela runs an application on her device called Study Buddy.

Here's what the application does: As Pamela begins her evening study session, she launches the Study Buddy system and views the display. Study Buddy congratulates her for studying for the third time that day, meeting the goal she set at the beginning of the academic quarter. The device suggests that Pamela start her study session with a five-minute review of her biology vocabulary words, then read the two chapters assigned for tomorrow's sociology lecture.

As Pamela reviews biology, the Study Buddy screen shows a cluster of shapes, which represent her classmates who are currently studying. This motivates her to continue studying.

Later that evening, as Pamela wraps up her work, she's curious about her mentor, Jean, so she turns to Study Buddy for information. Jean also subscribes to the Study Buddy system and has invited Pamela into her "awareness group."[1] Pamela sees a symbol on the display that indicates Jean is currently in one of the campus libraries. Jean is a good role model; she's a senior who was recently admitted to a top graduate school. Being a study mentor means that Jean has agreed to let Pamela remotely view Jean's studying habits. Using Study Buddy, Jean can send simple sounds and tactile cues such as vibration patterns to Pamela, to encourage her to study.

HydroTech

For the last eight months of 2010, Phil has been training for the New York City Marathon. He's made good progress, guided by his coach, Michael. The marathon is six weeks away, and Phil has increased his training level to about 50 miles per week in preparation. He's right on track. However, Michael suspects that Phil isn't drinking enough fluids to get the most out of his training runs, especially the two 20-mile runs he'll be doing over the next four weeks.

Based on Michael's recommendation, Phil gets a tiny device implanted just under the skin of his forearm. The device measures Phil's hydration level and transmits the data for display on Phil's running watch, which contains an embedded sensor and tracking software. Because the watch is aware of when Phil has planned his workout, it can also cue him to drink the right amount of water and sports drinks every day, and especially in the day before each long training run.

Phil knows his hydration data gets transmitted to his coach's mobile phone in real time, throughout the day and during his workouts, via the HydroTech system. This motivates Phil even more to stay on track with his water intake. He doesn't want to disappoint his coach.

An Emerging Frontier for Persuasive Technology

Although the preceding examples may never become actual products, the scenarios illustrate how the mobile and connected qualities of the technologies depicted boost the potential for persuasion. The persuasive products described in the examples would be much less effective if they were designed to run only on a desktop computer.

The fact that the products are connected also creates new pathways to persuasion. The precise networking technology doesn't matter; it could be the Internet, the cellular phone network, or another network. What's important is that the device can exchange data with remote people and devices.

Mobility and networking represent an emerging frontier for persuasive technology. This chapter will explore how and why mobile and connected devices can be so effective in persuading people to change their attitudes and behavior.

Although mobility and connectivity work well together, they don't always go hand in hand. To make my points about each quality clear, I'll address each area separately. First, I'll discuss persuasive technology products that are mobile; then I'll describe how and why connected, or networked, products increase the potential for persuasion.

Persuasion through Mobile Technology

In the last few years, the idea of mobile commerce has been a darling of technology companies, marketing agencies, and the news media. Some forms of mobile commerce are taking shape in Asia and Europe while the U.S. lags behind. One vision for mobile commerce is to provide people with opportunities to buy things conveniently and when the need arises. (Is it starting to rain unexpectedly? Your mobile device can tell you where to pick up the closest umbrella.) My vision for mobile persuasion goes beyond using mobile devices to promote products and services. I believe mobile systems can and will be used to promote health, safety, community involvement, personal improvement, and more.

When you pack a mobile persuasive technology with you, you pack a source of influence. At any time (ideally, at the appropriate time), the device can suggest, encourage, and reward; it can track your performance or lead you through a process; or it can provide compelling factual evidence or insightful simulations.

As I write this chapter, my Stanford lab is working under a grant to study the potential of mobile persuasion. Our goal is to create insight into how mobile devices, specifically mobile phones, PDAs, and specialized devices such as pedometers, can play a role in motivating and influencing people. As part of this research, we are conducting experiments, conceptualizing new mobile persuasion products, and analyzing existing products. We still have much left to discover, but part of what we've learned so far can be shared here.[2]

Examining Mobile Health Applications

In the fall of 2001, two researchers in my Stanford lab, Cathy Soohoo and Katherine Woo, investigated the state of the art in mobile health applications, specifically applications created for PDAs, mobile phones, or pagers. They identified 72 different mobile health applications, almost all for PDAs. When they examined the applications, they were surprised to discover that although most were designed to motivate people to change their health behaviors, the products failed to incorporate influence strategies effectively. (We repeated this research in late 2002 and found essentially the same thing.) Three fairly mundane strategies were widely used, with little creativity in any of the 72 applications. The researchers found that 46 of the 72 applications used some form of tracking: the program helped people keep a log of health behavior, such as what they ate or how much they exercised. Of the 72 applications, 33 offered some form of analysis, such as calculations of blood alcohol level or calories burned during an exercise program. In addition, 26 of the 72 applications provided reference material: health information, definitions, charts, and other such items.

One conclusion from this research was that mobile health applications have a strong tendency to use similar approaches: providing tracking, analysis, and reference material. Our lab group concluded that a significant opportunity exists to make mobile health applications more motivating and persuasive.

The United States Lags in the Wireless Domain

While it's relatively easy to create applications for stand-alone mobile products, such as Palm OS handheld computers and Microsoft's Pocket PC devices, it's challenging to create applications that run on mobile phones in the United States. While Asia and Europe are moving forward with their own relatively coherent wireless standards and network carriers, the U.S. mobile phone landscape is a mess. We have multiple mobile phone standards (CDMA, TDMA, GSM, iDEN), different platforms for phones (Symbian, Microsoft's PPC Mobile Edition, Palm OS, J2ME, and others), and too many phones with different screen sizes and input capabilities. Trying to create a single application that will work across all these variables is difficult.[3]

Given these challenges in the United States, Asia and Europe are likely to roll out innovative applications for mobile phones before the United States and the rest of the world. (For example, in Japan today people can purchase items from vending machines using their mobile phones.) However, because the market for mobile applications is large, it's a safe bet to say these near-term problems will be resolved, making it easier to create a mobile persuasion application that can be used worldwide.

As discussed throughout this book, there are many ways to influence and motivate people. To help people achieve their goals, mobile health applications could leverage a wider range of influence strategies, from offering simulations that give insight to establishing a system of digital rewards to motivate users.

Mobile devices offer unique opportunities for persuasion. The most obvious and compelling is that the devices can travel with users throughout the day. As a constant companion, these devices are in a unique position to persuade. This persistent presence creates two factors that contribute to persuasion opportunities. I call these the "kairos factor" and the "convenience factor."

The Kairos Factor

As noted in Chapter 3, kairos is the principle of presenting your message at the opportune moment. The biggest advantage that mobile devices have in persuasion is the ability to leverage the kairos principle. Mobile technology makes

Figure 8.1

Leveraging the kairos principle.

Future mobile technology can determine

Your physical location

Your typical routine

The time of day

Your goals for the day

Your current task

Kairos: "opportune moment"

it easy to intervene at the opportune moment for persuasion, as the technology can travel with users wherever they go (Figure 8.1).

The mobile systems of the future will be able to identify opportune moments for influence more effectively than they do today. By knowing a user's goals, routine, current location, and current task, these mobile systems will be able to determine when the user would be most open to persuasion in the form of a reminder, suggestion, or simulated experience. (Ideally, the system would also consider the social context, intervening only when this would not be a distraction to people in close proximity to the user.) It may sense when the user has a need and step in to provide a solution.

Contrast this vision of graceful interactions and proactive interruptions with the way desktop systems work today. (At least my own computer always seems to interrupt important work to run a backup or have me renew my authenticated login.)

For an extreme example, imagine how eBay.com might develop its recommendation engine to such a degree that as you lingered in a museum to admire sculptures by Auguste Rodin, the site could identify your interest in this artist and send you a special offer to buy prints of Rodin's work, if you have opted to receive such information.

Principle of Kairos

> Mobile devices are ideally suited to leverage the principle of kairos—offering suggestions at opportune moments—to increase the potential to persuade.

The Convenience Factor

Applying the kairos principle, a mobile device proactively inserts itself into the user's world, initiating the interaction at an opportune moment, enhancing the potential to persuade. Mobile technology also makes it easier for the user to

Principle of Convenience

> Interactive experiences that are easy to access (ideally, just a click away on a mobile device) have greater opportunity to persuade.

initiate an interaction, furthering the potential for persuasion. The device is always available (it's near the user) and responsive (it's instantly on—almost no delay to boot up or load). I refer to this as the "convenience factor."

Even the busiest of people have moments of downtime—riding the train, standing in line, waiting for the doctor. If a person doesn't want to meditate or simply enjoy the mental white space, he or she can turn to mobile technology to fill the void. For some people I know, this is one reason they pack their mobile devices with them everywhere. It gives them a sense of control over situations in which they must wait for others or are otherwise unable to get things done. These empty gaps in schedules are times when people may be open to interactive experiences that influence them. Even the simplest activity can seem interesting when you're in a state I call "trapped in silence" (waiting at the airport or riding the bus home from work).

One of my student teams developed a good example of providing a persuasive activity for these moments of downtime, in the form of a conceptual design called Tetrash (Figure 8.2).[4] In this game, the user sorts trash into recycling bins as the trash—virtual bottles, cans, and newspapers—moves down the screen of the mobile phone. The challenge is to sort the objects correctly. Every so often during the game, a garbage truck drives across the screen with messages of congratulations or quirky facts about recycling.

From a persuasion standpoint, Tetrash helps people rehearse recycling behavior, making it an activity they are more likely to think about—and ideally, perform—in the real world. The positive reinforcement and the facts about recycling also contribute to the persuasive experience.

Figure 8.2

A concept for mobile platforms, the Tetrash game challenges people to sort recyclables.

If Tetrash were a game for Playstation or PC, it's unlikely that people would play it because there are better alternatives. But as a game on a mobile device, Tetrash is compelling enough to occupy time when standing in line or riding in a taxi. People might then choose to learn about and practice recycling. That's the power of the convenience factor.

Another example of leveraging the convenience factor can be found in a game by Astraware called Bejeweled. An adaptation of the popular game Diamond Mine, a trial version of Bejeweled comes preinstalled on some PDAs. The game itself has nothing to do with persuasion. But the makers have made the game compelling enough (and it's so readily available, right there on your PDA) that a large number of users are seduced into parting with $14.95 to "register" the game. This strategy of leveraging convenience, then weaving in persuasion, seems to work. According to Handango.com, a leading source for handheld software, Bejeweled was the #2 selling software in 2002 in all categories for the Palm OS (right after Vindigo).[5]

Simplifying Mobile Devices to Increase Persuasion Power

While mobile devices have some distinct advantages, as noted above, they also have some drawbacks. The main drawback in using mobile devices is their limited input and output capabilities. When working with these products, you encounter challenges some call "baby faces"[6]—the screen sizes are small—and "baby fingers"—it's hard to enter information into the devices. These are real limitations, but they don't rule out the potential to use the devices for persuasive ends.

In my lab's research on mobile persuasion, we've examined what makes some of the more popular mobile persuasion devices effective. For two products, at least, the key to success seems to lie in their simplicity, in overcoming the limitations of the devices' input and output capabilities.

LifeSign is a mobile device designed to help people stop smoking (Figure 8.3). A tunneling technology, the device steps users through the process of quitting smoking. For the first week, you simply push the big button on the device each time you smoke. After the week is over, you then smoke only when the device signals it is time. These periods become farther and farther apart. In this way, the device gradually weans you from your nicotine addiction.

Notice how simple the input and the output is on this device. Yet it helps people to gradually decrease their need to smoke. In one six-week program involving adolescent smokers who used the device, 29% of program partici-

Figure 8.3

A mobile device, LifeSign is simple to operate.

pants were no longer smoking at the end of the program, 59% had reduced their smoking by more than 50%, and 71% had reduced their smoking by more than 35%.[7]

Sportbrain (Figure 8.4) provides an even simpler experience. At the most basic level, it tracks how many steps you take each day. But it's more than a simple pedometer. It's designed so that when you snap the device into a cradle that plugs into your phone line, the cradle automatically uploads your data over the Internet to your personalized Sportbrain Web page (unfortunately for the many enthusiastic supporters of the product, as I write this the company is in the process of restructuring and attempting to reopen under new ownership). It's on the Sportbrain Web page where you see how many steps you've taken and gather other useful information to help you in your quest to increase your physical activity. There is no input or output on the device; you simply carry it with you. The technology inside the device records your movements and stamps the time on them. Even if you don't put your device in the cradle for days, the device remembers your movements from previous days.

As a pedometer, Sportbrain uses the strategy of tracking performance to motivate people. But the Web site was designed to include even more elements to motivate. It enabled users to set goals and compare their progress with how their friends are doing (I know two high-tech executives who were competing enthusiastically with each other through the Sportbrain system). Under the original owners, the company also offered baseball caps and other paraphernalia to users who reached certain goals.

Principle of Mobile Simplicity

Mobile applications that are easy to use will have greater potential to persuade.

Figure 8.4   Sportbrain is a simple mobile device that moves complexity to the Web.

As an overall system, Sportbrain is notable for skillfully migrating any complexity to the desktop. It's on the Web site where you do the setup, personalization, goal setting, feedback, social interactions, and more. Designers of other mobile systems would do well to follow Sportbrain's approach of moving complex interactions from the mobile device to the desktop.

Wedded to Mobile Technology

As I see it, people don't adopt mobile devices; they *marry* them. Some people spend more time with these devices than with any person in their lives, including their spouses. In Finland, which is ahead of the United States in the design and use of mobile systems, the younger generation has a special term for their mobile phones: *känny*. The term means "extension of the hand."

Principle of Mobile Loyalty

> Mobile applications that are perceived to serve the needs and wishes of the owner first, rather than those of an outside party, will have greater persuasive powers.

In my research lab, we've debated how people view their mobile devices (Figure 8.5). Are they simply a tool? Are they like a faithful companion? Or, as the Finnish term suggests, do owners view their mobile devices as appendages, as part of themselves?

If indeed people view their mobile phones as extensions of themselves—as an integral part of who they are and what they can do—those who create persuasion experiences for mobile devices need to take particular care. The experiences likely to be appreciated are those that help people

Figure 8.5

Ho do people view
their mobile devices?

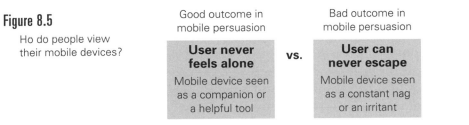

accomplish their *own* goals. Experiences that work against a person's goals or intrude into their lives may be viewed as a betrayal.

The media and some futurists have proclaimed the coming day when advertisers will push context-relevant messages to our mobile phones: as we walk by the Gap, we'll be offered 10% off on khaki slacks, or as we near the bakery, we'll get a message that cinnamon rolls are fresh out of the oven. My lab members and I are skeptical of this vision. Will people accept such intrusions into their mobile devices? We suspect not, unless the person gives permission to receive such information from specific sources.

At least in the United States, it seems there must be a compelling reason (such as a subsidy in service costs) for people to give up control of their most personal technology—their mobile devices—and let outside players intrude in this domain. The territoriality people may feel toward their mobile devices was nicely captured in a phrase one of my students recorded during a user study: "If my mobile phone ever did that, it would be a goner!"

Motivating Users to Achieve Their Own Goals

In contrast, mobile products that help motivate people to achieve their own goals are likely to be welcomed. For example, my students and I often discuss how mobile phones can influence users to stay in touch better with the people who are close to them. Specifically, the mobile phone can motivate users to place calls to people according to a schedule they have predetermined.

My student teams have prototyped various ways that mobile phones could help users set preferences for phone calls (essentially, these are goals for enhancing relationships), for showing how long it's been since the user last placed a call to a person, and to prompt the user to make a call at a designated time (birthdays and anniversaries, for example) and—finally—to reward the person for making the call (reaching the goal). On the one hand, this seems quite mechanical—having a computer run your social agenda for phone conversations. On the other hand, many people, especially those with hectic lives, seem to welcome this form of self-persuasion. The key point is that this persuasive technology concept is about helping people change behavior in ways that *they* choose.

Another example of a mobile technology helping people achieve their own goals, rather than someone else's, is the pedometer, or step counter. The Japanese have been pedometer enthusiasts for more than 30 years, and the adoption rate is remarkable: 3.2 pedometers per Japanese family.[8] Many people wear pedometers all day, every day. (I've talked to researchers who say that some people even wear pedometers to bed.) Most devices that count steps include simple computers (in the same way that digital watches and calculators are a type of computing product). The step counters can track your steps and calculate the distance walked and the calories you've burned in the process. Some can track your activity over the course of seven days and allow you to click back through the days to see the activity level. Pedometers can motivate people through self-monitoring (a principle discussed in Chapter 3); these devices make it easy for people to see if they are achieving their activity goals and boost their activity level if they are not (the widely recommended level is 10,000 steps each day).

The Importance of Experience Design

Principle of Mobile Marriage

Mobile applications designed to persuade should support an intensive, positive relationship (many interactions or interactions over a long time period) between the user and the product.

While mobility can leverage the kairos (opportune moment) and convenience factors, it also opens the door to a bad relationship with mobile devices, if applications are not designed well. More than anything else, interactions created for mobile devices should support an intensive, positive relationship between user and product. Otherwise, the relationship is likely to be terminated, as the device becomes "a goner." If you viewed a mobile device as part of you, you would expect it to serve you; serving someone else would be a type of betrayal—your device sold you out.

To create successful mobile persuasion experiences, designers need to design interactions that will weather well, like a long-standing, comfortable friendship.

Persuasion through Connected Technology

Just as mobile technologies open doors to persuasion, technologies that are networked or connected create opportunities to use influence effectively. A connected device is one that it is capable of exchanging data with remote devices and people through the Internet or another communication infrastructure.

Networked computing products can be more persuasive than those that aren't connected because they can provide better information, can leverage social influence strategies, and can tap into group-level intrinsic motivators. The remainder of this chapter will focus on these three attributes of connected devices, and how and why they can enhance persuasion.

Leveraging Current, Contingent, and Coordinated Information

In terms of information quality, connected devices have three advantages over nonnetworked devices: they can provide current, contingent, and coordinated information. These information characteristics enable experiences that can motivate and persuade.

Connected devices are able to gather and report the most current—and therefore the most persuasive—information. eBay leverages the power of current information to motivate and influence people bidding on an eBay item. With the introduction of its wireless notification service, eBay can send a message to your mobile phone, pager, or connected handheld device to inform you that you have been outbid. By providing this current information, eBay extends the excitement and competition of an online auction beyond the Web browser to bidders wherever they happen to be. This updated information keeps bidders interested, reminds them of items they've bid on that might have slipped their minds, and eliminates the need to check the eBay site over and over to ensure they still have the leading bid.

When eBay customers have the latest information delivered to them, connecting them to their auction wherever they are, this changes the eBay customer's experience. With this current information, bidders are invited back to the virtual auction and prompted to respond to being outbid. The currency of the information seduces people back into the eBay world, even when they're away from their Web browsers. Of course, this service of providing the latest information ultimately benefits eBay by stimulating higher prices on items sold and by increasing the customer's engagement with eBay.

On the U.S. TV show *Will & Grace,* actor Sean Hayes portrays how motivating it can be to receive the latest information from eBay on a mobile device. As part of the comedy, he becomes obsessed about winning eBay auctions for a Ricky Martin scooter and Britney Spears platform shoes.[9] His character announces: "Guess what I just got off eBay? . . . I got this scooter, which happens to be autographed by Ricky Martin. But the best part is, I outbid my archrival, Dr. Dangerous, to get it."

Connected products also are more persuasive because they can provide contingent information—that is, information that takes into account variables that are relevant to users, their goals, and their contexts. Think of a product designed to promote smart commuting. It could account for immediate personal needs ("I've got to get to work by 9 a.m. today, and I don't need to run errands during lunch"), enduring preferences ("I like the idea of taking public transportation"), passing constraints ("This morning I have only four dollars to spend"), and environmental variables (the weather and traffic conditions). With these variables taken into account, the connected product can be more persuasive in proposing what commute option would be best for that day.

In addition to current and contingent information, connected products can coordinate information among various people and devices, further enhancing the products' potential to persuade. Suppose a 55-year-old man sets a goal of exercising 30 minutes each day and has enlisted the help of a connected device—a personal activity monitor—to help him achieve his fitness goal. By coordinating information among people and equipment, the technology can give the man considerable flexibility in how he achieves his goal. When he decides to take a rigorous lunchtime walk through the city, his personal activity monitor informs the fitness system at his health club. Later that evening, when he arrives at his health club for his usual workout, the system already knows he's had cardiovascular exercise for the day, so it suggests a different type of workout, perhaps focusing on strength or flexibility. The adaptability that comes with coordinated information can make the intervention more effective, and it would likely increase a person's confidence in the persuasive technology.

Principle of Information Quality

Computing technology that delivers current, relevant, and well-coordinated information has greater potential to create attitude or behavior change.

Connected Products: Leveraging Social Influence

Why do people join support groups, aerobics classes, or study groups? One reason is that other people play a key role in motivation and persuasion. People can generally achieve a greater degree of attitude and behavior change working together than working alone.[10] That's the power of social influence.

Because of their networking capability, connected products can create many opportunities for social influence from both peers and experts. This gives connected products another important advantage when it comes to persuasion.

The study of social influence includes many theories and perspectives. In the next sections I'll touch on four prominent theories—social facilitation, social comparison, conformity, and social learning theory—and show how they can be applied to connected persuasive technologies.

Persuading through Social Facilitation

When I'm training for a big swim meet, I join a master's swim club and train as part of a team. I can work out fine alone, but when I'm swimming with a team, I find that my workouts are much better and I progress faster. I'm not alone. Since the late 1800s, sport psychologists have observed this same phenomenon: Most people exercise more effectively when they are with other people.[11]

Principle of Social Facilitation

People are more likely to perform a well-learned target behavior if they know they are being observed via computing technology, or if they can discern via technology that others are performing the behavior along with them.

The principle of social facilitation suggests that people perform better—more, longer, harder—when other people are present, participating, or observing.[12] Connected products can leverage this principle by creating new opportunities to generate social facilitation effects.

Because connected products can allow other people to be virtually present, the products can be used to motivate better performance by creating a virtual social group.[13] If a person is performing a well-learned activity—such as running on a treadmill—he or she will likely perform better if a connected product shows that other people are virtually present, performing the same activity.[14] You could even envision a completely virtual fitness facility: You work out at home, but through connected technology you can see others doing the same thing, and you know they can see you.[15] This virtual presence would likely produce some of the same beneficial social facilitation effects of working out at a regular gym. This approach might also be used to inspire better performance from workers in remote locations, motivate students as they prepare for college entrance exams, or encourage higher bidding in online auctions.

To generate social facilitation effects, the representation of others doesn't need to be realistic at all.[16] Simple avatars could represent other people. Abstract shapes would probably work in some cases, as I described earlier in the Study Buddy scenario at the start of this chapter. Even bar graphs might effectively represent the presence and performance of others.

Although computer scientists and game designers have created various ways to represent other people's presence and performance,[17] no one has yet performed a controlled study that documents how virtual representations of other people lead to social facilitation effects. But the research that exists suggests that the effect is real.[18]

The Power of Social Comparison

Principle of Social Comparison

People will have greater motivation to perform a target behavior if they are given information, via computing technology, about how their performance compares with the performance of others, especially others who are similar to themselves.

Connected products also can change behaviors and attitudes through a phenomenon known as social comparison. Social comparison theory holds that people seek to know the attitudes and behaviors of others in forming their own attitudes and behaviors. (This is not the same as peer pressure, which I'll discuss later in this chapter.) According to social comparison theory,[19] people seek information about others to determine how they compare and what they should be thinking or doing. In essence, we use people as a comparison point or a reality check.

To attract and involve readers, certain magazines engage people's natural drive for social comparison. The magazines offer surveys on health, safety, relationships, and other topics, each with a title like "How do you measure up?" or "What's your safety IQ?" Such quizzes enable people to compare their knowledge, attitudes, or behavior against what the editors say is normal or desirable. Social comparison is all about benchmarking your performance, reactions, attitudes, or behaviors against those of others.

Social comparison has many practical applications. One study demonstrates that people experiencing pain benefited from social comparison.[20] When patients could compare their pain reaction to that of others who were coping well with pain, the perception of their own pain decreased. Information about another person's pain response not only caused patients to report feeling less pain, but physiological measures indicated that the patients actually experienced less pain. Social comparison is so powerful it sometimes can change physiological responses.

This principle can be applied to connected products. Suppose a cancer patient is going through painful treatment. A connected computing system could link this patient to other patients who are coping well with pain. In theory, this would reduce the perception of pain and the need for pain medication.

The Study Buddy application uses social comparison as one of its strategies to promote better study habits. The connected device lets the student know when her classmates are studying. The point of this information isn't to put peer pressure on the user; instead, it's providing information about similar others—information that helps shape decisions and behaviors.

The social comparison effect is strengthened when it allows people to compare themselves with *similar* others. In other words, the motivation people feel from social comparison is stronger when they can compare themselves to those who are similar to themselves in terms of age, ability, ethnicity, or another key attribute.[21]

Leveraging Conformity—and Resistance

Social comparison leverages the persuasive power of information about what others are thinking or doing. *Normative influence* works through a different process, exploiting peer pressure, or what psychologists refer to as "pressures to conform." Research on conformity shows that people tend to change attitudes and behaviors to match the expectations, attitudes, and behaviors of classmates, a team, a family, a work group, or other groups.[22] The psychology literature refers to these as "in-groups."

Sometimes the pressure to conform is explicit: people badger or belittle those who don't fit in with the rest of the group. In other cases the pressure is more subtle, such as not inviting "unfashionable" people to a party, failing to greet people as they walk by, or ignoring their contributions to a conversation. Even when not consciously aware of the pressure to conform, people tend to change their attitudes and behaviors to match the expectations of their in-group.[23]

Connected products can create situations that leverage normative influence to change people's attitudes and behavior. A product simply has to track a person's behavior and, in some form, share the results with the person's in-group.

A product could track and share how promptly you return phone calls or emails. Or, a product could monitor seat belt use or recycling habits, and share the results among community members. If you're below the norm for your in-group, you may feel pressure to reply faster, use your seat belt, or do more recycling. Making people's behavior visible to their in-groups will affect what they do.

The examples above produce benign behavioral outcomes: returning phone calls, wearing seatbelts, and recycling. Other uses of technology to leverage peer pressure might not be so benign. A technology to motivate online filing of taxes would seem quite dark if it leverages peer pressure. A product to promote quality time with your children would seem unethical and intrusive if it gained its persuasive power from peer pressure.

In addition to leveraging peer pressure, connected products can be used to undermine it, to help people resist the pressure to conform. People are more capable of resisting group conformity influence when at least one person defies the group. In other words, one "deviant" (the term used in the research) will make it easier for others to resist the pressure to conform.[24] The deviant doesn't even have to be physically present; just the knowledge that someone else is not following the group helps other people to dissent as well.

What does this mean for connected persuasive technologies? Suppose a teen were facing pressure to conform with her group norm of smoking cigarettes. If a technology could convincingly show her that at least one other person in her in-group had successfully resisted the pressure to start smoking—maybe someone she doesn't even know well—she would be less likely to give in to group pressure.

Continuing the example, a health organization could set up a system that allows people to share their views on smoking with one other. Even if this sharing were anonymous, a teen who wants to resist pressures to smoke would find

Principle of Normative Influence

> Computing technology can leverage normative influence (peer pressure) to increase the likelihood that a person will adopt or will avoid performing a target behavior.

support and comfort in a message or a real-time chat with someone she perceives as a member of her in-group. She may find that her impression about teen smoking—that everyone who is cool does it—is biased. The networked technology would allow her to expand her horizon and safely go outside her immediate circle of friends.

Another example (although not a networked product) is Alcohol 101, which uses social comparison to promote saner drinking practices among college students. Described in the Introduction, Alcohol 101 is an interactive CD-ROM game that simulates a college party and provides college students with data about how much their peers actually drink. A large percentage of students who play the game find the actual statistics on drinking to be lower than they expected, and this has a positive impact on their attitudes toward drinking.[25]

In sum, while connected technologies can leverage conformity dynamics, they also can undermine the pressure to conform by providing potential nonconformists with an awareness of others who have resisted this pressure. This is a liberating use of persuasive technology, helping people choose what they want to choose—not what a peer group chooses for them.

Applying Social Learning Theory

The final theory I want to introduce represents one of the most popular and effective ways for changing attitudes and behaviors: social learning theory.[26] Developed by psychologist Albert Bandura,[27] the theory is broad in scope, but one aspect is especially relevant to connected technologies: the power of modeling.[28]

Research on social learning theory has shown that people learn new attitudes and behaviors by observing others' actions and then noting the consequences of those actions. If an observer notices someone is being rewarded for his or her behavior, the observer is much more likely to perform that behavior. People tend to observe and learn most when behavior is modeled by others who are similar to themselves but somewhat older or more experienced.[29]

Principle of Social Learning

> A person will be more motivated to perform a target behavior if he or she can use computing technology to observe others performing the behavior and being rewarded for it.

Modeling Behavior at QuitNet.com

QuitNet.com (Figure 8.6), a site devoted to helping people stop smoking, taps into the power of social learning theory by celebrating people who are quitting successfully. As you go into the site, one of the most prominent (and reportedly well-used) areas of the site is the "Community" area. Here you will find a celebration of quit-date anniversaries, with links to people who have stopped smoking for two days, seven days, on up to years.

As you continue inside QuitNet.com, you'll find "Forums," "Clubs," "Buddies," and more. While the strong focus on community brings the power of social support to the difficult task of quitting smoking, the site seems specifically designed to highlight successes, and it rewards people who are succeeding, thus setting up the social learning dynamic: people who see others being rewarded for a behavior are more likely to perform that behavior.

The rewards on this site seem compelling. In the QuitNet Forum area, quitters have threaded discussions all about one person who is succeeding in quitting, usually on an anniversary date. For example, one of the community members sees that Julie has a four-month anniversary, so he starts the thread with a note of congratulations (sometimes the person starts the thread herself,

Figure 8.6

QuitNet.com is a stop-smoking site that effectively leverages elements of social learning theory.

Figure 8.6

(Continued)

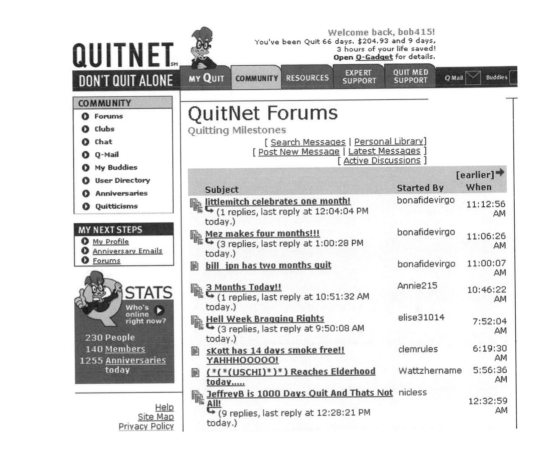

unself-consciously proclaiming "Hooray for me!"). Other community members chime in, adding to the thread and offering their own words of encouragement and praise.

This kind of warm response and attention would be rewarding for anyone, but these public messages provide motivation to the outside reader by making the modeled behavior seem achievable and by showing the rewards that will follow.

As QuitNet.com makes clear, the ability to see how others succeed, to watch their progress over time, and even interact with them, is now quite easy thanks to connected technologies. When people are connected, even in a time-shifted medium such as threaded discussions, social influence dynamics come into play in ways that are not possible with stand-alone technologies or via traditional media, such as books or television.

Modeling at epinions.com

Some Web sites rely on contributions from outsiders for their very existence. eBay is perhaps the most prominent example. Another site that depends on outside contributions is epinions.com, which relies on users to review products and services—the main purpose of the site. Persuading users to post quality content on the site is essential to the success of epinions.

Modeling is one method the site uses to motivate people to contribute high-quality content. The site rewards those who contribute good reviews and makes these rewards public, setting up the dynamics of social learning theory. As you click on a reviewer's name, you are taken to a list of all their reviews. This page includes the dates the reviewer posted the content, the topic, and the rating of how much others liked this review, among other things. People who contribute at least 100 opinions that are well regarded by others (users rate the reviews) receive a "Top Reviewer" designation, which appears next to their name at all their reviews. These reviews also are listed at the top of the page, ahead of reviewers who have not done as well.

Being designated as a top reviewer is a status symbol, akin to being a media pundit (albeit at a less prestigious level). Reviewers also can receive the "Advisor" designation, which means they have a particular area of expertise, such as musical instruments. Other designations: "Editor," "Featured Member," and "Most Popular Reviewers." (Note: These designations are not just about status. Valued reviewers also receive a share of royalties from the epinions site. So there is a profit motive as well as a social status reward.)

By observing this system of rewards, observers will be more likely to contribute high-quality content to epinions.com. This is a good example of how social learning theory can be leveraged to change people's attitudes and behavior in cyberspace.

Persuading through Intrinsic Motivation

The three group-level intrinsic motivators are competition, cooperation, and recognition.

In addition to extending the power of social influence principles, connected products can leverage the power of intrinsic motivation, a type of energizing force that arises directly from an activity or situation. Certain activities—playing the guitar, writing poetry, swimming at a lake—are inherently rewarding. Many people don't need external pressure or rewards to do these things; the rewards are built in, or intrinsic.

Principle of Competition

> Computing technology can motivate users to adopt a target attitude or behavior by leveraging human beings' natural drive to compete.

Principle of Cooperation

> Computing technology can motivate users to adopt a target attitude or behavior by leveraging human beings' natural drive to cooperate.

Principle of Recognition

> By offering public recognition (individual or group), computing technology can increase the likelihood that a person or group will adopt a target attitude or behavior.

MIT's Tom Malone and Stanford's Mark Lepper have outlined seven types of intrinsic motivators.[30] Three of these motivators—competition, cooperation, and recognition—involve interaction among people; they are group-level intrinsic motivators. Because connected products can link people together over time and space, they can leverage group-level intrinsic motivators to influence users.

Competition is perhaps the most powerful group-level intrinsic motivator. When you set up a competition, people become energized. They invest time and effort. They care about the outcome. You don't even need to offer a prize (an extrinsic motivator) to the winner. Not everyone is competitive by nature, but in many situations and for most people, competition is energizing and motivating.

Cooperation is another motivator, one that seems to be built into human nature. When people belong to a work group, most of them cooperate. Whenever there is a pressing need, a call for cooperation will naturally motivate most people to help out.

Finally, people are intrinsically motivated by recognition. Many organizations leverage the power of recognition. Employers create "employee of the month" awards, blood banks give out "I've donated" stickers for people to wear, and top students get listed on the honor roll. These and many other programs leverage the motivating power of recognition.

Recognition can motivate groups as well as individuals. High school students who know their artwork will be on display will work longer and harder to create something they can be proud of. A hometown baseball league that prints scores in the newspaper is likely to develop players and teams that are more motivated to achieve.

Because networked products can connect people over space and time, they can also create group situations that leverage group-level intrinsic motivators. To show how these intrinsic motivators might work in connected persuasive technologies, I'll describe a hypothetical system named AlternaTV that could use one or any combination of the intrinsic motivators.

AlternaTV: Leveraging Group-Level Intrinsic Motivators

Televisions in the future are likely to become not just passive boxes that receive signals but interactive devices that send out data over a network and run applications above and beyond broadcast programming.

If individuals and organizations can somehow decide what kind of interactive experiences happen through TV (as opposed to the broadcast giants controlling this decision), it's not hard to imagine that future software for interactive TVs might be created to motivate people, especially school kids, to watch less TV. This type of connected persuasive technology could leverage the power of group-level intrinsic motivators—competition, cooperation, and recognition—to persuade kids to spend less time in front of the television.

Here's how it might work: In the AlternaTV program, school kids are encouraged to watch less than five hours of TV per week during the school year. That's the behavioral objective. To motivate kids to comply with the program, each participating household becomes an "AlternaTV family." This means they agree that the number of hours they watch TV gets recorded and reported to a central database.

The first intrinsic motivator in the AlternaTV system is competition. The competition takes place on various levels. School districts compete against other school districts to see who watches the least TV. Schools compete against other schools. Classrooms compete against other classrooms. Having a technology that simply provides a way for this competition to happen would increase the motivation of the kids to watch less TV. In this scenario there doesn't need to be a prize; there doesn't need to be any external incentive. Simply having a competition may be sufficiently motivating for many people.

The next intrinsic motivator would be cooperation. The AlternaTV system would advocate that kids in one classroom cooperate with each other to reach their goals of watching less TV. Perhaps the system would allow one student to send a message to the TV screen of another who is watching a lot of TV, asking that person to watch less to help out the entire class. This type of cooperation could also take place on other levels, such as cooperation within an entire school.

Recognition would be the third intrinsic motivator integrated into the AlternaTV system. At the simplest level, the winning classroom, school, or district would be listed on the screen of all the AlternaTVs in the program (or perhaps in a special window on all the school's computer monitors). Another type of recognition would be to simply list all the AlternaTV households who are reaching their goal of less than five hours of TV each week. In this way, each household can be motivated by the idea of recognition, even if other students in their class or school are not curbing their TV watching.

The intrinsic motivators work nicely together in the AlternaTV system. Of course, each of the intrinsic motivators would have an effect alone, independent of the other two. However, in this example, the system is more interesting, compelling, and persuasive with the intrinsic motivators working together.

The AlternaTV system could be effective using only the three intrinsic motivators as persuasion strategies. But other influence strategies could be incorporated into the system: AlternaTV could suggest other activities kids could do; it could require physical effort (such as pedaling a stationary bike) in order to watch TV; or it could quiz kids on their homework, allowing access to broadcast TV only when they pass the material.

There's significant potential in using the principles of intrinsic motivation in connected products to change attitudes and behaviors for positive purposes (unfortunately, as with all persuasive technology, psychological principles can be leveraged for negative or unethical purposes as well). When interactive technologies are networked, they can be designed to use competition, cooperation, and recognition as motivating forces. In this way, connected computing products gain power to persuade.

The Future of Mobile and Connected Persuasive Technology

Today, products that are both mobile and connected are few, and the products that do exist are limited in what applications they run. But this will change. In the future we're likely to see a wide range of devices and applications, including those designed to motivate and persuade.

Although examples of mobile persuasion are few today, many will emerge in the coming years, especially as mobile phone systems allow people and companies to easily create and deploy applications. While mobile persuasion in the service of mobile commerce will receive lots of attention and funding, a clear win for individuals is using mobile technology to help people achieve their own goals. The kairos and convenience factors make mobile persuasion one of the most promising frontiers in persuasive technology.

Notes and References

For updates on the topics presented in this chapter, visit *www.persuasivetech.info.*

1. For an idea of how simple this representation can be, see Thomas Erickson, Christine Halverson, Wendy A. Kellogg, Mark Laff, and Tracee Wolf, Social Translucence: Designing Social Infrastructures That Make Collective Activity Visible, *Communications of the ACM,* 45(4): 40–44 (April 2002).

2. It's frustrating to write this section on mobile persuasion while a number of lab studies are in process. I considered hypothesizing about what we'll find in these studies but decided it's better to wait rather than speculate. By the time you read this chapter, it's likely you'll be able to find pointers to our latest mobile persuasion research at *www. captology.org.*

3. *Handspring Treo Design and the Challenges of Becoming a Wireless Company.* Presentation given by Peter Skillman, Director of Product Design, Handspring, Inc. at American Center for Design's Wireless Seminar, April 5, 2002, Berkeley, California.

4. Tetrash was conceptualized by Stanford students Ling Kong, Sarah Jasper, and Caroline Campbell.

5. As of June 2002, per handango.com. In addition to gaining commercial success in terms of sales, Bejeweled has charmed the reviewers at Cnet.com; in June 2002 they described the game as "extremely popular" and listed it first in the Cnet.com section on "Top 10 must-have Palm OS games." (See *http://computers.cnet.com/hardware/0-1087-8-9081112-1.html.*)

6. I learned this term from Aaron Marcus of Aaron Marcus and Associates.

7. LifeSign uses a behavior change strategy that has proven effective in a number of studies. For a description of the program involving adolescent smokers and for information about other studies, see *http://www.lifesign.com/114.html.*

8. L. Schnirring, Can exercise gadgets motivate patients? *The Physician and Sports Medicine,* 29(1): (2001).

9. Season 3, Episode 56; original airdate: Thursday, January 11, 2001.

10. For a discussion of the power of groups in persuasion, see J. C. Turner, *Social Influence,* (Buckingham, U.K.: Open University Press, 1991).

11. Glyn C. Roberts, Kevin S. Spink, and Cynthia L. Pemberton, *Learning Experiences in Sport Psychology,* 2nd ed. (Champaign, IL: Human Kinetics, 1999).

12. R. Zajonc, Social facilitation, *Science,* 149: 269–274 (1965). See also J. R. Aiello and E. A. Douthitt, Social facilitation from Triplett to electronic performance monitoring, *Group Dynamics: Theory, Research, and Practice,* 5(3): 163–180 (2001).

For other research on virtual social facilitation, see J. R. Aiello and C. M. Svec, Computer monitoring of work performance: Social facilitation and electronic presense, *Journal of Applied Social Psychology,* 23(7): 537–548 (1993). For research on the topic of virtual environments and social influence, including social facilitation, see the work of U.C. Santa Barbara's James Blascovich and colleagues at *http://www.psych.ucsb.edu/research/recveb/.*

13. For more about how social influence dynamics can play out virtually, see the work of U.C. Santa Barbara's James Blascovich. One of his most recent publications is J. Blascovich, Social influence within immersive virtual environments, in R. Schroeder (ed.), *The Social Life of Avatars* (New York: Springer-Verlag, 2002), pp. 127–145.

    Web presence: *http://www.psych.ucsb.edu/fac/blasc98.htm.*

14. For activities that are not well learned, the presence of others will *decrease* performance. In other words, you will do worse when learning a new skill if you know that others are observing you.

15. Although not directed toward fitness, researchers at IBM have been working on how to use computer technology to virtually represent co-workers who are in a remote location but also working. See

    Thomas Erickson, Christine Halverson, Wendy A. Kellogg, Mark Laff, and Tracee Wolf, *Social Translucence: Designing Social Infrastructures That Make Collective Activity Visible,* Communications of the ACM, 45(4): 40–44 (April 2002).

16. The IBM researchers use simple circles to represent people in their system. Ibid.

17. M. Ackerman and B. Starr, *Proceedings of the ACM Symposium on User Interface Software and Technology, www.ics.uci.edu/~ackerman/docs/uist95/uist95* (1995).

18. For some intriguing research in this area, see the work of U.C. Santa Barbara's James J. Blascovich and colleagues at *http://www.psych.ucsb.edu/research/recveb/.*

19. This was first articulated by L. Festinger, A theory of social comparison process, *Human Relations,* 7: 117–140 (1954).

20. K. Craig and K. Prkachin, Social modeling influences on sensory decision theory and psychophysiological indexes of pain, *Journal of Personality and Social Psychology,* 36: 805–815 (1978).

21. The classic work in social comparison supports the idea that similarity matters. L. Festinger, A theory of social comparison process, *Human Relations,* 7: 117–140 (1954).

    A recent discussion (and review) of social comparison and how similarity figures into this process is by J. Suls, R. Martin, and W. Wheeler, Responding to the social world: Explicit and implicit processes in social judgments and decisions, Chapter for Fifth Annual Sydney Symposium of Social Psychology, March 20–22, 2002. Available online at *http://www.sydneysymposium.unsw.edu.au/2002/papers/* (click on "Suls chapter").

22. For a readable academic book on social forces in conformity, see J. Turner, *Social Influence* (Pacific Grove, CA: Brooks/Cole, 1991). See also

   a. C. McGarty, S. A. Haslam, K. J. Hutchinson, and J. C. Turner, The effects of salient group memberships on persuasion, *Small Group Research, 25:* 267–293 (1994).

   b. J. C. Turner, M. A. Hogg, P. J. Oakes, S. D. Reicher, and M. S. Wetherell, *Rediscovering the Social Group: A Self-Categorization Theory* (Oxford: Blackwell, 1987).

23. J. Turner, *Social Influence* (Pacific Grove, CA: Brooks/Cole, 1991).

24. Solomon Asch's work explored the effects of nonconformists in group situations. See

   a. S. Asch, Effects of group pressure upon the modification and distortion of judgments, in H. Gvetzkow (ed.), *Groups, Leadership and Men* (Pittsburgh: Carnegie Press, 1991).

   b. S. E. Asch, *Social Psychology* (New York: Prentice Hall, 1952).

   c. S. E. Asch, Studies of independence and conformity: A minority of one against a unanimous majority, *Psychological Monographs*, 9:70 (1956).

   For a more recent discussion of this area, see J. Turner, *Social Influence* (Pacific Grove, CA: Brooks/Cole, 1991).

25. The use of "positive norming" has been an important persuasive element in Alcohol 101. Janet Reis, Ph.D., a professor of Community Health at the University of Illinois–Urbana-Champaign, has been instrumental in the creation and evaluation of this product. The research results for various studies involving Alcohol 101 can be found at *http://www.centurycouncil.org/campus/a101/research/demresults.cfm.*

26. Social Learning Theory goes by other names, including Social Cognitive Theory.

27. A. Bandura, *Social Foundations of Thought and Action: A Social Cognitive Theory* (Englewood Cliffs, NJ: Prentice Hall, 1986).

28. Bandura doesn't use all the same terms I use here, but the concepts are the same.

29. A. Bandura, *Self-Efficacy: The Exercise of Self-Control* (New York: W.H. Freeman, 1997).

30. As described by Malone and Lepper, the seven intrinsic motivators are fantasy, curiosity, challenge, control, competition, cooperation, and recognition. See T. Malone and M. Lepper, Making learning fun: A taxonomy of intrinsic motivation for learning, in R. E. Snow and M. J. Farr (eds.), *Aptitude, Learning, and Instruction* (Hillsdale, NJ: Lawrence Earlbaum, 1987).

chapter **9**

The Ethics of Persuasive Technology

An advertising agency creates a Web site that lets children play games online with virtual characters. To progress, kids must answer questions[1] such as, "What is your favorite TV show?" and "How many bathrooms are in your house?"[2] Kids provide these answers quickly in their quest to continue playing.[3]

Kim's portable device helps her choose affordable products made by companies with good environmental records. In advising Kim on buying a new printer, the system suggests a more expensive product than she wanted. It shows how the company has a much better environmental record. Kim buys the recommended printer. The system fails to point out that the printer she bought will probably break down more often.

Julie has been growing her retirement fund for almost 20 years. To optimize her investment strategy, she signs up for a Web-based service that reportedly can give her individualized expert advice. Using dramatic visual simulations and citing expert opinion, the system persuades Julie to invest more in the stock market and strongly recommends a particular stock. Two months later, the stock drops dramatically and Julie loses much of her hard-earned retirement money. Although the system has information about risk, the information isn't prominently displayed. Nor is the fact that the site is operated by a company with a major financial investment in the company issuing the stock.

211

Mark is finally getting back into shape. At the gym he's using a computerized fitness system that outlines his training routines, monitors each exercise, and acknowledges his progress. The system encourages people to use a full range of motion when lifting weights. Unfortunately, the range of motion it suggests is too extreme for Mark, and he injures his back.

As the hypothetical scenarios above suggest, persuasive technology can raise a number of ethical concerns. It combines two controversial domains—persuasion and technology—each with its own history of moral debate. Debate over the ethics of persuasion dates back to Aristotle and other classical rhetoricians, and the discussion continues to this day. As for technology and ethics, people have expressed misgivings about certain computer applications[4] at least since Joseph Weizenbaum created ELIZA, the computer "therapist" described in Chapter 5.[5]

Examining ethical issues is a key component of captology, the study of persuasive technology. When is persuasive technology ethical and when is it not? Because values vary from one culture to the next, there is no easy answer that will satisfy everyone, no single ethical system or set of guidelines that will serve in all cases. The key for those who design, study, or use persuasive technologies is to become sensitive to the range of ethical issues involved. The purpose of this chapter is to provide a foundation for identifying and examining those issues.

> *Is* persuasion unethical? That depends. *Can* it be unethical? Clearly, the answer is yes.

Is Persuasion Unethical?

Is persuasion inherently unethical? The answer to this question depends on whom you ask. Some people believe that attempting to change another person's attitudes or behaviors always is unethical, or at least questionable. In the extreme, this view holds that persuasion can lead to indoctrination, coercion, brainwashing, and other undesirable outcomes. Even some notable health promotion experts have questioned the foundation of their work, wondering what right they have to tell others how to live and what to believe.[6]

Other people view persuasion as fundamentally good. To some, persuasion is the foundation of ethical leadership,[7] while others see persuasion as essential for participatory democracy.[8]

Can persuasion be unethical? The answer clearly is yes. People can use persuasion to promote outcomes that we as a culture find unacceptable: persuading teens to smoke, advocating that people use addictive drugs,[9] persuading people to harm those who are different in race, gender, or belief. Persuasion also is clearly unethical when the tactics used to persuade are deceptive or compromise other positive values. I'll revisit both of these concepts later in this chapter.

In the end, the answer to the question "Is persuasion unethical?" is neither yes nor no. It depends on how persuasion is used.

Unique Ethical Concerns Related to Persuasive Technology

Because persuasion is a value-laden activity, creating an interactive technology designed to persuade also is value laden.

I teach a module on the ethics of persuasive technology in my courses at Stanford. One assignment I give students is to work in small teams to develop a conceptual design for an ethically questionable persuasive technology—the more unethical the better. The purpose is to let students explore the dark side of persuasive technology to help them understand the implications of future technology and how to prevent unethical applications or mitigate their impact. After teaching this course for a number of years, I've come to see certain patterns in the ethical concerns that arise. The information I offer in this chapter comes from working with students in this way, as well as from my own observations of the marketplace and investigations into the possibilities of future technologies.

For the most part, the ethical issues relating to persuasive technologies are similar to those for persuasion in general. However, because interactive technology is a new avenue of persuasion, it raises a handful of ethical issues that are unique. Below are six key issues, each of which has implications for assessing the ethics of persuasive technology.

1. The Novelty of the Technology Can Mask Its Persuasive Intent

While people have been persuaded by other forms of media for generations, most people are relative novices when it comes to dealing with persuasion

Figure 9.1

Volvo Ozone Eater
is a simulation game
wherein Volvos convert
ozone into oxygen.

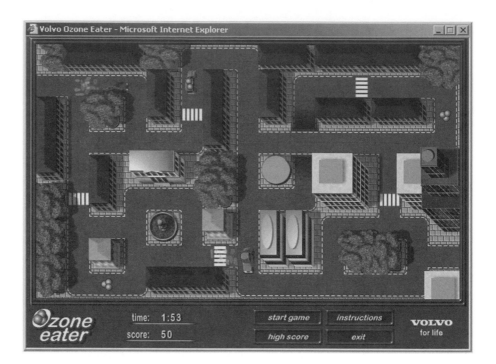

from interactive computing systems—in part because the technologies themselves are so new. As a result, people may be unaware of the ways in which
interactive computer technology can be designed to influence them, and they
may not know how to identify or respond to persuasion tactics applied by the
technology.

Sometimes the tactics can be subtle. Volvo Ozone Eater (Figure 9.1), an
online game produced for the Swedish automaker, provides an example. In this
Pacman-like game, players direct a blue Volvo around a city block. Other cars
in the simulation give off exhaust and leave pink molecules behind—ozone.
As the Volvo drives over the pink molecules, it converts them into blue molecules—oxygen.

The point of the game is to drive the Volvo through as many ozone areas as
possible, cleaning up the city by producing oxygen. This simple simulation
game suggests that driving a Volvo will remove ozone from the air and convert
it to oxygen. The truth is that only Volvos containing a special radiator called
PremAir can convert ozone to oxygen, and then only ground-level ozone. (The
implications of such designer bias were discussed in Chapter 4.) But I hypothesize that those who play the game often enough are likely to start viewing all
Volvos as machines that can clean the air.[10] Even if their rational minds don't

accept the claim, a less rational element that views the simulation and enjoys playing the game is likely to affect their opinions.[11] It's subtle but effective.

Ethical issues are especially prominent when computer technology uses novelty as a distraction to increase persuasion. When dealing with a novel experience, people not only lack expertise but they are distracted by the experience, which impedes their ability to focus on the content presented.[12] This makes it possible for new applications or online games such as Volvo Ozone Eater to deliver persuasive messages that users may not scrutinize because they are focusing on other aspects of the experience.

Another example of distraction at work: If you want to sign up for a particular Web site, the site could make the process so complicated and lengthy that all your mental resources are focused on the registration process. As a result, you may not be entirely aware of all of the ways you are being influenced or manipulated, such as numerous prechecked "default" preferences that you may not want but may overlook to get the registration job done as quickly as possible.

Some Web sites capitalize on users' relative inexperience to influence them to do things they might not if they were better informed. For instance, some sites have attempted to expand their reach through "pop-up downloads," which ask users via a pop-up screen if they want to download software. Once they agree—as many people do, sometimes without realizing what they're agreeing to—a whole range of software might be downloaded to their computers. The software may or may not be legitimate. For instance, it could be used to point users to adult Web sites, created unwanted dial-up accounts, or even interfere with the computer's operations.[13] At a minimum, these virtual Trojan horses use up computer resources and may require significant time and effort to uninstall.

In summary, being in a novel situation can make people more vulnerable because they are distracted by the newness or complexity of the interaction.

2. Persuasive Technology Can Exploit the Positive Reputation of Computers

When it comes to persuasion, computers also benefit from their traditional reputation of being intelligent and fair, making them seem credible sources of information and advice. While this reputation isn't always warranted (especially when it comes to Web credibility, as noted in Chapter 7), it can lead people to accept information and advice too readily from technology systems. Ethical concerns arise when persuasive technologies leverage the traditional reputation of computers as being credible in cases where that reputation isn't deserved.

If you are looking for a chiropractor in the Yellow Pages, you may find that some display ads mention computers to make this sometimes controversial healing art appear more credible. In my phone book, one ad reads like this:

> *No "cracking" or "snapping." Your adjustments are done with a computerized technology advancement that virtually eliminates the guesswork.*

It's hard to judge whether the claim is accurate or not, but it's clear that this chiropractor—and many others like her in a wide range of professions—are leveraging the positive reputation of computers to promote their own goals.

3. Computers Can Be Proactively Persistent

Another advantage of computers is persistence. Unlike human persuaders, computers don't get tired; they can implement their persuasive strategies over and over. One notable example is TreeLoot.com, which pops up messages again and again to motivate users to keep playing the online game and visit site sponsors (Figure 9.2). The requests for compliance never end, and users may finally give in.

Not only can computers persist in persuading you while you are using an application, they also can be persistent when you are not. Persuasive messages can pop up on your desktop or be streamed to your email inbox on a frequent basis. Such proactive attempts to persuade can have a greater impact than other persistent media. You can always set aside a direct-mail solicitation, but a pop-up screen is hard to avoid; it's literally in your face.

4. Computers Control the Interactive Possibilities

A fourth area of ethical uniqueness lies in how people interact with computing technology. When you deal with human persuaders, you can stop the persuasion process and ask for clarification, you can argue, debate, and negotiate. By contrast, when you interact with computing technology, the technology ultimately controls how the interaction unfolds. You can choose either to continue

Figure 9.2

TreeLoot.com is persistent in its attempts to persuade users to keep playing and to visit sponsors.

or stop the interaction, but you can't go down a path the computer hasn't been programmed to accept.

5. Computers Can Affect Emotions But Can't Be Affected by Them

The next ethical issue has to do with emotional cues. In human persuasion, the process proceeds more smoothly when people use emotional cues. A coach can sense when you're frustrated and modify her motivational strategy. A salesperson may give subtle signals that he's exaggerating a bit. These cues help persuasive exchanges reach more equitable and ethical outcomes.

By contrast, computing products don't (yet) read subtle cues from people,[14] but they do offer emotional cues, which can be applied to persuade. This imbalance puts humans at a relative disadvantage. We are emotional beings, especially when it comes to issues of influence. We expect ethical persuasion to include elements of empathy and reciprocity. But when dealing with interactive technology, there is no emotional reciprocity.

6. Computers Cannot Shoulder Responsibility

The final ethical issue unique to interactive technology involves taking responsibility for errors. To be an ethical agent of persuasion, I believe you must be able to take responsibility for your actions and at least partial responsibility for what happens to those whom you persuade. Computers cannot take responsibility in the same way.[15] As persuasive entities they can advise, motivate, and badger people, but if computers lead people down the wrong path, computers can't really shoulder the blame; they are not moral agents. (Consider the last anecdote at the start of this chapter. Who could blame the computerized fitness system for Mark's injury?)

Making restitution for wrongdoings (or at least being appropriately punished) has been part of the moral code of all major civilizations. But if computers work autonomously from humans, perhaps persuading people down treacherous paths, the computers themselves can't be punished or follow any paths to make restitution.

The creators of these products may be tempted to absolve themselves of their creations. Or, they may be nowhere to be found (the company has folded, the project leader has a different job), yet their creations continue to interact with people. Especially now with the Internet, software doesn't necessarily go away when the creators leave or after the company abandons the product. It still may exist somewhere in cyberspace.

This changes the playing field of persuasion in ways that raise potential ethical concerns: one party in the interaction (the computer product) has the power to persuade but is unable to accept responsibility if things go awry. Imagine a Web-based therapy program that was abandoned by its developer but continues to exist on the Internet. Now imagine a distraught person stumbling upon the site, engaging in an online session of computer-based therapy,

Ethical Issues in Conducting Research

Ethical issues arise when doing research and evaluation on persuasive technology products. These issues are similar to, but more acute than, those for studies on products designed solely for information (like news Web sites) or straightforward transactions (such as e-commerce sites). Because persuasive technologies set out to change attitudes or behaviors, they may have a greater impact on the participants involved in the studies. And the impact won't always be positive. As a result, researchers and evaluators should take care when setting up the research experience; they should follow accepted standards in the way they recruit, involve, and debrief participants.

Academic institutions usually have a board that formally reviews proposed research to help prevent abuses of study participants and unplanned outcomes. At Stanford, it typically takes about six to eight weeks for my study protocols to receive approval. To win approval, I must complete a rather involved online application (which is much easier than the old method with paper forms). I outline the purpose of the study, describe what will happen during the experience, explain recruitment procedures, list the research personnel involved, outline the sources of funding (conflict of interest check), and more. I submit examples of the stimuli and the instrument for collecting the measurements (such as questionnaires). A few things complicate the application: involving children as participants, collecting data on video, or using deception as part of the study. In our lab we rarely do any of those things, and if we do, we must carefully describe how we will address and overcome any ethical concerns.

A number of weeks after I submit the application, I hear back from the panel, either giving the okay to move forward or asking for further information. Each time I receive the official approval letter from the Stanford review board, I pass it around at my weekly lab meeting. I want the other researchers in my lab to understand how the research approval system operates, and I want them to know that I consider institutional approval a necessary step in our research process. While the procedure for winning approval from the Stanford board slows down the research cycle, it clearly serves a useful purpose, protecting both the study participants and the researchers.

(continued)

In my work at technology companies, I also seek approval from review committees. However, in some companies research approval systems don't exist. It's up to the individuals designing and conducting the research to assure that participants are treated with respect—that they understand the nature of the study, give their specific consent, are allowed to withdraw at any time, and are given a way to contact the responsible institution later. In my view, these are the basic steps required to protect participants when conducting research involving persuasive technology products.

requiring additional help from a human being, but being unable to get a referral from the now-abandoned computer therapist.

Alone or in combination, the six factors outlined above give interactive computing technology an advantage when it comes to persuasion. Said another way, these factors put users of the technology at a relative disadvantage, and this is where the ethical issues arise. These six areas provide a solid starting point for expanding our inquiry into the ethics of persuasive technologies.

Intentions, Methods, and Outcomes: Three Areas Worthy of Inquiry

Many ethical issues involving persuasive technologies fall into one of three categories: intentions, methods, and outcomes. By examining the intentions of the people or the organization that created the persuasive technology, the methods used to persuade, and the outcomes of using the technology, it is possible to assess the ethical implications.

Intentions: Why Was the Product Created?

One reasonable approach to assessing the ethics of a persuasive technology product is to examine what its designers hoped to accomplish. Some forms of intentions are almost always good, such as intending to promote health, safety, or education. Technologies designed to persuade in these areas can be highly ethical.

The designer's intent, methods of persuasion, and outcomes help to determine the ethics of persuasive technology.

Other intentions may be less clearly ethical. One common intention behind a growing number of persuasive technologies is to sell products or services. While many people would not consider this intent inherently unethical, others may equate it with less ethical goals such as promoting wasteful consumption. Then there are the clearly unethical intentions, such as advocating violence.

To assess intent, you can examine a persuasive product and make an informed guess. According to its creators, the intent of Baby Think It Over (described in Chapter 4) is to teach teens about the responsibilities of parenthood—an intention that most people would consider ethical. Similarly, the intent of Chemical Scorecard (discussed in Chapter 3) would appear to be ethical to most people. Its purpose appears to be mobilizing citizens to contact their political representatives about problems with polluters in their neighborhoods. On the other hand, you could reasonably propose that Volvo commissioned the Volvo Ozone Eater game as a way to sell more cars to people who are concerned about the environment. For some people, this intent may be questionable.

Identifying intent is a key step in making evaluations about ethics. If the designer's intention is unethical, the interactive product is likely to be unethical as well.

Methods of Persuasion

Examining the methods an interactive technology uses to persuade is another means of establishing intent and assessing ethics. Some methods are clearly unethical, with the most questionable strategies falling outside a strict definition of persuasion. These strategies include making threats, providing skewed information, and backing people into a corner. In contrast, other influence strategies, such as highlighting cause-and-effect relationships, can be ethically sound if they are factual and empower individuals to make good decisions for themselves.

How can you determine if a computer's influence methods are ethical? The first step is to take technology out of the picture to get a clearer view. Simply ask yourself, "If a human were using this strategy to persuade me, would it be ethical?"

Recall CodeWarriorU.com, a Web site discussed in Chapter 1. While the goals of the online learning site include customer acquisition and retention, the influence methods include offering testimonials, repeatedly asking potential students to sign up, putting students on a schedule for completing their work in each course, and tracking student progress. Most people would agree that these methods would be acceptable ways to influence if they were used by a person. So when it comes to this first step of examining ethical methods of influence by interactive technology, CodeWarriorU.com earns a passing grade.

Now consider another example: a Web banner ad promises information, but after clicking on it you are swept away to someplace completely unexpected. A similar bait-and-switch tactic in the brick-and-mortar world would be misleading and unethical. The cyber version, too, is unethical. (Not only is the approach unethical, it's also likely to backfire as Web surfers become more familiar with the trickery.[16])

Using Emotions to Persuade

Making the technology disappear is a good first step in examining the ethics of persuasion strategies. However, it doesn't reveal one ethical gray area that is unique to human-computer interactions: the expression of emotions.

Because humans respond so readily to emotions, it's likely that computers that express "emotions" can influence people. When a computer expresses sentiments such as "You're my best friend," or "I'm happy to see you," it is posturing to have human emotions. Both of these statements are uttered by ActiMates Barney, the interactive plush toy by Microsoft that I described in Chapter 5.

The ethical nature of Barney has been the subject of debate.[17] When I monitored a panel discussion of the ethics of the product, I found that panelists were divided into two camps. Some viewed the product as ethically questionable because it lies to kids, saying things that imply emotions and motives, and presenting statements that are not true or accurate, such as "I'm happy to see you." Others argued that kids know it is only a toy without emotions or motives, part of a fantasy that kids understand.

The social dynamics leveraged by ActiMates characters can make for engaging play, which is probably harmless and may be helpful in teaching children social rules and behaviors.[18] But social dynamics could be used in interactive toys to influence in a negative or exploitative way what children think and do, and this raises ethical questions.

My own view is that the use of emotions in persuasive technology is unethical or ethically questionable only when its intent is to exploit users or when it preys on people's naturally strong reactions to negative emotions or threaten-

Figure 9.3

A TreeLoot.com character expresses negative emotions to motivate users

ing information expressed by others.[19] For instance, if you play at the Web site TreeLoot.com, discussed earlier in this chapter, you might encounter a character who says he is angry with you for not visiting the site's sponsors (Figure 9.3).

Because the TreeLoot site is so simple and the ruse is so apparent, you may think this use of emotion is hardly cause for concern. And it's probably not. But what if the TreeLoot system were much more sophisticated, to the point where users couldn't tell if the message came from a human or a computer, as in the case of a sophisticated chat bot? Or what if the users believed the computer system that expressed anger had the power to punish them? The ethics of that approach would be more questionable.

The point is that the use of emotions to persuade has unique ethical implications when computers rather than humans are expressing emotions. In addition to the potential ethical problems with products such as ActiMates Barney and TreeLoot.com, there is the problem discussed earlier in this chapter: while computers may convey emotions, they cannot react to emotions, giving them an unfair advantage in persuasion.

Methods That Always Are Unethical

Whether used by a person or a computer system, some methods for changing attitudes and behaviors are almost always unethical. Although they do not fall into the category of persuasion per se, two methods deserve mention here

Figure 9.4

This banner ad claims it's checking qualifications—a deception (when you click on the ad, you are simply sent to a gambling site).

because they are easy to incorporate into computing products: deception and coercion.

Web ads are perhaps the most common example of computer-based deception. Some banner ads (Figure 9.4) seem to do whatever it takes to get you to click on them. They may offer money, sound false alarms about computer problems, or, as noted earlier, promise information that never gets delivered. The unethical nature of these ads is clear. If the Web were not so new, it's unlikely we'd tolerate these deceptive methods.[20]

Besides deception, computers can use coercion to change people's behaviors. Software installation programs provide one example. Some installation programs require you to install additional software you may not need but that is bundled as part of the overall product. In other situations, the new software may change your default settings to preferences that benefit the manufacturer rather than the user, affecting how you work in the future (some media players are set up to do this when installed). In many cases, users may feel they are at the mercy of the installation program. This raises ethical questions because the computer product may be intentionally designed to limit user choice for the benefit of the manufacturer.

Methods That Raise Red Flags

While it's clear that deception and coercion are unethical in technology products, two behavior change strategies that fit into a broad definition of persuasion—operant conditioning and surveillance—are not as clearly ethical or unethical, depending on how the strategies are applied.

Operant Conditioning

Operant conditioning, described in Chapter 3, consists mainly of using reinforcement or punishment to promote certain behavior. Although few technology products outside of games have used operant conditioning to any great extent, one could imagine a future where operant conditioning is commonly used to change people's behavior, sometimes without their direct consent or without them realizing what's going on—and here is where the ethical concerns arise.

For instance, a company could create a Web browser that uses operant conditioning to change people's Web surfing behavior without their awareness. If the browser were programmed to give faster page downloads to certain Web sites—say, those affiliated with the company's strategic partners—and delay the download of other sites, users would be subtly rewarded for accessing certain sites and punished for visiting others. In my view, this strategy would be unethical.

Less commonly, operant conditioning uses punishment to reduce the instances of a behavior. As I noted in Chapter 3, I believe this approach is generally fraught with ethical problems and is not an appropriate use of conditioning technology.

Having said that, operant conditioning that incorporates punishment could be ethical, if the user is informed and the punishment is innocuous. For instance, after a trial period, some downloaded software is designed to take progressively longer to launch. If users do not register the software, they are informed that they will have to wait longer and longer for the program to become functional. This innocuous form of punishment (or negative reinforcement, depending on your perspective) is ethical, as long as the user is informed. Another form of innocuous and ethical punishment: shareware programs that bring up screens, often called "nag screens," to remind users they should register and pay for the product.

Now, suppose a system were created with a stronger form of punishment for failure to register: crashing the computer on the subsequent startup, locking up frequently used documents and holding them for ransom, sending email to the person's contact list pointing out that they are using software they have not paid for. Such technology clearly would be unethical.

In general, operant conditioning can be an ethical strategy when incorporated into a persuasive technology if it is overt and harmless. If it violates either of those constraints, however, it must be considered unethical.

Another area of concern is when technologies use punishment—or threats of punishment—to shape behaviors. Technically speaking, punishment is a negative consequence that leads people to perform a behavior less often. A typical example is spanking a child. Punishment is an effective way to change outward behaviors in the short term,[21] but punishment has limited outcomes beyond changing observable behavior.

Surveillance

Surveillance is another method of persuasion that can raise a red flag. Think back to Hygiene Guard, the surveillance system to monitor employees' hand washing, described in Chapter 3. Is this an ethical system? Is it unethical? Both sides could be argued. At first glance, Hygiene Guard may seem intrusive, a violation of personal privacy. But its purpose is a positive one: to protect public health. Many institutions that install Hygiene Guard belong to the healthcare and food service industries. They use the system to protect their patients and patrons.

So is Hygiene Guard ethical or unethical? In my view, it depends on how it is used. As the system monitors users, it could give gentle reminders if they try to leave the restroom without washing their hands. Or it could be set up mainly to identify infractions and punish people. I view the former use of the technology as ethical and the latter application as unethical.

The Hygiene Guard example brings up an important point about the ethics of surveillance technology in general: it makes a huge difference *how* a system works—the nature and tone of the human-machine interaction. In general, if surveillance is intended to be supportive or helpful rather than punitive, it may be ethical. However, if it is intended mainly to punish, I believe it is unethical.

Whether or not a surveillance technology is ethical also depends on the context in which it is applied. Think back to AutoWatch, the system described in Chapter 3 that enables parents to track how their teenagers are driving.[22] This surveillance may be a "no confidence" vote in a teenager, but it's not unethical, since parents are ultimately responsible for their teens' driving, and the product helps them to fulfill this responsibility.

The same could be said for employers that implement such a system in their company cars. They have the responsibility (financially and legally, if not morally) to see that their employees drive safely while on company time. I believe this is an acceptable use of the technology (although it is not one that I endorse). However, if the company were to install a system to monitor employees' driving or other activities while they were not on company time, this would be an invasion of privacy and clearly an unethical use of technology.

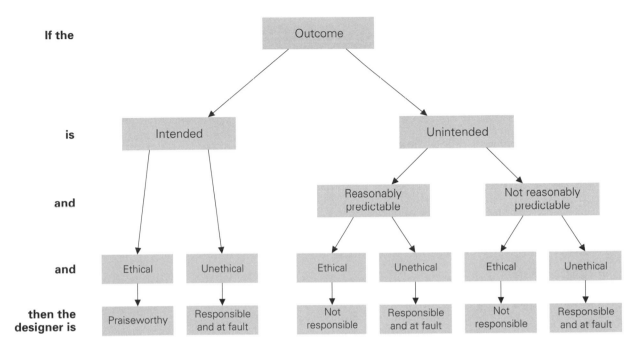

Figure 9.5   The ethical nature of a persuasive technology can hinge on whether or not the outcome was intended.

Outcomes: Intended and Unintended

In addition to examining intentions and methods, you can also investigate the outcomes of persuasive technology systems to assess the ethics of a given system, as shown in Figure 9.5. (This line of thinking originated with two of my former students: Eric Neuenschwander and Daniel Berdichevsky.)

If the intended outcome of a persuasive technology is benign, generally there is no significant ethical concern. Many technologies designed for selling legitimate products and strengthening brand loyalty fall into this category.

The intended outcomes of other technologies may raise ethical concerns. Think back to Banana-Rama, the high-tech slot machine described in Chapter 5. This device uses onscreen characters, an ape and a monkey, to motivate players to continue gambling. When you win, the characters celebrate. When you hesitate to drop in more of your money to continue playing, the characters' expressions change from supportive to impatient.

Figure 9.6

The MOPy screen saver (no longer promoted by Hewlett-Packard) motivates people to make original prints, consuming disposable ink cartridges.

Some people would find this product ethically objectionable because its intended outcome is to increase gambling, an activity that conflicts with the values of some individuals and cultures. Other people would not consider this intended outcome a cause for ethical alarm; gambling is an accepted part of many cultures and is often promoted by government groups. However, if Banana-Rama were wildly popular, with Las Vegas tourists lining up to lose their fortunes, the outcome may be significant enough to make it a major ethical issue.

Hewlett-Packard's MOPy (Multiple Original Printouts) is a digital pet screen saver that rewards users for printing on an HP printer (Figure 9.6). The point of the MOPy system is to motivate people to print out multiple originals rather than using a copy machine. As you make original prints, you earn points that can be redeemed for virtual plants and virtual toys for your virtual fish. In this way, people use up HP ink cartridges and will have to buy more sooner.

Some might argue that MOPy is unethical because its intended outcome is one that results in higher printing costs and environmental degradation. (To HP's credit, the company no longer promotes MOPy.)[23] Others could argue that there is no cause for ethical alarm because the personal or environmental impact of using the product is insignificant.

But suppose that Banana-Rama and MOPy were highly successful in achieving their intended outcomes: increasing gambling and the consumption of ink cartridges. If these products produced significant negative impacts—social, personal, and environmental—where would the ethical fault reside? Who should shoulder the blame?

In my view, three parties could be at fault when the outcome of a persuasive technology is ethically unsound: those who create, distribute, or use the product. I believe the balance of culpability shifts on a case-by-case basis.[24] The creators have responsibility because, in the case of MOPy, their work benefited a private company at the expense of individuals and the global environment. Likewise, distributors must also shoulder the ethical responsibility of making unethical technologies widely available.

Finally, users of ethically questionable persuasive technologies must bear at least some responsibility. In the cases of Banana-Rama and MOPy, despite the persuasive strategies in these products, individual users are typically voluntarily choosing to use the products, thus contributing to the outcomes that may be ethically questionable.

Responsibility for Unintended Outcomes

Persuasive technologies can produce *unintended* outcomes. Although captology focuses on intended outcomes, creators of persuasive technology must take responsibility for unintended unethical outcomes that can reasonably be foreseen.

To act ethically, the creators should carefully anticipate how their product might be used for an unplanned persuasive end, how it might be overused, or how it might be adopted by unintended users. Even if the unintended outcomes are not readily predictable, once the creators become aware of harmful outcomes, they should take action to mitigate them.

Designed to reduce speeding, the Speed Monitoring Awareness Radar Trailer, discussed in Chapter 3, seems to have unintended outcomes that may not have been easy to predict. Often when I discuss this technology with groups of college students, at least one male student will say that for him the SMART trailer has the opposite effect of what was intended: he speeds up to see how fast he can go.

As far as I can tell, law enforcement agencies have not addressed the possibility that people might actually speed up rather than slow down when these trailers are present. It may be the unintended outcome has not been recognized or is considered to apply to a relatively small number of people—mostly younger male drivers who seek challenges. In any case, if this unintended outcome were to result in a significant number of accidents and injuries, I believe the developers of the SMART trailer would have to take responsibility for removing or altering the system.

Some companies turn a blind eye to the unintentional, though reasonably predictable, outcomes of using their products. Consider the video game Mortal Kombat, which rewards players for virtual killing. In this game, players interact with other players through virtual hand-to-hand combat. This entertainment product can be highly compelling for some people.

Unfortunately, Mortal Kombat and other violent video games not only motivate people to keep playing, they also may have a negative effect on players' attitudes and behaviors in the real world. Social learning theory[25] suggests that practicing violent acts in a virtual world can lead to performing violent acts in the real world.[26] The effect of video game violence has been much debated for over a decade. After reviewing results of previous studies and presenting results of their own recent work, psychologists Craig Anderson and Karen Dill conclude:

> When the choice and action components of video games . . . is coupled with the games' reinforcing properties, a strong learning experience results. In a sense, violent video games provide a complete learning environment for aggression, with simultaneous exposure to modeling, reinforcement, and rehearsal of behaviors. This combination of learning strategies has been shown to be more powerful than any of these methods used singly.[27]

Although violent real-world behavior is not the intended outcome of the creators of video games such as Mortal Kombat, it is a reasonably predictable outcome of rewarding people for rehearsing violence, creating an ethical responsibility for the makers, distributors, and users of such violent games.

When Persuasion Targets Vulnerable Groups

Persuasive technology products can be designed to target vulnerable populations, people who are inordinately susceptible to influence. When they exploit vulnerable groups, the products are unethical.

The most obvious vulnerable group is children, who are the intended users of many of today's persuasive technology products.[28] It doesn't take much imagination to see how such technologies can take advantage of children's vulnerability to elicit private information, make an inappropriate sale, or promote a controversial ideology.

Figure 9.7

A conceptual design for an unethical computer game, by captology students Hannah Goldie, David Li, and Peter Westen.

How easy it is to exploit children through persuasive technology is evident from the classes I teach at Stanford in which I assign students to develop ethically questionable product concepts. One team made a simple prototype of a Web-based Pokémon game for kids. In the prototype, the team showed how this seemingly innocuous game could be designed to elicit personal information from children who play the game, using the popular Pokémon characters (Figure 9.7).

Are You Ready for "Behavioronics"?

The idea of embedding computing functionality in objects and environments is common, but it's less common to think about embedding computing devices into human bodies. How will we—or *should* we—respond when implantable interactive technologies are created to extend human capability far beyond the norm? Are we ready to discuss the ethics of the Bionic Human, especially when this is an elective procedure? ("Hey, I got my memory upgraded this weekend!") And how should we react when implantable devices are created not just to restore human ability but to change human behavior?

Some of these technologies raise ethical concerns. For example, in an effort to help drug-dependent people stay clean, these individuals might agree to—or be coerced into—having an implant put into their bodies that would detect the presence of the illegal substance and report it to authorities.

Who decides if and when it is ethical to use such technologies? Who should have access to the information produced? And who should control the functionality of the embedded devices? Important questions.

Unfortunately, our current understanding of what I call "behavioronics" is limited, so we don't have solid answers to these questions. Especially as we combine computing technology with pharmacological interventions, behavioronics is a frontier that should be explored carefully before we begin to settle the territory.

Children are perhaps the most visible vulnerable group, but there are many others, including the mentally disabled, the elderly, the bereaved, and people who are exceptionally lonely. With the growth of workplace technology, even employees can be considered a vulnerable group, as their jobs are at stake. Those who complain about having to use a surveillance system or other technology designed to motivate or influence them may not be treated well by their employers and could find that their jobs are in jeopardy.

Any technology that preys on the vulnerability of a particular group raises ethical concerns. Whether employers, other organizations, or individuals, those who use persuasive technologies to exploit vulnerable groups are not likely to be their own watchdogs. Outside organizations and individuals must take responsibility for ensuring that persuasive technologies are used ethically.

Stakeholder Analysis: A Methodology for Analyzing Ethics

Even if you are not formally trained in ethics, you can evaluate the ethical nature of a persuasive technology product by examining the intentions, methods, and outcomes of the product as well as the populations it targets, as outlined in this chapter. You also can rely on your intuition, your feeling for right and wrong, and your sense of what's fair and what's not. In many cases, this intuitive, unstructured approach can work well.

However, when examining the ethics of a complicated situation—or when collaborating with others—a more structured method may be required. One useful approach is to conduct a stakeholder analysis, to identify all those affected by a persuasive technology, and what each stakeholder in the technology stands to gain or lose. By conducting such an analysis, it is possible to identify ethical concerns in a systematic way.[29]

With that in mind, I propose applying the following general stakeholder analysis to identify ethical concerns. This seven-step analysis provides a framework for systematically examining the ethics of any persuasive technology product.

> To assess the ethics of a technology, identify each stakeholder and determine what each stands to gain or lose.

Step 1: List All of the Stakeholders

Make a list of all of the stakeholders associated with the technology. A stakeholder is anyone who has an interest in the use of the persuasive technology product. Stakeholders include creators, distributors, users, and sometimes those who are close to the users as well—their families, neighbors, and communities. It is important to be thorough in considering all those who may be affected by a product, not just the most obvious stakeholders.

Step 2: List What Each Stakeholder Has to Gain

List what each stakeholder has to gain when a person uses the persuasive technology product. The most obvious gain is financial profit, but gains can include other factors as well, such as learning, self-esteem, career success, power, or control.

Step 3: List What Each Stakeholder Has to Lose

List what each stakeholder has to lose by virtue of the technology, such as money, autonomy, privacy, reputation, power, or control.

Step 4: Evaluate Which Stakeholder Has the Most to Gain

Review the results of Steps 2 and 3 and decide which stakeholder has the most to gain from the persuasive technology product. You may want to rank all the stakeholders according to what each has to gain.

Step 5: Evaluate Which Stakeholder Has the Most to Lose

Now identify which stakeholder stands to lose the most. Again, losses aren't limited to time and money. They can include intangibles such as reputation, personal dignity, autonomy, and many other factors.

Step 6: Determine Ethics by Examining Gains and Losses in Terms of Values

Evaluate the gain or loss of each stakeholder relative to the other stakeholders. By identifying inequities in gains and losses, you can determine if the product is ethical or to what degree it raises ethical questions. This is where values, both personal and cultural, enter into the analysis.

Step 7: Acknowledge the Values and Assumptions You Bring to Your Analysis

The last step is perhaps the most difficult: identifying the values and assumptions underlying your analysis. Any investigation of ethics centers on the value system used in conducting the analysis. These values are often not explicit or obvious, so it's useful to identify the moral assumptions that informed the analysis.

These values and assumptions will not be the same for everyone. In most Western cultures, individual freedom and self-determination are valued over institutional efficiency or collective power. As a result, Westerners are likely to evaluate persuasive technology products as ethical when they enhance individual freedom and unethical when they empower institutions at the expense of individuals. Other cultures may assess the ethics of technology differently, valuing community needs over individual freedoms.

Education Is Key

This chapter has covered a range of ethical issues related to persuasive technologies. Some of these issues, such as the use of computers to convey emotions, represent new territory in the discussion of ethics. Other issues, such as using surveillance to change people's behaviors, are part of a familiar landscape. Whether new or familiar, these ethical issues should be better understood by those who design, distribute, and use persuasive technologies.

Ultimately, education is the key to more ethical persuasive technologies. Designers and distributors who understand the ethical issues outlined in this chapter will be in a better position to create and sell ethical persuasive technology products. Technology users will be better positioned to recognize when computer products are applying unethical or questionably ethical tactics to persuade them. The more educated we all become about the ethics of persuasive technology, the more likely technology products will be designed and used in ways that are ethically sound.

Notes and References

For updates on the topics presented in this chapter, visit *www.persuasivetech.info.*

1. Passed by Congress in 1998, the Children's Online Privacy Protection Act (COPPA) established strict privacy guidelines for child-oriented Web sites. Final rules on COPPA, drafted by the Federal Trade Commission (FTC) in 1999, became enforceable in April 2001. In April of 2002, the Federal Trade Commission reached a settlement with Etch-A-

Sketch, the toy manufacturer that was violating the Children's Online Privacy Protection Rule. Etch-A-Sketch agreed to modify its data collection practices and pay a civil penalty of $35,000. For more, see *http://www.ftc.gov/opa/2002/04/coppaanniv.htm*.

2. The number of bathrooms in a home is a rough indicator of socioeconomic status.

3. The idea for this concept came from Stanford captology students exploring the dark side of persuasive technologies. The students were Peter Westen, Hannah Goldie, and David Li.

4. See the following online bibliographies for information about computer ethics:

   http://courses.cs.vt.edu/~cs3604/lib/Bibliography/Biblio.acm.html

   http://www.rivier.edu/faculty/htavani/biblio.htm

   http://www.cs.mdx.ac.uk/harold/srf/justice.html.

   Professional societies have developed ethical codes for their members. Below are some codes relating to psychology and to computer science:

   American Psychological Association (APA) Ethics Code Draft for Comment: *http://anastasi.apa.org/draftethicscode/draftcode.cfm#toc*

   American Psychological Association (APA) Ethics Code (1992): *http://www.apa.org/ethics/code.html*

   Association for Computing Machinery (ACM) Code of Ethics and Professional Conduct: *http://www.acm.org/constitution/code.html*

   Australian Computer Society (ACS) Code of Ethics: *http://www.acs.org.au/national/pospaper/acs131.htm*

   For printed material on computer ethics, see the following:

   a. B. Friedman, *Human Values and the Design of Computer Technology* (Stanford, CA: CSLI Publications, 1997).

   b. D. Gotterbarn, K. Miller, and S. Rogerson, Software engineering code of ethics, *Communications of the ACM,* 40(11): 110–118 (1997).

5. Joseph Weizenbaum, *Computer Power and Human Reason: From Judgment to Calculation* (San Francisco, CA: W.H. Freeman, 1976).

6. Health interventions, Guttman (1997) argues, can do damage when experts imply that others have weak character, when experts compromise individual autonomy, or when they impose middle-class values. As Guttman writes, "Interventions by definition raise ethical concerns" (p. 109). Guttman further states that ethical problems arise when "values emphasized in the intervention [are] not fully compatible with values related to cultural customs, traditions, and some people's conceptions of what is enjoyable or acceptable" (p. 102). In short, persuasion can become paternalism. See N. Guttman, Beyond strategic research: A value-centered approach to health communication interventions, *Communication Theory,* 7(2): 95–124 (1997).

For more on the ethics of interventions, see the following:

    a. C. T. Salmon, Campaigns for social "improvement": An overview of values, rationales, and impacts," in C. T. Salmon (ed.), *Information Campaigns: Balancing Social Values and Social Change* (Newbury Park, CA: Sage, 1989).

    b. K. Witte, The manipulative nature of health communication research: Ethical issues and guidelines, *American Behavioral Scientist,* 38(2): 285–293 (1994).

7. R. Greenleaf, *Servant* (Peterborough, NH: Windy Row Press, 1980).

8. R. D. Barney and J. Black, Ethics and professional persuasive communications, *Public Relations Review,* 20(3): 233–248 (1994).

9. For example, Opioids.com is a site that at one time rationally argued for use of controlled substances.

10. At the time of this writing, the Volvo car game is available at *http://fibreplay.com/other/portfolio_en.html#.*

11. There are at least three arguments that the Volvo interactive simulation will make an impact on users. First, users are essentially role playing the part of the Volvo. The psychology research on role playing and persuasion suggests that playing roles, even roles we don't believe or endorse, influences our thinking. For a review of the classic studies in role playing and persuasion, see R. Petty and J. Cacioppo, *Attitudes and Persuasion: Classic and Contemporary Approaches* (Dubuque, IA: Brown, 1981).

    Second, the message processing literature suggests that people have a tendency to forget the source of a message but remember the message, a phenomenon called the "sleeper effect." In this situation, the message is that Volvo cars clean the air, which people may remember after they have forgotten that the simple simulation was the source of the message. Research on the sleeper effect goes back to the 1930s. For a deeper exploration of this phenomenon, see D. Hannah and B. Sternthal, Detecting and explaining the sleeper effect, *Journal of Consumer Research,* 11 (Sept.): 632–642 (1984).

    Finally, the marketing literature on demonstrations show that showing product benefits in dramatic ways can influence buying decisions. For example, see R. N. Laczniak and D. D. Muehling, Toward a better understanding of the role of advertising message involvement in ad processing, *Psychology and Marketing,* 10(4): 301–319 (1993). Also see Amir Heiman and Eitan Muller, Using demonstration to increase new product acceptance: Controlling demonstration time, *Journal of Marketing Research,* 33: 1–11 (1996).

12. The classic study in distraction and persuasion is J. Freedman and D. Sears, Warning, distraction, and resistance to influence, *Journal of Personality & Social Psychology,* 1(3): 262–266 (1965).

13. S. Olson, Web surfers brace for pop-up downloads, CNET news.com, April 8, 2002. Available online at *http://news.com.com/2100-1023-877568.html.*

14. The most notable research in the area of computers and emotion has been done by Rosalind Picard's Affective Computing group at MIT Media Lab (see *http://affect.media. mit.edu*). Thanks to research in this lab and elsewhere, someday computers may deal in emotions, opening new paths for captology.

15. For more on this issue, see B. Friedman, *Human Values and the Design of Computer Technology* (Stanford, CA: CSLI Publications, 1997).

16. See "Do they need a "trick" to make us click?," a pilot study that examines a new technique used to boost click-through, by David R. Thompson, Ph.D., *Columbia Daily Tribune*, and Birgit Wassmuth, Ph.D., University of Missouri. Study conducted September 1998. Paper presented at the annual Association for Education in Journalism and Mass Communication Convention, August 4–7, 1999, New Orleans, Louisiana.

17. At the 1999 ACM SIGCHI Conference, I organized and moderated a panel discussion on the ethical issues related to high-tech children's plush toys, including Barney. This panel included the person who led the development of the Microsoft ActiMates products (including Barney) and other specialists in children's technology. The panelists were Allen Cypher, Stagecast Software; Allison Druin, University of Maryland; Batya Friedman, Colby College; and Erik Strommen, Microsoft Corporation.

    You can find a newspaper story of the event at *http://www.post-gazette.com/businessnews/ 19990521barney1.asp*.

18. E. Strommen and K. Alexander, Emotional interfaces for interactive aardvarks: Designing affect into social interfaces for children, *Proceeding of the CHI 99 Conference on Human Factors in Computing Systems*, 528–535 (1999).

19. In an article reviewing various studies on self-affirmation, Claude Steele discusses his research that showed higher compliance rates from people who were insulted than from people who were flattered. In both cases, the compliance rates were high, but the people receiving the negative assessments about themselves before the request for compliance had significantly higher rates of compliance. See C. M. Steele, The psychology of self-affirmation: Sustaining the integrity of the self, in L. Berkowitz (ed.), *Advances in Experimental Social Psychology*, 21: 261–302 (1988).

    For a more recent exploration of compliance after threat, see Amy Kaplan and Joachim Krueger, Compliance after threat: Self-affirmation or self-presentation?, *Current Research in Social Psychology*, 2:15–22 (1999). *http://www.uiowa.edu/~grpproc*. (This is an online journal. The article is available at *http://www.uiowa.edu/~grpproc/crisp/crisp.4.7.htm*.)

    Also, Pamela Shoemaker makes a compelling argument that humans are naturally geared to pay more attention to negative, threatening information than positive, affirming information. See Pamela Shoemaker, Hardwired for news: Using biological and cultural evolution to explain the surveillance function, *Journal of Communication*, 46(2), Spring (1996).

20. For a statement about the "Wild West" nature of the Web in 1998, see R. Kilgore, Publishers must set rules to preserve credibility, *Advertising Age*, 69 (48): 31 (1998).

21. For book-length and readable discussions about how discipline works (or doesn't work) with children in changing behavior, see

    a. I. Hyman, *The Case Against Spanking: How to Discipline Your Child without Hitting* (San Francisco: Jossey-Bass Psychology Series, 1997).

    b. J. Maag, *Parenting without Punishment: Making Problem Behavior Work for You* (Philadelphia, PA: The Charles Press, 1996).

22. To read about the suggested rationale for AutoWatch, see the archived version at *http://web.archive.org/web/19990221041908/http://www.easesim.com/autowatchparents.htm.*

23. While Hewlett-Packard no longer supports MOPy, you can still find information online at the following sites:

    http://formen.ign.com/news/16154.html

    http://cna.mediacorpnews.com/technology/bytesites/virtualpet2.htm

24. Others suggest that all parties involved are equally at fault. For example, see K. Andersen, *Persuasion Theory and Practice* (Boston: Allyn and Bacon, 1971).

25. A. Bandura, *Self-Efficacy: The Exercise of Control* (New York: Freeman, 1997).

26. C. A. Anderson and K. E. Dill, Video games and aggressive thoughts, feelings, and behavior in the laboratory and in life, *Journal of Personality and Social Psychology*, 78 (4): 772–790 (2000). This study, which includes an excellent bibliography, can be found at *http://www.apa.org/journals/psp/psp784772.html.*

27. Other related writings on video games and violence include the following:

    a. D. Grossman, *On Killing* (New York: Little Brown and Company, 1996). (Summarized at *http://www.mediaandthefamily.org/research/vgrc/1998-2.shtml.*)

    b. Steven J. Kirsh, Seeing the world through "Mortal Kombat" colored glasses: Violent video games and hostile attribution bias. Poster presented at the biennial meeting of the Society for Research in Child Development, Washington, D.C., ED 413 986, April 1997. This paper now also available: Steven J. Kirsh, Seeing the world through "Mortal Kombat" colored glasses: Violent video games and hostile attribution bias, *Childhood*, 5(2): 177–184 (1998).

28. P. King and J. Tester, Landscape of persuasive technologies, *Communications of the ACM*, 42(5): 31–38 (1999).

29. The stakeholder approach I present in this chapter brings together techniques I've compiled during my years of teaching and research. I'm grateful to Professor June Flora for introducing me to the concept in early 1994. The stakeholder approach originated with a business management book: R. E. Freeman, *Strategic Management: A Stakeholder Approach* (Boston: Pitman, 1984).

    Later work refined stakeholder theory. For example, see K. Goodpaster, Business ethics and stakeholder analysis, *Business Ethics Quarterly*, 1(1): 53–73 (1991).

chapter 10

Captology
Looking Forward

The previous chapters have taken you through the fundamentals of captology, the study of computers as persuasive technologies. My goal has been to give you the resources for researching, designing, using, or simply understanding persuasive technology products, present and future. In these pages I've offered frameworks, such as the functional triad and the Web Credibility Grid, for conceptually organizing this dynamic area.

We're just now witnessing the dawn of persuasive technology, in theory and in practice. Because captology is new, not only are some frameworks in this book likely to change or evolve, but many of the examples offered here represent pioneering experiments, not mature products. It's difficult to judge the potential or pitfalls of persuasive technology on the basis of these early examples alone. Much like the early designs for flying machines, the early designs for persuasive technologies are likely to have a high failure rate. As the theory and practice of captology matures, those early examples will be replaced by far more sophisticated applications.

Competency in persuasive technology is likely to grow at a rapid rate in the coming years, due to advances in computing power and the considerable money at stake.[1] Research in persuasive technology should progress rapidly as well, because technology will change the way research is conducted.

In the past, studying persuasion was laborious and slow. A single study could take years to complete. Even "quick" laboratory experiments required at least a few months. And once a study was completed and documented, the results might not appear in print for a year or two, the time it takes for scholarly

As we learn how computers persuade people, we'll create new insights into how *people* persuade other people.

peer reviews, revisions, editing, typesetting, production, and so on. As a result, for the last century the scientific study of persuasion has plodded forward at a painstaking pace.

All that is changing. Today, the Internet and other computing technologies enable us to research persuasion quickly, setting up studies, recruiting participants on a large scale, collecting and analyzing data, and sharing the results online. Using these new technology systems, it is possible to conduct a study and report the results in a matter of days rather than years.[2]

There are potential drawbacks to such rapid research-and-reporting cycles, including the temptation to launch a study quickly, without a well-thought-out design; lack of time to carefully consider the results; and a rush to share results without sufficient peer review. In addition, the Internet makes it possible for anyone—not just those who are well qualified—to conduct research; there is no governing body that oversees online research efforts. The Internet also makes it easier to recruit large numbers of study participants, presenting the danger that studies will be evaluated based on the quantity of participants rather than the quality of the research.

Nevertheless, I believe the speed and relative ease of conducting research using interactive technology will change the study of persuasion forever. For better, and sometimes for worse, this new technology will spawn a new breed of researcher who will not settle for the steady but slow methods of the previous century.

Because captology is both theoretical and practical, efforts to research and design persuasive technologies are likely to become intertwined processes. Research will provide a foundation for designing new persuasive technology products, and design will serve as stimulus and inspiration for new research.

As I see it, the greatest contributions to our understanding of persuasive technology won't come from a research lab that pursues only theory or from a gifted designer working alone. Rather, the greatest contributions will come from researchers and designers who value each others' work and know how to work together effectively.

As we develop a deeper understanding of how computing systems can be designed to change attitudes and behaviors, I predict we'll see a remarkable shift: knowledge about how computers persuade people will create new insights into how *people* persuade other people.

Let me elaborate: To date, captology has drawn on various disciplines, most notably social psychology, to predict the potential that computers have for influencing people. For example, my early hypotheses about the persuasive effects of praise from computers grew out of the social psychology research about praise from people.[3] Although in the past, psychology and other disciplines have shed light on persuasive technology, I'm proposing that the flow of information could reverse.

In the future, we may well discover new influence dynamics by first studying *computer*-based persuasion. Then, researchers will perform tests to determine if these new dynamics apply when only humans are involved. In other words, new knowledge about computer-human persuasion may give significant insight into human-human persuasion.[4] Although speculative, if this approach succeeds, it would offer practical advantages: we could learn how coaches, teachers, salespeople, and even parents could be more effective persuaders by first trying out influence strategies using computing systems.

Five Future Trends in Captology

My assertion about reversing the flow of persuasion theory is speculative, but other issues in captology seem quite clear. In the next few years, I anticipate five emerging trends in the study and design of computers as persuasive technologies.

Trend 1: Pervasive Persuasive Technologies

In the future, persuasive technology systems will become numerous, eventually becoming part of our everyday lives, at home and at work. Throughout history, the art of persuasion has helped people and groups reach their goals. That won't change, and persuasion will continue to be pervasive in human life. What will change is how the persuasion takes place: increasingly, people will be persuaded via interactive technology.

Computer-based influence strategies will not only appear in typical desktop and Web applications, but they will be designed into everyday consumer products: cars, kitchen appliances, perhaps even clothing. Technology researchers and visionaries have predicted how computing systems will alter the ordinary objects and environments in our lives.[5] In the future, we'll use a variety of smart products and work and live in smart environments. What I add to that vision is this: the smart products and environments of the future won't just be about productivity or entertainment; they also will be about influencing and motivating people.

In the Persuasive Technology Lab, my students and I have explored how smart lamps and high-tech blankets could motivate energy conservation, how next-generation couches and home heating systems might encourage social interactions, and how future automobiles and neighborhood street signs could motivate safer driving. While the vast majority of such concepts will never become actual products, some will.

This future will take time to emerge; creating smart, persuasive products and environments presents significant technological and economic challenges. However, it seems clear that one platform will start running persuasive applications in the near future: mobile phones. In Chapter 8 I discussed the potential of mobile devices to enhance persuasion. I believe that, more than any other near-term innovation, introducing applications to promote e-commerce and self-help via mobile phones will make persuasive technologies commonplace.

The pervasiveness of persuasive technologies has direct implications for high-tech designers. Because many interactive systems will have persuasive elements, most high-tech designers will need to be at least somewhat familiar with captology, just as most designers are now familiar with usability. And like usability, captology may become part of a standard curriculum for people learning to design interactive computing systems.

Trend 2: Growth Beyond Buying and Branding

The second major trend deals with application areas for captology. Of the 12 domains for persuasive technologies outlined in Chapter 1,[6] the largest growth area in the near term is commerce—buying and branding through interactive systems. Already companies have shown their eagerness to promote their products, services, and brands via Web technology. As of this writing, many of these attempts are shoddy (using overwrought graphics, text, or animation; trapping users by disabling the "back" button on their browsers; tedious FAQs instead of real customer support; trick banner ads), not yet well developed (online characters designed to promote products or services), or just plain annoying (blizzards of junk mail filling your inbox, a requirement to register at a news site before you can view its streaming video content). The successful implementations of persuasive technology for e-commerce and for online promotion will live on and replicate, while unsuccessful approaches will fade away. Over time, the promotion of buying and branding through interactive systems of many types—not just the Web—will become more sophisticated and more effective.

In the future, companies that have had little to do with interactive technology will begin to leverage its potential. Specifically, companies that have core competencies in finance, fitness, personal relationships, environmental preservation, and more will see that they can accomplish their corporate goals better by using technology as a means of motivation and influence.

Already we are seeing examples of nontechnology companies offering or considering persuasive technology products. Weight Watchers has produced a pedometer to motivate fitness activity. Insurance companies are exploring the potential for using in-car surveillance systems as a way to motivate safer driving, with the lure of lower insurance rates. Merck, a pharmaceutical company that sells a drug to slow hair loss, provides an online simulation to help people see what they will look like with less hair.[7] Companies with established interest in a vertical market will increasingly use interactive technologies to achieve their goals. In addition, governments and politicians are sure to get more sophisticated in their use of technology to gain power through persuasion.

Healthcare

Healthcare is one of the vertical markets that is most likely to leverage persuasive technology. Today, you can find a large number of interactive systems designed to support health, but relatively few of these products actively motivate or persuade people to live healthier lives (the Weight Watchers pedometer is one example). We're still in the early stages of using interactive technology for health.[8]

Although still in the early stages, I believe we will see many innovations in the health arena. The driver for using persuasive technology in this arena will come from insurance companies and healthcare providers that see the potential for financial gain. These institutions know that many health problems have behavioral components: smoking contributes to heart disease, unprotected sex increases risk for contracting HIV, failure to manage diabetes leads to a host of health problems. By helping people change behaviors in these and other areas, insurance companies and healthcare providers can save money and boost their profits in the process. For this reason alone, I predict that as understanding of captology increases, stakeholders in healthcare will make significant investments to develop interactive technologies that proactively promote health.

Education

Another persuasive technology domain positioned for imminent growth is education. From the classroom to the workplace, educational designers will create computing applications that deeply motivate people to acquire new knowledge and skills. Persuasive technology can motivate people to initiate a learning process, to stay on task, and then to review material as needed.[9] Some interactive learning systems already incorporate influence principles, most notably in titles considered "edutainment." The vision for educational technology is sure to expand. As sophistication increases, we'll see adaptive education and training products that tailor motivational approaches to match each individual learner—motivating "accommodators" to learn through cause-and-effect simulations, or providing "convergers" with rewards for performance on interactive problem sets and quizzes.[10] Perhaps even more significant will be interactive systems designed to teach people at the right time and place—nutrition education while buying groceries, or information on etiquette just before meeting with people from a different culture.

Healthcare and education are two domains of persuasive technology that are likely to grow quickly because of their financial potential. Other important domains that don't offer immediate monetary gain, such as environmental conservation, are likely to grow only as quickly as altruistic individuals and foundations can provide the resources—which, unfortunately, will be slow compared to the pace of industry innovation.

Trend 3: Increase in Specialized Persuasive Devices

Another trend in captology will be the proliferation of devices created specifically for persuasive purposes. Today, a relative handful of such devices exist, ranging from Baby Think It Over to the Pokémon Pikachu pedometer. However, I predict that within a few years, you'll be able to find scores of interactive devices designed to influence and motivate. The purpose of these devices will become quite narrow, using influence strategies to target a specific audience in a limited domain.

One day we could see a device that motivates college students to donate blood, or a device that helps teenagers overcome shyness. In the commercial domain, we'll probably see innovations such as a device that motivates parents to visit a toy store as they're driving near a mall or a device that persuades high school students to visit a certain clothing or music store once a week. Most of these specialized devices will be mobile, so they can be in the right time and place to be most effective in changing what people think or do.

The proliferation of specialized devices will result from three factors converging. First, organizations will begin to understand the potential for creating persuasive interactive devices. Once news hits the front page about a persuasive device changing the financial fortunes of a company, decision makers will start investigating possibilities for their own companies.

The next factor is cost. In the coming years, it will become significantly cheaper to create persuasive devices. Other consumer electronic devices, such as PDAs and digital pets, have experienced dramatic declines in cost over time. The same will hold true for persuasive interactive devices, as the cost factors to produce such devices (mainly, cheaper offshore labor, strong global competition, and more efficient design methods) are similar to those for producing productivity or entertainment devices.

The third factor that will drive the proliferation of persuasive devices is progress in network connectivity. Today, creating user-friendly mobile devices that access the Internet is not trivial. At least in the United States, a unified wireless data infrastructure is not yet in place; various standards and schemes are competing, with no clear winner in sight.[11] This should change over the next few years. As wireless technology advances and wireless standards emerge, it will become much easier to create mobile devices—or applications for these devices—that share data over a network. When connectivity becomes a trivial task, the idea of producing persuasive mobile devices will become all the more compelling.

Trend 4: Increased Focus on Influence Strategies

The fourth trend has to do with the nature of captology itself. In the coming years, the study of computers as persuasive technologies will focus more directly on computer-based influence strategies[12] wherever they occur—in Web sites, desktop productivity software, specialized devices, or in smart environments. As attempts to influence people via computing technology become more common, it will become less important to distinguish between two types of interactive products: those designed exclusively for persuasion (macrosuasion) and those that incorporate influence strategies as part of a larger application (microsuasion).

As captology matures, the influence strategy, not the interactive product, will be the unit of analysis, the basic building block. This shift will expand the scope of captology. It's my view that virtually all mature end-user applications—whether on the desktop, mobile, or Web-based—will eventually incorporate elements of motivation and persuasion.

We're already witnessing this shift. Mature desktop applications that were once clearly about productivity, such as Intuit's Quicken software, are evolving to include elements of coaching, monitoring, advising, even cross-selling (TurboTax, also made by Intuit, tries to persuade users to try Quicken).

Web sites are applying persuasion to keep visitors coming back. Iwon.com gives users an incentive to make it their default homepage. CNN attempts to persuade browsers to register for its premium content. The list of other applications and sites that apply persuasion is rapidly growing.

Two factors are driving this trend toward incorporating persuasion into technology products. One factor is that as applications mature, companies begin to focus not on one-time transactions but on building brand loyalty, on selling more products and services to existing customers. Designing persuasion into interactive technology products can help companies to achieve those goals.

The second driver is that, as a result of technology advances, companies are able to improve the user experience of their interactive products, extending their products' basic functionality to provide a much broader range of services.

Quicken isn't just a fancy calculator to balance your checkbook; it's a personal finance adviser. Norton Utilities isn't just a software tonic you apply when something goes wrong with your computer; it's a proactive maintenance service. These and other products are increasingly being designed to help end users be successful in a certain domain, such as personal finance—and in the process, strengthen brand loyalty.

Focusing on influence strategies rather than on products may be inevitable for another reason: many products are no longer discrete units—a single application you install or a device you carry around. Computing products are extending beyond their former boundaries; more and more, desktop software will link to Web services, Internet content will appear on your TV screen, and portable devices will deliver real-time data from third parties. This blurring of boundaries will create new opportunities for researchers and designers of persuasive technology. Those who understand persuasive technology from the perspective of influence strategies will be able to apply their skills across the wide range of existing and emerging product categories.

Trend 5: A New Focus on Influence Tactics

As captology focuses more on influence strategies, another trend will emerge: a focus on influence *tactics*. By "tactics" I mean the specific implementations of influence strategies. Praise is an influence *strategy*. Exactly how you implement the strategy of praise in a computing product is a *tactic*. When it comes to computer-based praise, tactics could include a dialog box that says, "You're doing a good job," a music clip from the James Bond theme song "Nobody Does It Better," or animated lizards dancing the samba across the screen in celebration. Hundreds of other tactics are possible.

While the number of influence strategies is finite, the number of potential tactics for implementing strategies is almost limitless. With new computing capabilities come more possibilities for new tactics. This is one thing that makes captology so interesting: as long as interactive technology advances, new tactics will emerge for changing people's attitudes and behaviors.

For designers of persuasive technologies, choosing the right influence tactics is critical to the success of a product. Suppose you are designing a technology to increase compliance with an exercise program, and you determine that tracking is an important influence strategy. How will you implement the tracking strategy? Will users input their own compliance data, or will the system sense and record compliance automatically? What is the appropriate frequency for tracking each act of compliance? Daily? Weekly? What tracking metaphor will work best? Check boxes? Awarding points? How can users view their performance records? These questions might have different answers for different target behaviors and for different audiences. Choosing the correct answers—the correct tactics—will determine the product's effectiveness in persuasion.

As captology moves forward, researchers and designers both will pay more attention to influence tactics, to determining which tactics work in which situations for what types of users. Tactics will become central to the practical world of persuasive technology in other ways. Companies are likely to create core competencies in developing specific types of technology-based tactics to influence people. A company could lay claim to being the best in creating persuasive simulations for small screens, such as those on mobile phones. Another company might focus on creating a repertoire of verbal audio elements that convey messages of praise or encouragement. Yet another company may create a system for suggesting purchases at the opportune time and place.[13]

Influence tactics also will become more important when it comes to patents. You can't patent an influence strategy, but you can patent a specific implementation of that strategy—a tactic. One of the notable cases in the arena of persuasive technology is Amazon's hotly contested patent for "one-click shopping," which the company was awarded in 1999.[14] The idea of one-click shopping is based on the strategy of reduction—reducing a complex activity to a simple one—to increase persuasive power.

The issue of Amazon's patent for one-click shopping is still a debated topic among people in the Internet world and people involved in intellectual property rights.[15] It's likely that interactive influence tactics will eventually generate dozens if not hundreds of patents (and inevitably, many lawsuits), creating significant intellectual property related to captology.

Finally, persuasion tactics are likely to come under increasing scrutiny of policymakers because of their potential impact on the public.[16] The previous chapter on ethics pointed out how some uses of persuasive technology can be harmful to individuals and society. In the future, certain interactive influence tactics are likely to raise ethical concerns, if not public outrage. It's not hard to imagine that stricter regulations will guard against certain tactics, such as using a gaming platform for motivating children to divulge private information about themselves and their families.[17] Policymakers can't outlaw the use of game dynamics such as creating simulations, awarding points, or using other means to influence people, but they could ban specific implementations for specific audiences.

Looking Forward Responsibly

The five trends outlined above preview the next stages of captology. Some of these trends may fade and others may emerge; it's never been an easy task to predict where technology is headed. It becomes even more challenging to foresee the future in a domain that is relatively new and that hinges on multiple factors: academic research, economic vitality, technology innovations, and more.

One thing is certain: As computing technology becomes more deeply embedded in everyday life, new possibilities for persuasion will emerge. Whatever the form of the technology, from a desktop computer to a smart car interior to a mobile phone, it can be designed to change attitudes and behaviors—in ways we can't fully predict.

We don't yet appreciate all the possibilities or pitfalls associated with computers as persuasive technologies; the domain of captology is still in its infancy.

But persuasive technologies will grow and mature. The precise growth path will depend, in part, on those familiar enough with persuasive technologies to help guide this developing domain.

My main purpose in writing this book was to enhance the collective understanding of persuasive technology so computing products can be created to influence people in ways that enhance quality of life. This will require at least three things: raising awareness of persuasive technologies among the general public, encouraging designers to follow guidelines for creating ethical interactive products, and taking action against individuals and organizations that use persuasive technology for exploitation. I hope this book will contribute to these worthy goals.

Notes and References

For updates on the topics presented in this chapter, visit *www.persuasivetech.info.*

1. Currently there are no solid financial projections for persuasive technologies, but the market is likely to be enormous. One slice of this market, mobile commerce in Europe, gives an indication. According to the Mobile Commerce site supported by KPMG, "[a]nalysts are estimating that the European mobile commerce market alone could be worth $60 billion by 2003." See *http://www.mcommcentral.com/.*

2. For example, in my lab we are now running rapid studies from our research site, *webresearch.org.*

3. B. J. Fogg and C. I. Nass, Silicon sycophants: The effects of computers that flatter, *International Journal of Human-Computer Studies,* 46(5): 551–561 (1997).

4. This has already happened to a limited extent. My research on human-computer persuasion uncovered persuasion dynamics never before shown in human-human studies. Specifically, in studying the persuasive effects of affiliation, Professor Clifford Nass and I separated the affiliation construct into two elements: interdependence (people would receive the same reward or punishment as another entity) and identity (people were assigned to the same group). In essence, what we found was that interdependence, not identity, was the element that led to conformity with others and positive disposition toward others. The first few studies in this line of research involved people working with computers. After these studies showed interesting results, we replicated the study with people working with other people. We got the same results in the human-human studies.

   I expect to see more of this as the pace of persuasion research quickens and as computer systems provide a way to run experiments in highly controlled ways.

5. For visions of how computing technologies of the future will be part of ordinary objects and environments, see

   a. Don Norman, *The Invisible Computer* (Cambridge, MA: MIT Press, 1998).

   b. Neil A. Gershenfeld, *When Things Start to Think* (New York: Henry Holt & Company, 1999).

   c. M. L. Dertouzos, *What Will Be: How the New World of Information Will Change Our Lives* (New York: HarperCollins Publishers, 1997).

6. I discuss these in Chapter 1. The 12 domains are commerce—buying and branding; education, learning, and training; safety; environmental conservation; occupational productivity; preventative health care; fitness; disease management; personal finance; and community involvement/activism.

7. *http://www.merck.com/product/usa/propecia/cns/morph/morph2.html.*

8. A 2001 report on the status of eHealth laments how little this field has developed. See T. R. Eng, *The eHealth Landscape: A Terrain Map of Emerging Information and Communication Technologies in Health and Health Care* (Princeton, NJ: The Robert Wood Johnson Foundation, 2001). See *http://www.rwjf.org/app/rw_publications_and_links/publicationsPdfs/eHealth.pdf.*

9. For a short article that describes how computer games motivate people in a training situation, see M. Feldstein and D. Kruse, The power of multimedia games, *Training & Development,* 52(2): 62–63 (1998).

10. There are various approaches to learning styles. The approach I'm referring to here is based on David Kolb's theory of learning styles. In Kolb's model, the four learning styles are Diverger, Assimilator, Converger, and Accommodator.

11. Asia and Europe are far ahead of the United States in some aspects of wireless data standards.

12. You'll find examples of influence strategies throughout this book. For example, Chapter 3 discusses strategies of tailoring, self-monitoring, and surveillance, among others; Chapter 4 explains the strategies of simulating cause and effect and more; and Chapter 5 explains the persuasive impact of attractiveness, similarity, and more.

13. The specialization of companies in creating or enabling influence tactics is already taking place to some extent.

14. For an overview of the controversy, see *http://www.noamazon.com/.*

15. One of the most notable opponents of Amazon's one-click patent is Tim O'Reilly, a prominent computer trade book publisher. (See *http://www.bookmarket.com/fame.html.*) O'Reilly has offered a bounty to people who can find evidence of prior art and others conceptualizing or using one-click ordering before Amazon. In March 2001, he awarded the bounty to three different people. (See *http://www.oreillynet.com/pub/a/policy/2001/03/14/bounty.html.*)

For a long list of prior art for one-click, see *http://bountyquest.com/patentinfo/oneclickart.htm#no22thru24 29.*

Even Jeff Bezos of Amazon has responded to the uproar by advocating a revision of the patent system. The main issue now in the Internet community is not whether Amazon should be issued the patent (that's a done deal) but about any steps Amazon takes to enforce its patent. That's where people want to put pressure on Amazon to step back.

An interesting blow-by-blow account of the Amazon patent story can be found at *http://btl.bus.utexas.edu/IBM%20Course%20modules/bizmethpatents1.pdf.*

16. Passed by Congress in 1998, the Children's Online Privacy Protection Act (COPPA) established strict privacy guidelines for child-oriented Web sites. Final rules on COPPA, drafted by the Federal Trade Commission (FTC) in 1999, became enforceable in April 2001. For more on this, see *http://www.ftc.gov/bcp/conline/edcams/coppa/index.htm.*

17. There are some regulations about the privacy of kids online. To find out more about the Children's Online Privacy Protection Rule, see the FTC Web page at *http://www.ftc.gov/bcp/conline/pubs/buspubs/coppa.htm.*

Appendix
Summary of Principles

Chapter 3: Computers as Persuasive Tools

Principle of Reduction

> Using computing technology to reduce complex behavior to simple tasks increases the benefit/cost ratio of the behavior and influences users to perform the behavior.

Principle of Tunneling

> Using computing technology to guide users through a process or experience provides opportunities to persuade along the way.

Principle of Tailoring

> Information provided by computing technology will be more persuasive if it is tailored to the individual's needs, interests, personality, usage context, or other factors relevant to the individual.

Principle of Suggestion

> A computing technology will have greater persuasive power if it offers suggestions at opportune moments.

Principle of Self-Monitoring

Applying computing technology to eliminate the tedium of tracking performance or status helps people to achieve predetermined goals or outcomes.

Principle of Surveillance

Applying computing technology to observe others' behavior increases the likelihood of achieving a desired outcome.

Principle of Conditioning

Computing technology can use positive reinforcement to shape complex behavior or transform existing behaviors into habits.

Chapter 4: Computers as Persuasive Media: Simulation

Principle of Cause and Effect

Simulations can persuade people to change their attitudes or behaviors by enabling them to observe immediately the link between cause and effects.

Principle of Virtual Rehearsal

Providing a motivating simulated environment in which to rehearse a behavior can enable people to change their attitudes or behavior in the real world.

Principle of Virtual Rewards

Computer simulations that reward target behaviors in a virtual world, such as giving virtual rewards for exercising, can influence people to perform the target behavior more frequently and effectively in the real world.

Principle of Simulations in Real-World Contexts

Portable simulation technologies designed for use during everyday routines can highlight the impact of certain behaviors and motivate behavior or attitude change.

Chapter 5: Computers as Persuasive Social Actors

Principle of Attractiveness

A computing technology that is visually attractive to target users is likely to be more persuasive as well.

Principle of Similarity

People are more readily persuaded by computing technology products that are similar to themselves in some way.

Principle of Praise

By offering praise, via words, images, symbols, or sounds, computing technology can lead users to be more open to persuasion.

Principle of Reciprocity

People will feel the need to reciprocate when computing technology has done a favor for them.

Principle of Authority

Computing technology that assumes roles of authority will have enhanced powers of persuasion.

Chapter 6: Credibility and Computers

Principle of Trustworthiness

Computing technology that is viewed as trustworthy (truthful, fair, and unbiased) will have increased powers of persuasion.

Principle of Expertise

Computing technology that is viewed as incorporating expertise (knowledge, experience, and competence) will have increased powers of persuasion.

Principle of Presumed Credibility

People approach computing technology with a preconceived notion about credibility, based on general assumptions about what is and is not believable.

Principle of Surface Credibility

People make initial assessments of the credibility of computing technology based on firsthand inspection of surface traits like layout and density of ads.

Principle of Reputed Credibility

Third-party endorsements, especially from respected sources, boost perceptions of credibility of computing technology.

Principle of Earned Credibility

Credibility can be strengthened over time if computing technology performs consistently in accordance with the user's expectations.

Principle of (Near) Perfection

Computing technology will be more persuasive if it never (or rarely) commits what users perceive as errors.

Chapter 7: Credibility and the World Wide Web

Principle of "Real-World Feel"

A Web site will have more credibility if it highlights the people or organization behind the content and services it provides.

Principle of Easy Verifiability

Credibility perceptions will be enhanced if a Web site makes it easy for users to check outside sources to verify the accuracy of site content.

Principle of Fulfillment

A Web site will have increased credibility when it fulfills users' positive expectations.

Principle of Ease-of-Use

A Web site wins credibility points by being easy to use.

Principle of Personalization

Web sites that offer personalized content and services get a boost in credibility.

Principle of Responsiveness

The more responsive to users, the greater the perceived credibility of a Web site.

Chapter 8: Increasing Persuasion through Mobility and Connectivity

Principle of Kairos

Mobile devices are ideally suited to leverage the principle of kairos—offering suggestions at opportune moments—to increase the potential to persuade.

Principle of Convenience

Interactive experiences that are easy to access (ideally, just a click away on a mobile device) have greater opportunity to persuade.

Principle of Mobile Simplicity

Mobile applications that are easy to use will have greater potential to persuade.

Principle of Mobile Loyalty

Mobile applications that are perceived to serve the needs and wishes of the owner first, rather than those of an outside party, will have greater persuasive powers.

Principle of Mobile Marriage

Mobile applications designed to persuade should support an intensive, positive relationship (many interactions or interactions over a long time period) between the user and the product.

Principle of Information Quality

Computing technology that delivers current, relevant, and well-coordinated information has greater potential to create attitude or behavior change.

Principle of Social Facilitation

People are more likely to perform a well-learned target behavior if they know they are being observed via computing technology, or if they can discern via technology that others are performing the behavior along with them.

Principle of Social Comparison

People will have greater motivation to perform a target behavior if they are given information, via computing technology, about how their performance compares with the performance of others, especially others who are similar to themselves.

Principle of Normative Influence

Computing technology can leverage normative influence (peer pressure) to increase the likelihood that a person will adopt or will avoid performing a target behavior.

Principle of Social Learning

A person will be more motivated to perform a target behavior if he or she can use computing technology to observe others performing the behavior and being rewarded for it.

Principle of Competition

Computing technology can motivate users to adopt a target attitude or behavior by leveraging human beings' natural drive to compete.

Principle of Cooperation

Computing technology can motivate users to adopt a target attitude or behavior by leveraging human beings' natural drive to cooperate.

Principle of Recognition

By offering public recognition (individual or group), computing technology can increase the likelihood that a person or group will adopt a target attitude or behavior.

Figure Credits

Figure 3.2 courtesy of Capitol Advantage, *http://www.capwiz.com*.

Figure 3.3 from the Environmental Defense Web site, *http://www.scorecard.org*.

Figure 3.4 from the Mountain Home, Idaho, Police Department Web site, *http://www.mhpd.net/traffic_enforcement.htm*.

Figure 3.5 from the Polar Heart Rate Monitors Web site, *http://www.polar.fi*.

Figure 3.7 from the former Hygiene Guard Web site, *http://www.hygieneguard.com*.

Figure 3.9 from the TreeLoot Web site, *http://www.treeloot.com*.

Figures 4.2 and 4.3 from the Albathion Web site, *http://www.albathion.com*.

Figure 4.4 from Rockett's New School by Purple Moon, a subsidiary of Mattel, Inc.

Figure 4.5 courtesy of Life Fitness, a Brunswick Corporation, *http://www.lifefitness.com*.

Figure 4.6 from the former Tectrix Web site, *http://www.tectrix.com*. Tectrix is now owned by Cybex International, Inc.

Figure 4.7 from the Video Game Museum Web site, *http://www.vgmuseum.com/images/snes01/01/bronkie.html*. Bronkie the Bronchiasaurus is a video game by Raya Systems, now known as Health Hero Network, Inc.

Figure 4.8 courtesy of UW HITlab, *http://www.hitl.washington.edu/people/hunter*.

Figure 4.9 from a story appearing on the CNN Web site, *http://www.cnn.com.health/ 9809/25/virtual.reality.cancer.*

Figure 4.10 © BTIO, Inc. Photo of Caucasian Girl Standing Up, diapering RealCare® Baby.

Figure 4.11 courtesy of Davison Community Schools Driver Education Web site, *http://www.davison.k12.mi.us/neon/neon.htm.*

Figure 5.3 from the former Silicon Gaming Web site, *http://www.silicongaming.com.*

Figure 5.4 from multiple Web sites, in order from left to right: *http://www.speech .kth.se/multimodal, http://mambo.ucsc.edu/psl/pslfan.html,* and *http://www .lce.hut.fi/research/face/demo.html.*

Figure 5.5 courtesy of Quicken © 1997–2002 Intuit, Inc.

Figure 5.8 courtesy of Eudora © 1999, 2000, 2001 QUALCOMM, Inc.

Figure 5.9 from The Learning Company Web site, *http://store.learningservicesinc .com/cgi-bin/lscatalog/swt09040-mpcs.html.*

Figure 5.10 from the Ask Jeeves Web site, *http://www.askjeeves.com.*

Figure 5.11 from "Virtual PAT: A Virtual Personal Aerobics Trainer" by James W. Davis and Aaron F. Bobick, posted on the NEC Research Index Web site, *http:// citeseer.nj.nec.com/10057.html.*

Figure 6.3, top image, from the Oxygen Web site, *http://thriveonline.oxygen.com* and bottom image from the National Institutes of Health (NIH) Web site, *http:// www.nih.gov.*

Figure 7.5 from multiple Web sites, in order from left to right: *http://www .pointcom .com, http://www.pcmagazine.com, http://www.kn.pacbell.com/wired/ bluewebn/hot.html,* and *http://www.pointcom.com.*

Figure 7.6, left image, from *http://www.truste.org* and right image from *http:// verisign.com/index.html.*

Figure 7.7 courtesy of Aetna InteliHealth, *http://www.intelihealth.com.*

Figure 8.3 courtesy of Personal Improvement Computer Systems, Inc., *http://www .lifesign.com.*

Figure 8.4 from the Sportbrain Web site, *http://www.sportbrain.com.*

Figure 8.6 courtesy of the QuitNet.com, Inc. Web site, *http://www.quitnet.com.*

Figure 9.1 from the Fibreplay Web site, *http://fibreplay.com/other/portfolio_en.html.*

Figures 9.2 and 9.3 from the TreeLoot Web site, *http://www.treeloot.com.*

Figure 9.4 from the former Bali Casino Web site *http://www.balicasino.com.*

Index

About the Author

After earning his Ph.D. from Stanford University, B. J. Fogg launched the Stanford Persuasive Technology Lab, a research and design center that explores how interactive technology can motivate and influence people. Since 1993, Dr. Fogg's research in the area of persuasive technology has involved more than 6,500 participants in lab experiments, field studies, online investigations, and design explorations.

An experimental psychologist, Dr. Fogg has been appointed to Stanford's consulting faculty in both the School of Engineering and the School of Education. Each year he teaches graduate-level courses in persuasive technology for the Computer Science Department and for Stanford's Learning, Design, and Technology Program.

In addition to his academic endeavors, Dr. Fogg plans and directs projects for companies seeking new uses for technology. Most recently, he was the Senior Director of Research and Innovation at Casio's U.S. Research and Development Center. Previously, he led strategic innovation efforts at HP Labs, Interval Research, and Sun Microsystems.

Dr. Fogg holds seven patents for his innovations in user interface design. For more information about his background and research, visit *www.bjfogg.info*.